Handbook of Medical Tourism Program Development

Developing Globally Integrated Health Systems

Endorsements for *Handbook of Medical Tourism Program Development*
Maria K. Todd

More praise for *Handbook of Medical Tourism Program Development: Developing Globally Integrated Health Systems*

"The medical tourism industry has a great but, as of yet, unrealized potential to transform the way global health-care is delivered. After much press and many start ups, no one has yet developed the ideal system to connect patients and providers on a global basis. Perhaps, had her book been available earlier on, the Medical Travel Industry would look completely different today.

Dr. Todd writes with much wit and grace and explains the elements required to succeed in this difficult but essential business. Following her suggestions and implementing her ideas are as important to Medical Tourism as following a detailed recipe is to cake making. In either situation, the end result can be very tasty or a disaster. My experience tells me there are many bad cooks in the medical tourism arena. Dr. Todd is a top-notch chef among chefs in this industry. To be a successful medical tourism cook, I recommend a short course in her kitchen!"

Armando Baez, FLMI
General Manager—China
Global Benefits Group/"Insurance Without Borders"
Board Member—Self Insurance Institute of America

"Maria crafted this hands-on guideline from the insight lesson that she learned and her wide-ranging proficient experiences in both clinical and non-clinical aspects, from the view of a patient, a consumer, a health administrator, and a marketing person. This handbook, therefore, demonstrates a concrete practical roadmap in developing true "medical tourism health delivery systems" in the real world that puts an emphasis on patient safety, quality, service, and accountability."

Chatree Duangnet, MD, FAAP
Chief Executive Officer
Bangkok Hospital Medical Center
Bangkok Dusit Medical Services, Plc., Thailand

"The handbook provides the reader with detailed information and practical tools on program development, all conveyed with the author's unique wit. Ms. Todd shows that, if understood and implemented correctly, all stakeholders in international medical travel can have their cake and eat it too."

Margaret A. Bengzon
Group Head—Strategic Services
The Medical City (TMC)
Pasig City, Philippine

"Maria Todd has written the A-Z handbook for the medical tourism industry, and there is no one more qualified to do it."

Ruben Toral
Founder and CEO
Medeguide

"Great instructional resource for healthcare providers looking to explore the international market. I love the bakery analogy and the market survey is a great tool! It's an easy read and a must-have "cookbook" for those entering the healthcare travel arena!"

Patty Urban, LHRM, CASC
Administrator
Nucci Medical Clinic, LLC

"Maria has taken a complex and completely misunderstood subject and transformed it into a concise, easily read training guide for anyone even considering the possibility of participating in medical tourism. She has removed the guesswork from medical tourism assessment and development by providing the critical and concise answers to the questions you didn't know you needed to ask."

Jackie Hodges
President
HRC Strategies, LLC

"Maria Todd addresses one of the tremendous growth areas in healthcare as it is known today. Truly, this book should serve as an anthem to any and all who wish to understand, engage, develop, and execute their strategic medical tourism offering. As a rising champion for Medical Tourism, Maria provides an informed, insightful and authoritative perspective. The *Handbook of Medical Tourism Program Development* gives you the tools and framework necessary to create success."

Rhett Stover, M.H.A.
Vice President, GlobalHealth, Inc.

"Medical tourism is a vast new field of healthcare. The needs are great but the providers that can meet the demands and/or needs of the patients are few. The patients will first look at price and/or availability. They will then quickly compare the quality to their expectations (which are usually formed in their native land). The healthcare team must provide an environment that puts the needs of the patients first. The patient's needs start with their decision to seek options, to travel for their healthcare and it ends when they return home, their post-procedure bodies are mended and the restoration is complete. It is like an airline. It starts when you decide to travel by air, search for an airline, purchase tickets, travel, and then return home. It again only ends when the luggage is put away."

Dato' Teddric Mohr, FACHE
Chief Executive Officer
Penang Adventist Hospital—Malaysia

"From cover to cover this book about medical tourism includes practical advice and first-hand knowledge when designing a patient-centered experience— both domestically and internationally. Like me, it will transform your thinking about selecting and participating in an accreditation program that aligns with your organization's purpose and strategic goals, thereby, developing processes that result in quantifiable outcomes. It's a must-read guide for any professional in healthcare who cares about patient safety!"

Donna Goestenkors, CPMSM
Credentialing & Privileging Consultant

"Dr. Todd's new book is critically important to clarify health travel from medical tourism, the latter a concept that is poorly understood in America but pretty well understood internationally. Maria shows how medical tourism bridges the gap between the hospitality and healthcare delivery industries in ways that are far more specific than previously understood, particularly in America. Similarly, Maria also shows the need for global integration of healthcare services that are hospitality-friendly, which is vitally important to the needs of globalized employers and purchasers of services, and to the need for American healthcare delivery and tour operators to be receptive to the needs of a globalized customer base. A vitally important work, *Handbook of Medical Tourism Program Development* is a necessity for the future of medical tourism and health travel now and in the immediate future."

David I. Samuels, FHFMA
Author of Managed Health Care in the New Millennium
President, EthiCare Breakthrough Solutions

Handbook of Medical Tourism Program Development

Developing Globally Integrated Health Systems

Maria K. Todd

Foreword by Keith Pollard, International Medical Travel Journal

CRC Press
Taylor & Francis Group
Boca Raton   London   New York

CRC Press is an imprint of the
Taylor & Francis Group, an **informa** business

A PRODUCTIVITY PRESS BOOK

CRC Press
Taylor & Francis Group
6000 Broken Sound Parkway NW, Suite 300
Boca Raton, FL 33487-2742

© 2012 by Taylor & Francis Group, LLC
CRC Press is an imprint of Taylor & Francis Group, an Informa business

No claim to original U.S. Government works

Printed in the United States of America on acid-free paper
Version Date: 20111028

International Standard Book Number: 978-1-4398-1314-0 (Paperback)

Visit the Taylor & Francis Web site at
http://www.taylorandfrancis.com

and the CRC Press Web site at
http://www.crcpress.com

Contents

SECTION III   NICHE MARKET OPPORTUNITIES

SECTION IV   WELLNESS AND MEDICAL TOURISM

Foreword

Back in the 1990s, before someone, somewhere, coined the term "medical tourism," I was a marketing director with an American-owned hospital company running private hospitals in the United Kingdom. More than 50% of the revenues in our biggest London hospitals were derived from what was then known as the "international patient business." Patients from the Middle East, India, Pakistan, Greece, and Turkey came to London in large numbers for healthcare that wasn't readily available in their own country. They still do.

One day, I got a call from a headhunter, promising big money for a job opportunity that surely I wouldn't want to miss. Here's how the conversation went:

Headhunter: We've got these American investors who are planning to spend millions of dollars on a brand new 500-bed state-of-the-art private hospital in the UK. It's going to be an 'international medical center' attracting patients from all over the world.

Me: Sounds interesting. Where are they going to build it?

Headhunter: On Clydebank. It's going to be massive.

Me: Clydebank..... You mean Clydebank.... in Scotland....near Glasgow?

Headhunter: Yes, that's right. It'll be close to the airport so people will be able to fly in from all over the world. Labor costs for hospital workers in Scotland are much lower than they are in America. It's backed by some U.S. doctors and investors. They're going to create a medical city.

Me: Are you serious? Or is this a bad joke?

I didn't take the job. ... The hospital was built and opened with fanfare. But occupancy never got above more than 20 or so of the 500 planned beds. The "if we build it (in Scotland!), they will come" approach was a disaster. Receivership followed and ownership changed hands. A group of investors from the Middle East then came in with big ideas of creating a medical tourism flagship for patients from that region—a second disaster ensued.

Today, the hospital is owned by the Scottish National Health Service and is treating domestic patients. The NHS bought it at a knock-down price when the second, Arab-funded medical tourism venture failed.

If Maria Todd had been on the board of these two medical tourism ventures, I doubt that either group of investors would have poured millions of dollars into a medical tourism black hole. They probably wouldn't have gotten past the initial concept.

I have known Maria for the last five years, and have been impressed by her conference presentations, workshops, and her writings. Ask Maria what she thinks of your medical tourism program, idea or business venture, and she won't pull punches. She will give you insight and an honest opinion that will focus your thinking, and ensure that you don't make the same mistakes as many others in the medical tourism sector.

Around the world, there are investors, governments, health departments, hospitals and healthcare businesses that continue to make ill-advised decisions on developing medical tourism programs. I advise them to read this book before they gamble away their first thousand, ten thousand, or ten million dollars. They won't regret it.

Keith Pollard
International Medical Travel Journal—www.imtj.com
Treatment Abroad—www.treatmentabroad.com

Preface

As a former professional musician who was reared in a musical family of composers, arrangers, musicians, actors, and vocalists, music is a core element of what makes me who I am. I relate many experiences to music, use many analogies to describe my impressions and how I process the world around me. Therefore, it is no surprise that as I travel the world inspecting hospitals and health systems and assessing their readiness for "medical tourism" business, I am reminded of an American pop music song hit[1] from the 1950s, *If I Knew You Were Comin' I'd've Baked a Cake* (1950, Hoffman, Merrill, and Watts, National Records). As I walk the halls of hospital after hospital and attend meetings and presentations by the hospital executives, physicians, marketing staff, government tourism officials, and others, the melody floats in my stream of consciousness, and transforms into an image that is worth thousands of words. It is that stream of consciousness that motivated me to propose this book to my publisher, Productivity Press, and I use it to organize the contents of this book because the song's lyrics evoke easier access and construction to my verbal musings than if I were to sit down and just write.

My undergraduate education focused on music, educational psychology, and biology, so I am keenly aware of the theory of *positive transfer*. With more than 2,600 professional presentations including speeches, keynotes, workshops, lectures, training sessions, and webinars, I incorporate the learning theories of Piaget, Ellis (1965), Thorndike, and Woodworth (1938), each of whom explored how individuals transfer learning in one context to another context that shares a similar characteristic. No one else that I know of has given that many presentations around the world on healthcare reimbursement, managed care, or health travel and medical tourism administration topics, so I would assume it is safe to say that my teaching and presentation style is effective. Postpresentation evaluations consistently range in the first quartile of attendee satisfaction in all metrics, so I assume that I am successful in achieving my objective of teaching and learning transfer, rather than selling from the podium or campaigning for a cause. Because I tend to use what works, I use this same technique in this book.

So if you hear a relaxed, almost conversational tone in your mind's ear as you read the contents, I've succeeded in my first objective, which is that I want you to read this book and not memorize facts and figures, but instead glean a conceptual framework for the development of a medical tourism or health travel business model and not memorize rote facts, figures, statistics, rules, and history. As such, the book is not meant to be read cover to cover. I have also developed each chapter more or less to stand alone as an independent topic, affording the reader the convenience of reading up on a topic of interest at the moment. Ultimately they are all related to the development of a medical tourism or health travel program and the myriad directions the program might take.

One might ask why I have been using this dual nomenclature of medical tourism and health travel. I see them as entirely different pursuits. I delve into the definition more deeply in Chapter 1; however, I am convinced that medical tourism is when one intentionally pairs up a health service to be undertaken in conjunction with leisure or adventure travel, and that health travel is when there is a *de novo* departure for the sole purpose of accessing healthcare, without a leisure or touristic itinerary in conjunction with the mission. As the health travel market matures and evolves into that which is reimbursed by insurers or employer self-funded health benefit trusts and self-insurance plans, they will react negatively if one mentions "tourism" as part of the episode of care for which they have undertaken the financial responsibility for payment as a claims risk.

This book looks forward to what can be, and doesn't focus much on medical tourism business traffic and trends; I am an achiever, not necessarily a researcher. As a business owner and strategist in this domain, I have followed the works of Dr. Paul Keckley, executive director for the Deloitte Center for Health Solutions (DCHS)[2] who analyzes trends that affect health systems and focuses on emerging sectors or business models, and his competitors at McKinsey[3] (Ehrbeck, Guevara, and Mango, 2008), each of whom published articles in 2008 that sought to project the market size and opportunity of medical tourism. I also subscribe to various industry newsletters published formally and informally, and blogs, and attend many industry conferences. As a speaker at a significant number of those conferences, I am constantly updating my materials, facts, figures, slides, and presentation notes.

In order to be achievers, together with our managing directors and executive team, we are responsible for the direction of training and development for employees and affiliates, and the board of directors of Mercury Healthcare. In this role, I am responsible for providing weekly industry updates, observations, impressions, clarifications, and my best interpretations of market developments to our brokers and agents, who interact daily with employers, insurers, and third-party administrators, my board of directors (who often grant me leniency in entrepreneurial decision making and calculated risk taking), and our staff located worldwide, who take their corporate culture cues from me, our medical directors, and our domain experts and consulting affiliates at Mercury Healthcare Advisory Group, a subsidiary of Mercury Healthcare International.

Sitting around the hotel lobbies and meeting rooms, we've all chuckled a time or two at the outcomes of Dr. Keckley's team and the predictions in their 2008 publication, but in fairness and out of respect for the effort that went into the research, we are about four years out now, and I have the benefit of hindsight that they did not have as authors and researchers at the time of publication. We all have opinions and impressions of each of the works. Those opinions don't really matter. Regardless of whether they were correct or incorrect as predictions, one has to give them credit for taking the risk to go first in such projects, for they contributed to the stimulation of market development, awareness, and interest in medical tourism, and ultimately for me personally, the advancement of my now trademarked model of globally integrated healthcare delivery. For that, I properly acknowledge and thank them.

But, I digress, so let's go back to the learning theory, the positive transfer, and my defense for this chosen organization of the information, along with why I disclosed my music history to you. No, it was not a case of TMI (too much information) but instead, reliance upon a well-known fact that studies have shown medical schools take a higher percentage of applying music majors than even biochemistry majors. (66 to 44%, see "The Case for Music in the Schools," *Phi Delta Kappan*, Feb. 1994). Why? That part is easy! Music majors graduating with a Bachelor of Arts or science degree (like any other degree) are required to take a dozen or so "general" courses designed to give them a well-rounded education. This includes classes in the hard sciences (chemistry, physics,

250-300 г
колбаса.

лук 1/3 головы.
1 перец ост.
1/3 длинны кабач.
1ст.л растит. масло
1/4 л. молоко
уксус
(...)
соль.
3ст.л. воды.

П.І.Б. пац. _____

Ціна

biology), soft sciences (philosophy, psychology, sociology, humanities), math, history, literature, foreign languages, performing arts, and so on. That means that a music major will have to take many of the classes they would have to take as any other major, and can usually easily take the prerequisite courses to apply for a graduate program in other subjects. They also have to manage multiple priorities, manage practice time in order to perform as musicians, and still maintain their grades in the hard sciences in order to pass the entrance exams and have the grade point average to gain entry into the various programs. (Call it "Multitasking 1.0.")

Therefore, music is likely a common thread that serves as an easy point of positive transfer between many of us in the healthcare industry, and even more relevant when one attempts to develop a program such as medical tourism within an already existing workflow of health delivery for local patients and clientele. It requires the use of creativity, logic, data assessments, research, and developing and implementing a strategy that meets performance objectives, achieving clinical and revenue outcomes, demonstrating technique in direct patient care, refining marketing strategies, and finding one's differentiation and unique selling proposition (USP) concurrently, while already engaged in the business of healthcare and the art of healing ("Multitasking 2.0"). You are all smart people, and many of you are probably musicians who can relate to how sometimes we process the world around us through an association with a melody or certain lyrics. This is one of those cases.

Now, let's go back to the song. On an interesting side note, when the song became too big a hit for National to handle, it arranged with Mercury Records to help with distribution.[4] No, that's not why I named our company Mercury Healthcare (but that's an entirely different subject, and I do not digress further at this time)! In fact, I had no idea about the Mercury Records involvement when the song started floating through my head, but I do like the fact that an entity named Mercury stepped in to handle the call for assistance.

The lyrics (Figure 1) to the first three verses of the song are even funnier (at least they are to me) when I compare them to medical tourism and health travel program development in the sense that some patients come unannounced (second verse) and find providers unprepared or surprised by their arrival, whereas others seem to elect a medical tourism or health travel option as a last

If I knew you were comin' I'd've baked a cake, baked
 a cake, baked a cake
If I knew you were comin' I'd've baked a cake
Howdya do, yowdya do, howdya do?

Had you dropped me a letter, I'd a hired a band,
 grandest band in the land
Had you dropped me a letter, I'd a-hired a band
And spread the welcome mat for you

Oh, I don't know where you came from 'cause I don't
 know where you've been
But it really doesn't matter
Grab a chair and fill your platter
And dig, dig, dig right in

Figure 1   Lyrics from "If I Knew You Were Comin' I'd've Baked a Cake." (Written by Al Hoffman, Bob Merrill, and Clem Watts, 1950.)

resort because the care available locally is nonexistent, insufficient, inaccessible, unaffordable, or was unsuccessful (third verse).

Similarities between Baking Cakes and Organizational Development

Cake baking has a tremendous significance here as well: Cakes are a common frame of reference because it is difficult to imagine anyone unfamiliar with the essential ingredients (Figure 2) of a traditional cake: flour, salt, sugar, eggs, and some ingredient to create a unique flavor and color. It is also difficult for me to imagine anyone being unfamiliar with the process of baking a cake, but I am going to break it down for you perhaps to a level that is more fundamental:

1. Determine the recipe to be used
2. Assemble ingredients
3. Warm oven
4. Mix ingredients in a bowl
5. Bake
6. Cool
7. Frost or decorate
8. Serve

The reason that it requires a deeper breakdown is because each of the above steps assumes quite a bit that goes into each phrase.

For example, determining the recipe requires a consensus on what kind of cake everybody wants to eat, unless, of course you are eating alone. If you eat a whole cake alone, well, psychiatry is down the hall and to the left. I'm afraid you have some preliminary "issues" to resolve that this book won't address. Put the book down and go there now. The book will be here later when you are ready to assimilate the material covered within it. The rest of us should continue on while the

Figure 2   Common cake ingredients.

Table 1 Comparison of Cake Baking to Medical Tourism Program Development Stages

Basic Cake-Baking	*Medical Tourism Program Development*
Determine the recipe to be used	Program concept, strategy, uniqueness
Assemble ingredients	Stakeholder involvement and role definition, including collaborators from outside the organization
Warm oven	Process development, workflow design
Mix ingredients in a bowl	Actual program development
Bake	Implementation
Testing for "doneness"	Testing, mock delivery rehearsal, refinement
Cool	The gap between readiness of the deliverable and market arrival
Frost or decorate	Marketing, promotion and packaging
Serve	Customer service
Critique	Clinical outcomes and customer delight measurement

would-be overeaters go to therapy. If they don't go now, we'll see them later in the bariatric program we create, which is not a bad thing, I suppose, if the book were only focused on developing market share for your program.

Let us review a few very high-level parallels as shown in Table 1. In actuality, there is so much more to both activities.

For every chef, professional baker, or home baker, there is a certain pride in the creativity of designing a unique "signature" recipe for one's cake. It is a very different orientation to the task when one bakes a cake "from scratch" (for readers whose first language is other than English, this means "from the beginning, especially without relying on resources or other advantages") and adjusts the recipe to taste, versus the baker who follows directions for prepackaged, commercial cake mixes (a developed nation invention of convenience). But even if one uses the prepackaged commercial cake mix, there are variations based, for example, on elevation, oven temperature regulation, following the ingredients to the letter, and so on. For example, I reside in Denver, Colorado, where the elevation is 5,280 feet above sea level (1,609 m).

If I make a cake from a prepackaged mix and don't add a little extra time and flour to the mix, my cake-baking attempt will be an anticipated failure. But wait, there are lot more refinements necessary, and technical issues other than simply time and flour. For example, I make sure to have all ingredients at room temperature, with any ingredients such as berries, or other produce washed using lukewarm water, not hot or cold (product design, preparation, strategy).

Furthermore, if I am directed to bake at 400°F or 425°F for a recipe designed to be followed at sea level, I have to decrease it by 25°F in higher elevations. Doing so prevents the outside from over-baking and drying out before the center has a chance to catch up in temperature. I also need to permit the cake to bake just a few more minutes than directed (methodology, research, admonitions and lessons learned from others).

I have to know my equipment. All ovens cook and heat differently. Therefore I have to check for doneness prior to removing the cake from the oven. To do this, I insert a toothpick or knife into the center of the cake, and if crumbs are attached when the knife or toothpick is removed, then it needs a few more minutes to bake. This is never an exact science (working with physicians—sorry, ladies and gents—you are a wildly temperamental bunch and although you hold a special place in my heart, your creative and autonomous natures and egos make development of these attempts at integrated health delivery "interesting" but worthy challenges)!

I have to be aware of adjustment ratios: depending on the altitude at which I am to bake the cake, I need to add an extra 1.5–2 rounded tablespoons of flour per cup; if above 10,000 feet add 2–2.5 tablespoons of flour per cup. I also will be required to add an extra 1.5–2 tablespoons per cup of liquid (not oils); if above 10,000 feet add 2–2.5 extra tablespoons of liquid. I also need to decrease sugar by 2 teaspoons per cup; above 10,000 feet, decrease by 1 tablespoon per cup. Because I am not at 10,000 feet above sea level, but only about half that, I have to rely upon my training in basic chemistry and balancing equations. This is after all, food chemistry, is it not (altitude physiology and medical travel considerations)?

I could go on, but let's fast forward to the end of this process. One of the most difficult aspects in high-altitude baking is retaining the moisture in a cake once fully baked because when baking at high altitude, where the atmosphere is much dryer, I want to retain as much moisture as possible. Therefore, upon removal from the oven, I have to wrap my cake in cellophane or place it in a plastic container within the first 3–10 minutes after removing it from the oven (sustainability, outcomes).

These are things I have to take into consideration whether I choose to create a cake from scratch or use a commercial mix.

Okay, so here is the point where you are allowed to say either, "She is starting to make sense with this analogy," or, alternatively, "Now I want some cake."

Consultants and Medical Tourism Development Projects: Caveat Emptor!

For some developers of medical tourism program initiatives, no truer words were spoken than when someone once said *caveat emptor* (let the buyer beware) of the many self-declared experts posing as consultants (see Figure 3). In my professional opinion, millions of dollars have been "wasted" (a strong but carefully chosen verb) in this industry on nonexperts with great marketing and self-promotion skills. They were hired to bake a cake from a commercial prepackaged mix. What is most disappointing is that the client impulsively purchased a "one flavor and texture fits all" solution that was applied to every one of the consultant's engagements regardless of location, ingredients, or outcomes.

As most of you know, prepackaged cake mixes come in a variety of qualities, brands, and some contain nonessential ingredients called "fillers." For example, many of these mixes also contain chemicals/preservatives, and may contain hydrogenated oils/trans fats. Similarly, some individuals who are not really professional consultants with any special training, work experience, or process knowledge, have profited from unsuspecting hospitals' and other providers' and governments' hope, enthusiasm, and naïveté, and have charged a great deal of money to build a medical tourism "cluster" or program, whatever that means.

Most have failed miserably in their objective of creating something that works to attract patients to the providers. But, in fairness to these salespersons, lest I offend my professional colleagues by including these individuals, they most likely crafted contracts with a carefully stated deliverable, which was performed to the letter, even if the deliverable was what was available to

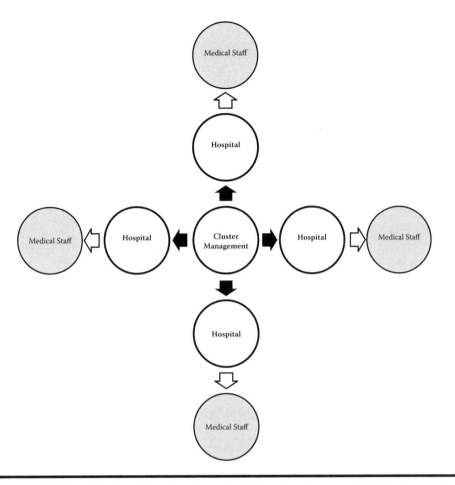

Figure 3 Typical regional and national medical tourism clusters built by inexperienced consultants.

be sold rather than what was really needed by the client. It is tantamount to going to the bakery, comparing what is available for sale with what one originally went to the bakery to purchase. On arrival the baker says, "I have no *Gâteau Parisien*, which is a rich, moist, almond-infused cake with a praline buttercream center, and coated with a crunchy topping, but I do have this plain yellow cake that was made from a prepackaged mix, and it has a buttercream center and some sprinkled almond bits on top. After all, cake is cake, and at least you'll have a dessert to serve."

The mix offers simplicity, seemingly rapid completion, and an immediate solution, but often contains few necessary functional ingredients, and sometimes substitutes certain easily available ingredients as equivalents for the best quality ingredients, but which may not achieve the objective of a creative, great-tasting, great-selling product that might have been possible with another flavor and texture approach and different ingredients and a distinctively different recipe.

I've seen a variety of opportunists posing as consultants, in some cases attorneys, marketing experts, or business management generalists, who are neither experts nor possess hands-on experience in healthcare administration, operations of healthcare organizations, or tourism and travel management. They have traveled to market after unsuspecting market, extracting large sums of money from the local, regional, or national government agency to sell advice to organizers of the program. They then extract huge additional consulting fees for the project from the hospitals and other stakeholders.

As the commercialism and popularity increase in this sector, more often it resembles the Wild West.[5] It angers me greatly to watch this because these salespeople pose as legitimate subject matter experts, authorities, or experienced developers and sell the "fast track" to medical tourism business. The "fast track" to what? Unfortunately, many of the consulting contracts were written such that the deliverable was the cluster itself, not the sustainable competitive advantage and the successful product performance or a functioning infrastructure of the cluster. Therefore, performance on the contract deliverable was complete; it was simply for the wrong deliverable. As a result, upon completion of the project, the entire stakeholder group sits around the conference table with its brand new cluster and a lighter wallet, only to look around the room and say, "OK, now we are a cluster. How come we don't have patients queuing up to be treated by us?"

My primary criticism is the unrealized potential of the stakeholders in these clusters. Despite the talent, resources, and creativity of the program operators, the cluster cakes "taste" no different from the other prepackaged, commercially developed clusters. They are all like plain yellow cakes on the baker's shelf.

Worse yet, most were likely more expensive to develop than a cake baked from scratch, and that concerns me as a corporate buyer. I can safely assume that in order to recover the costs to develop their program, they will likely want to charge more than other home-baked cakes for their product because it cost more to bring to market. To me, if there's no advantage to using a consultant to help create your unique cake recipe, and all it does is add layers of costs that do not provide value or utility (empty calories and fillers), our clients, the employers and insurers and consumers, don't really want to pay for them. I probably won't be able to resell those cakes anyway, even if they are sold to me wholesale.

What is even worse is that every one of these clusters lacks a proven recipe that creates any market distinction beyond the consultants' logo on it and in every case has failed to meet what should be the primary objectives of: (a) a functional, integrated health delivery system, (b) brand development (and don't get me started on the misuse and overuse of the term "branding" at this point), (c) capitalizing on a unique selling proposal that differentiates one provider from another to the extent that a consumer can make a prudent choice to select a provider, and (d) generating referral volumes, rather than simply having a cluster created. I believe I've made my point here. As a professional consultant for over 30 years, please, *caveat emptor*!

A true medical tourism or health travel project consultant is one who can take time with the client and brainstorm about what the client possesses in its unique ingredients (its location, its resources, including leadership, investment capital and supply chain, among others) and helps the client to determine the flavor, texture, appearance (marketing, promotion) and the amount of cake to be baked, the anticipated consumers of the cake, the selling price of the cake in order to meet profit objectives, the quality of the cake, the safety of the ingredients' handling (eggs, salmonella, uh-oh, there goes my microbiology positive transfer again!).

I have personally consulted on more than 100 medical tourism projects, and many have called our specialized team of health administration, clinical, and tourism industry experts, and international hospital accreditation preparation experts in after the cluster bombed, but we have had to keep our impressions and opinions to ourselves, lest we appear unprofessional, or give rise to a threat of litigation for disparagement. Besides, what matters ultimately is if we can help the client recover from the mistake they made prior to engaging us?

One thing about me that you will find is that I am unrelenting in my directness and my approach to accountability. You are responsible adults and you made a business decision in your choice of consultant. There was no duress to choose them; you perceived value in your choice of consultants, evaluated their proposal, approved their contracted deliverable, hired them, followed their instructions, and probably got what you contracted for. There are no "victims" of consultants, rather there are poor decisions made on

- Relative value for money for the price of the consulting
- Failure to recognize the lack of legitimate authority and expertise
- Failures on "what to buy" as a deliverable
- The perceived prestige of the consultant's "brand or logo" affixed on reports and product marketing
- A host of other failures

In most cases, we have had to essentially rebuild the project in its entirety and redirect the scope and add functionality and business process, only we've had to do it with a smaller budget and sensitivity to the client's previous experience of having been "burned" by our predecessors. Sadly, some very promising projects have been abandoned because the financial devastation that resulted from the predecessor's burns were fatal and the organization did not have the financial means to undertake a "do-over."

Endnotes

1. According to music historian Joel Whitburn, the record first reached the *Billboard* magazine charts on March 3, 1950 and lasted 15 weeks on the chart, peaking at #1.
2. "Medical Tourism: Consumers in Search of Value," a 2008 report from the Deloitte Center for Health Solutions, part of Deloitte LLP, examines the growth of medical tourism, the hot spots for outbound and inbound programs and factors important to the attractiveness of both. http://www.deloitte.com/assets/Dcom-UnitedStates/Local%20Assets/Documents/us_chs_MedicalTourismStudy%283%29.pdf
3. http://www.mckinseyquarterly.com/Mapping_the_market_for_travel_2134
4. http://tinyurl.com/3jg68n3
5. A term used to describe the western United States during the period of its settlement, especially with reference to its lawlessness and absence of regulation or expected business protocols.

Acknowledgments

I am thrilled to wrap up this manuscript. It has been a labor of love for the industry, my colleagues, and you, my readers. My publisher, Kristine Rynne-Mednansky, has been patient beyond that which I deserve. She and the team at Productivity Press let me write, speak, travel, inspect hospitals, spas, and build Mercury Healthcare in parallel.

This subject is well known to me, not just from a theoretical standpoint, but from a practical standpoint. I have given hundreds of lectures, presentations, and webinars, and written numerous white papers, strategic plans for clients, and participated in consultations to more than 100 medical tourism projects. Making the commitment to write what I have learned, experienced, and witnessed was by far the hardest task. Sorting through my myriad experiences and choosing the most beneficial information has been a tremendous but worthwhile challenge. Therefore, putting these options in print is a task that I am glad is behind me.

Today's senior hospital executives are now articulating that this new business of medical tourism and health travel is upon us, and in a process of transformation that no government has really sorted out yet, no one hospital has developed all the answers, and no consulting firm or association is yet the official authority.

Somewhere along the way we've come to understand that this market change is now a permanent part of our lives, and one that is moving faster every day. No one can manage a business or plan a strategy without being able to anticipate where technology, demographics, and other transforming forces will lead us. Unfortunately, making successful forecasts, and anticipating successful business models has been a tough skill to learn, not only because the task itself is challenging, but because few specific resources have been available to help with the task.

That only the author gets to place her name on the book's cover is one of life's inequities. invariably there are many others whose contributions deserve equally public acclaim.

Robin Lloyd-Starkes, my skilled and patient editor at Productivity Press, whose guidance and encouragement were critical factors in bringing this effort to fruition.

Nick Brooks, MBA, MSc Fin, managing director of Mercury Healthcare, Ltd, in our London office, whose generosity in sharing his unique insights into the leisure, travel, and tourism industry helped to round out the tourism side of the subject matter. As a sounding board, he's come (kicking and screaming, mind you) to learn the healthcare side of the medical tourism industry. He and I coined a new definition for an acronym NaCL, which most of you know as table salt. We use it on familiarization (fam) tours of hospitals to mean "Not Another Cath Lab!").

Mark I. Bentkower, CISSP, who reviewed the chapter on Internet privacy and security for accuracy, and always stands ready to answer questions.

Lionel Bentkower, Mark's father, who is our resident expert on all things payment card industry data security standard (PCI) compliance, for his review of the chapter and pointing me in the direction of source materials for review.

Susanne Sapa, RN-BC, CCM, is a nurse, certified case manager and entrepreneur and medical tourism facilitator, whose help and counsel I respect and treasure.

Carol L. Boyer, RN (*deceased*) a dear friend since childhood and nurse whose counsel I treasured as our senior case manager. You were always there for me. I am saddened by your untimely and unexpected passing. I hear your voice in every case, every critical analysis, and I hear your compassion and patience and resolve when things get crazy. I promise to do my best by our patients as a tribute to you. I so wanted you to be there with us at the hour of our success. Thank you my dear friend.

No doubt many others should be listed here, and I apologize for their omission. My thanks to them all. Working with consultants can be just as challenging as working with physicians. Each is fiercely autonomous, busy, and has many priorities. Originally the book was proposed as a collaborative project involving 14 other authors. In the end, two, Lisa Beichl, MBA and Tracy H. Simons pulled through with their assigned chapters. I appreciate your contributions. Thanks, ladies!

Finally, I owe a debt of thanks to Alan Burch, MBA, my wonderful husband, partner, confidante, chief information officer, and strategist. He has traveled with me, stayed home as I traveled on business, fixed computers, written programs to automate data sorting for me, cooked dinners, washed clothes, and put up with my absence from our bed in the wee hours of the morning as I worked. He's watched TV alone at night, fed cats, made shopping lists, handled grocery shopping, run dry cleaning errands, tended my vegetable garden, and brought normalcy to my hectic life. He complained much less than most men would have through these last four books. I have just one more to write and then no more books for at least a year! I promise.

Introduction

Medical tourism and health travel are not just subjects for a book to me. My experiences as a patient, consumer, former surgical nurse, health administrator, and disaster management coordinator, and my work experience as a professional travel agent back in the 1970s have shaped and contributed to my orientation to patient safety, quality, service, and accountability.

This book has been a labor of love. It is a subject for which I have deep passion on several levels. I've been a patient and a victim of patient care that was "anything but" patient-centered, and in my opinion lacked compassion, quality, safety, and effective best practices. These events, over several years include

- On one occasion, I was awakened at 6:00 a.m. by a nurse who tried to inject me with my roommate's insulin. My name is Maria. Her name is Mary. In a half-awake stupor, I protested as my arm was being swabbed with an alcohol wipe for the injection. Why would a nurse give insulin without a finger-stick glucometry first, and an I.D. check?
- On another occasion, a covering physician came in looking like he'd been on an all-night drinking binge. Without introducing himself, he started pressing on my belly after surgery. That was tantamount to battery. He had no right to touch me without my consent.
- After an event of chest pain following extensive travel, I was subjected to an extensive diagnostic workup including cardiac angiography upon equivocal findings of some anomaly on a CT scan. In being interviewed by the nurse on duty and charged with my postprocedure pain management, she asked if I wanted pain medication to which I answered yes. She brought a syringe to my bedside that contained medication. When I questioned what it was, she stated rather condescendingly, "It's what your doctor ordered for you." When I insisted I be told what the name of the medication was, she told me. It was a drug to which I am allergic. When I asked why she would follow an order to inject a medication that I was allergic to, she stated, "Your doctor ordered it and I don't have time to review your chart." That particular hospital, part of a huge award-winning American chain of hospitals, accredited by a who's who of professional organizations and medical societies, has a website that touts its "strength" of putting patients first, as well as having top-notch personnel, cutting-edge techniques, superior facilities and an unparalleled level of care. Such marketing babble!

To err may be human, but that response from that nurse was downright unprofessional and dangerous. When I complained to hospital executives who are members of a professional association in which we are both members, they reacted poorly by responding that I shouldn't give my unsolicited opinion of corrective action plans.

After that experience, I sent registered mail to all my family's personal physicians with a directive to be placed in our charts that states, "If necessary, you are directed to use this hospital for stabilization only and then without delay please transfer us to a safer patient care environment if continued inpatient confinement is necessary." That hospital is also on a Mercury Healthcare "do not use" except in the case of absolute emergency list, and then the orders in the database are to arrange stabilization and transport out. Hell must freeze over before I will allow execution of a contract with that hospital for network inclusion. It competes with eight hospitals within a 10-mile radius, so rarely is there a reason to go there.

My Own Medical Tourism-Related Misadventure

On another occasion, while on a medical tourism familiarization tour in a foreign country, I acquired an infection that advanced so rapidly that I had to be admitted to hospital. Much to my chagrin, I had a chance to find out what the proletariat expatriate patients would be subjected to in the "non-VIP" section of the hospital. Not because I was uninsured. I had both major medical insurance with a Blue Cross Blue Shield® franchise and a travel illness and accident policy with HTH®, but because I needed to be on that floor for infection control. Never mind that each morning and afternoon, they hauled me across four huge buildings, to the ophthalmology department to visit the doctors in that department, exposing everyone we encountered along the way to the infection that it was necessary to control.

The Nursing Care

The nurses on any shift spoke no English, and I didn't speak their language (other than hello and thank you). I repeatedly asked for the light to be turned off, as I was photophobic, and the only switch on the wall was red, the international, "Don't touch this or you might accidentally call a Code," symbol, so the light remained on for three days. Another red flip-switch was over the sink outside the ensuite bathroom, but the toilet and shower area were dark, so I had to do my business in the dark for three days. That was actually funny because when the lights were sorted out, I could finally see the sign that advised me to call the nurse to avoid falls.

I was in pain and undermedicated, but the Wong–Baker* pain scale face pictographs were not available for use to let them know I needed more medicine. I was at about 8/10.

The Amenities

I was left in the bed for three days before a representative from the international department came back to check on me. Oh yes, I was given their business card, but it listed a mobile phone, and the bedside phone was restricted from calling mobile phones because in that country that costs extra.

Despite having a VIP ward and bragging about continental menus, I was fed local cuisine morning, noon, and night. I cannot tell you what it was lest I reveal the location. I can tell you that the hospital had a convenience store and a food court but the food court refused to sell to me, but was unable to articulate their reasons in English.

---

* From Wong D.L., Hockenberry-Eaton M., Wilson D., Winkelstein M.L., Schwartz P.: *Wong's Essentials of Pediatric Nursing*, 6/e, St. Louis, 2001, p. 1301.

During the familiarization (fam) tour, we inquired as a group about television broadcasts in English and were told, "Of course." I found out that each channel broadcasted a program here and there and then went back to local language, so I had to play the game of channel surfing to locate another program on another channel to be able to watch English speaking programs.

The room air conditioner was set at 25°Celsius (77°F) and could not be controlled by me. I was always too warm. I couldn't communicate with anyone to let them know that I wanted it cooler, so I woke up most nights drenched from perspiring under the covers and heavy hospital pajamas.

The hospitalwide Wi-Fi they bragged about during the familiarization tour didn't work in my proletariat room, and it wasn't until the nice man from international relations came to visit on my third day that I could even let my family know I was in the hospital. He stayed after hours and worked overtime to get me connected. Then I was finally able to communicate with friends and family via Skype®.

Medical Records

Also during the fam tour, I had inquired about the language of the medical records, and was told they would be translated to English for the patients. I was also reassured that my records would get home before I did via e-mail, so my doctor back home would be able to follow up with necessary aftercare. After 30 days, my hometown ophthalmologist was doing all he could to retain his composure as the infection was extremely recalcitrant; I was resistant to the antibiotics and we still had no records. When they finally arrived, they were in the other language.

Accreditation

All of these things happened in a JCI-accredited facility. But, having read the standards, much of what I encountered is not surveyed or required by JCI. Ask me what my opinion is of one brand of accreditation over another yawn and you will get the textbook facial expression for nonplussed. Still, I would reconsider this hospital for inclusion in our network if the situations I found were improved. I find it appalling, however, that most medical tourism facilitators include this hospital in their network, sight unseen, because its international department spokesperson and figurehead is an American physician and it is JCI-accredited. To me, in hindsight, it was a bill of goods. But what was worse is that when I had the chance to choose a hospital of the nine we visited in that country, I, too, independently chose that hospital, placing a high perceived value on both those features and its modern appearance for the parts of the hospital we were shown. Therefore, I cannot find too much fault with others in the medical tourism facilitation sector for doing likewise. They had the ingredients in raw form, but no fully developed product ready to sell.

The Journey Home

When it was time to travel home, the hospital was so far from the airport that I opted to book a hotel on the Internet that was adjacent to the airport, and had to take a taxi to the airport. The hospital left me to my own devices to get to the airport. I hired a taxi. Despite having an onboard global positioning system (GPS) in his taxi, he could not find this name-brand hotel that was closer than one mile from the airport terminal, and proceeded to drive around for well over an hour, in circles, with the meter running the entire time, until he called the hotel and had them guide us all the way to the front door, turn-by-turn.

I needed food and water, but he got me to the hotel so late that the restaurant was closed. My plan "B" was to forage for food in the concierge lounge, where I found…more local food. Oh well, a bottle of water and two Vicodin later, I didn't care anymore.

The next morning, I made my way on the hotel shuttle to the airport, only to find that the flight was cancelled. I had already given up my hotel room; the hotel was sold out so I had to find someplace else, and my business class, fly-flat, medically necessary seating arrangements were cancelled. In order to get a seat on an aircraft that had the fly-flat configuration, I had to wait another day. As a former travel agent, I knew what to do and how to make things happen, but I am horrified to think what would have happened if I had been just a layperson without the same training and experience.

My next challenge was hopping on a flight that was only a few hours to a much larger international hub, where I knew I could plead my case to someone to get me a fly-flat business class seat for the ride back to the States (now look, I am doing everything in my power not to tell you where I was, so quit trying to guess as it would embarrass their government medical tourism agency, the hospital, and many others!).

Airport Connections

During the airplane's preparation for landing in the United States, the changes in cabin pressurization caused the pain in my eye to crescendo to an unbearable level. I could not leave my seat on landing, so the staff had to call Customs onto the aircraft after the other passengers disembarked. I was in tears, with a cold compress over my eye. They authorized my re-entry into the country, and then had me taken off the aircraft on a stretcher by local ambulance and paramedics.

Having been a paramedic and firefighter earlier in my career, I know the drill. If they get you on the stretcher, they won't let you off without a big hassle. Besides, I was in indescribable pain, I was so upset that I could not help crying. The salt from my tears further irritated my red, painful swollen eye—not the best combination for paramedic negotiation—and the airline was not going to let me back on an aircraft anyway, so off to the local hospital I went.

Trip Interruption

On arrival at the local hospital, I was admitted to the emergency room, examined first by the emergency physician and second by the ophthalmologist who practiced in the medical office building across the street. I was given an injection of a large amount of hydromorphone for pain. I was then summarily discharged. Still wobbly, I was told to get my prescription filled at the local pharmacy two miles away. How?

Comparison: American Hospital Customer Service

Although I was stoned and walking funny, the nurse told me to "Get a hotel for the night." I only had foreign currency in my wallet. I had no personal vehicle, no one to call, a prescription to be filled, no luggage or fresh undergarments or personal toiletries, and had nothing to eat in several hours (opiates always make me hungry). I went to the gray-haired volunteer lady who was staffing the reception desk to beseech her for help. She handed me the telephone book and said she was too busy to help me. (There was not one other person in the waiting room!) I took a seat in the empty waiting room, and started searching for a hotel, a pharmacy, and a taxi service. Then, I reached for my cell phone. Dead! My cell phone battery died. Okay, now to ask the not so accommodating volunteer lady if I could use the telephone. She said it was against hospital policy to allow patients to use the telephones. My first thought was to say, "Okay lady, here are the numbers I need called!" but I didn't, after all she could have been my grandma! I had to show respect for my elders!

My negotiation training taught me to find a different way to phrase it but that if one does not ask, one does not get. So, I said something to the effect of, "Oh, I see. The problem I have (take ownership, it's not her problem) is that my cell phone has an exhausted battery and I cannot use it to make a call. I haven't any American currency to make a call from the public phone over there in the corner, because I was taken off the plane from an international flight by the paramedics, and I don't see a way to get any American currency. Would you be so kind as to make these brief telephone calls for me?"

Her answer: "I'm sorry, dear, but perhaps you can go to the automated teller machine (ATM) on the other side of the hospital and get some cash and then use the public phone."

"How far is the walk?" I inquired."

"Oh, it's a bit of a walk, as this emergency room is on one street, and the entrance of the hospital where the ATM is located is on the other street. You just have to follow the yellow line on the floor. It will be about a 10-minute walk."

Assuming an average walking speed of about 3 miles per hour, I would estimate a 10-minute walk to be about 2,600 feet, or roughly half a mile. Me—stoned drunk on narcotics, staggering, with a rollaboard suitcase and a computer bag in hand, and told to walk a half-mile or so because of a paper policy designed to maintain flow in a typically busy work environment, but that at the moment had no one but me present.

And then I saw it—no, it couldn't be—the really big, prideful banner, the one that says, "Congratulations to [name] hospital, voted in the Top 100 Hospitals' of Thomson Reuters' list of elite organizations that demonstrated high quality outcomes on key measures of clinical quality, efficiency, and patient satisfaction." Common decency prohibits me from writing the one word that flashed across my thoughts at that very moment.

So, I mustered one more sheepish smile and asked the lady nicely, "I am a bit wobbly from the narcotics they gave me for pain back in the treatment area. Is there someone who could take me to the ATM by wheelchair?" "Oh, I don't know, dear, I'd have to call someone" she said. At this point, I glared at her as if to say, "So why aren't you calling?" Perhaps her vision was impaired, because she didn't interpret my reaction and simply went back to the novel she was reading. So I asked, "Would it be terribly inconvenient for you to do that for me?"

About 30 minutes later, another volunteer came, wheelchair in hand, still nobody else in the waiting area. He surveyed the room, and then went to the volunteer to ask who needed the wheelchair. She pointed at me. He came closer, loaded me into the chair, placed my rollaboard on my lap, my computer bag on top of the rollaboard, and off we went. When we got to the ATM, it was out of order. At that point, I broke down in tears.

Failed in our mission, we headed back to the waiting area. The room was still empty, and she sat reading her book. (Now do you see why I don't want to tell you the name of this hospital? It would be sooooooo embarrassing for them!) The wheelchair pusher offloaded me into a chair. I opened my luggage, found my cell phone charger, found a wall receptacle, and plugged in my cell phone. Thirty minutes passed. The anesthetic effect of the pain medication, when injected, wears off sooner than tablets taken, and mine was starting to wear off. She was still reading, nobody came into their emergency room. (Perhaps the community knew something I didn't?) My cell phone had enough of a charge to be able to make my three calls.

First, I called the hotel. Did they have a room for me? The first two did not. The third not only had a room, but it offered a discount to people coming from that hospital. A Hyatt Regency with a $99 discount rate. I trusted I would be comfortable there and booked it. Next, I placed a call to the two local pharmacies. Did they have the medication I was prescribed? The first one, a CVS was out of stock. The second, a Walgreens, had the medication. I spoke with the pharmacist, told her my predicament, and asked if she could have it ready on arrival so that the taxi could simply wait for me. I also asked if she know of a nearby ATM close to their location. As luck would have it, my bank had a branch location in their parking lot and she had used it earlier that day and it had been in working order just hours before. Problems almost solved. Now to find a taxi to come and collect me.

I called a taxi company, spoke with the dispatcher, told them what I needed. In America, one can almost guarantee in most major cities, that taxi drivers come from elsewhere in the world and often have limited English proficiency. Therefore, I knew to tell the dispatcher the plan: ATM, pharmacy, wait for me, and on to the hotel. He communicated this to the driver in advance of the taxi's arrival. When the taxi arrived, he knew the itinerary, he spoke English, and he was pleasant. As he arrived and helped me with my suitcase and computer bag, the volunteer lady did not even look up from her book once to acknowledge my departure, say goodbye, good luck, or have a nice day. I was still the only one in that waiting room. Now it was completely empty.

We embarked on our planned itinerary, and as I sat in the rear seat of the taxi for the 10-minute drive ahead, my thoughts drifted to the advantage I had as an experienced civil defense disaster planner, medical tourism facilitator, logistical coordinator, informed and clinically trained patient, experienced traveler, and medical assistance case manager. Had it been someone else without all that training and experience, on narcotic medications, alone in a strange city, without local currency in a situation that required cash, and with a dead cell phone, would that person have been overwhelmed? What would have been their fate?

As for the hospital, here I was in America, in a major city, at a hospital closest to the international airport. Surely, I was not the first stranded, ill or injured passenger to be taken to their hospital. One would assume they were accustomed to this scenario, but given my experience, they either were not prepared, did not care, or I just encountered a volunteer and an emergency department nurse who were less than exemplary of my expectation (correct or incorrect) of a top-rated hospital. As I write this, they are also now pridefully boasting their designation by the Leapfrog Group as a "top hospital." It makes me think much less of both the Thomson Reuters' designation, the Leapfrog Group's designation, and the hospital's executive leadership and corporate culture.

I can tell you that I have witnessed better care, more compassion, more professionalism, and better efforts at patient delight and satisfaction at hospitals in poverty-stricken developing nations. Even more appalling was today's review of this particular hospital's website under the Services tab, where it says what almost every other hospital in the world's tab says: "When you visit one of our…campus locations you can expect to receive world class care. Expert physician specialists and caring clinical staff provide you with an exceptional health care experience."

I shudder to think that this hospital might solicit traveling patients for medical tourism or health travel, for it offers the requisite typical service lines of spine, cancer treatment, organ transplantation, cardiovascular, wellness, joint replacement, robotic and minimally invasive surgery, epilepsy surgery, and is also an externally designated bariatric center of excellence.

One thing is for sure, despite all these capabilities and accolades, I know that by established formally adopted policy, Mercury Healthcare will avoid this facility as an elective care option at all costs, because I initiated that policy and it will remain in effect for as long as I can exert influence on the company's operational policy. But, therein lies the heart of the matter: which hospitals should endeavor to develop a medical tourism or health travel program, how should the development be planned and implemented, and who will build a product that is good for the consumer, safe, and meant to thrive and financially survive?

As a final note on this epic, the hotel desk clerk was a young woman, probably in her early twenties, with a great deal of compassion. She registered me into the hotel, assigned a room, and then had a bellman assist me with what little luggage I had. Soon after I got settled in the room, I heard a knock at the door. It was a room service delivery person. She took it upon herself to order chicken noodle soup, hot tea, and a pitcher of water and have it sent to my room with her compliments. The following morning, the hotel shuttle drove me to the airport and I continued toward home.

The Aftercare

Thirty days and three follow-up visits passed before my ophthalmologist back home insisted that he receive the records from my hospital stay. I had been promised by the hospital that they would be e-mailed to me and likely arrive translated into English before I arrived home. When we received them a few days after my secretary called the hospital and complained, they were forwarded untranslated and therefore unintelligible and useless to my physician for my aftercare.

I have shared this epic not for amusement, but to commit to myself, this industry, and the patients that we hope to serve, that no one go through this unnecessarily, that we reduce medical errors, that we aim to deliver not satisfaction, but over-the-top customer delight, and that none of the healthcare professionals, administrators, and other stakeholders approach the responsibility of medical tourism program development with such cavalier attitudes.

Oh yes…one final jab…the foreign hospital is part of one of those aforementioned "clusters!"

Those for Whom This Book Is Meant

You ought to find this book useful if you match one or more of the following criteria:

- You are a hospital administrator or executive, service line manager, physician, or decision maker involved in medical tourism program development.
- You want a hands-on, practical guide to developing medical tourism health delivery systems in real-world projects. That's exactly what this book is all about.
- You're a hands-on learner, someone who gets a lot more out of interactive experimenting than from just reading a book. Despite the fact that this is indeed a book, it's been intentionally designed to let the reader "learn as if he or she were having a chat with the author."
- You've been meaning to work on the strategy and operational issues for some time now, but you keep putting it off because strategic planning is a large, complex subject, and you don't have a roadmap for how to get to the next level.

Those for Whom This Book Is Not Meant

■ You've never used or even seen or heard of medical tourism before. Although some basic terms are defined in the text, the assumption here is that the reader knows the basics of medical tourism, healthcare management, hospital administration, medicine, and business development. This book was not written with the beginner or lay medical tourism facilitator in mind.

■ You want to understand all of the subtleties of the theory of strategic planning, market research, and grasp the nuances of the process. There are now many books on the market that occupy that niche. The focus here is on demonstrating lessons learned that work.

■ You want a book that will tell you how to begin in medical tourism.

■ You've read my other works and hate the direct, accountable, personal, familiar tone I take in my writing. I promise you that my writing style has changed very little. It works for me and over 10,000 readers of my previous works.

Section I—Product Definition, Business Model, and Strategic Planning

In Chapter 1, I have defined medical tourism and briefly reviewed the stakeholders. We all know that medical tourism is a neologism (albeit a poor one) used to describe the scenario where a person leaves the place where they normally reside to obtain healthcare someplace else. It does not require cross-border healthcare; it can simply involve some amount of inordinate travel to access care, beyond the distance normally traveled to receive care locally. It is actually quite relative. For some places in the United States, care is inadequate within a 60-minute drive on paved roads, and the patient must travel to a city hours away by car or by air just to access routine primary care, and even farther to access specialty care. It is no different in some countries where care is inaccessible or inadequate for a variety of reasons.

Chapter 1 is a relatively short chapter, but necessary, because it reminds us of the origins of the marketplace and it points to its potential growth. Deloitte and McKinsey were not necessarily incorrect. I believe that the readers of those articles, for some unknown reason, perhaps read more into it and inferred that the numbers should have been interpreted as American patients, and then were disappointed that planeloads full of American medical tourists were not descending jet bridges in wheelchairs, on crutches, and with wrinkled faces, droopy jowls, crow's feet around their eyes, and saggy gluteal muscles wanting a cosmetic makeover.

Chapter 2—"Defining Your Medical Tourism or Health Travel Business Model" addresses the medical tourism program business model and strategy. I start out at the very fundamental level of what it is you wish to develop, offering a checklist of considerations including some preliminary thoughts on hospital accreditation, designation, certifications, and other award programs.

Chapter 3—"Succeeding with Bundled Pricing for Medical Tourism" details the fine points and pitfalls of pricing and billing.

In Chapter 4—"Integrated Health Delivery Systems," I've tried to explain the variations of integration and how they align with managed care systems and third-party reimbursement options that will eventually pay for health travel, although you may find resistance to insurers paying for "medical tourism."

In Chapter 5—"Calculating the ROI of JCI Accreditation" I include a critical opinion on branded hospital accreditations, and challenge readers to organize their thoughts with a questionnaire as the exercise. In this questionnaire, I assume that the reader has read the standards, and is attempting to make a commitment to undertake and fund one of a number of accreditation programs. The questionnaire guides the reader through some open-ended questions to require consideration on the return on investment (ROI) of international hospital accreditation through any particular program.

In Chapter 6—"Shaping and Managing Your Medical Tourism/Health Travel Product Offering," I continue my focus on marketing and product development. Here I discuss the shaping and managing of the medical tourism or health travel "product." Like determining what cakes you will sell in a bakery, you have to determine the recipe, texture, flavor, and uniqueness that make this yours and yours alone, not a replica product of what everyone else in the other bakeries both near and far offer for sale to the market.

In Chapter 7—"Planning and Conducting Familiarization Tours," I review two formats to be used for conducting fam tours. One is for facilitators who will manage the referrals of consumers, and the other is for managing the fam tour for insurers and employers who seek to contract with you through a network such as ours, or directly.

In Chapter 8—"Quality and Safety Transparency" my colleague Lisa Beichl, MBA, who is an esteemed affiliate member of our consultancy group discusses quality and safety transparency in medical tourism. Successful business enterprises typically provide smart solutions to fill a market demand. Lisa's background in healthcare, quality measurement, and documentation shine through in this chapter. Her background and work experience with Milliman and several global insurers can be appreciated in the undertones of the material presented in this chapter.

In Chapter 9—"Risk Management and Liability Mitigation in the Medical Travel Industry," my colleague Tracy H. Simons examines liability issues that medical tourism/health travel professionals must consider.

In Chapter 10—"Introduce Your Program to the Media," I explain proper marketing techniques that enhance the reputaton of your business.

Sustainable solutions not only meet market demand, but also provide high perceived quality. In healthcare, quality-focused and patient safety practices yielding positive medical outcomes have become the hallmark of successful hospital strategies. As hospitals consider expanding into the medical tourism market, transitioning from a traditional domestic strategy to global outreach requires a fundamental shift from a focus on purely domestic quality agendas to expand and include strategies that proactively address cultural bias, social/psychological preferences, travel constraints, and effective transitions of care to the locally based provider.

Section II—Collaboration with Other Parts of the Medical Tourism/Health Travel Supply Chain

In Chapter 11—"Working with Case Managers," I address some nuances I have found in working with registered nurse case managers and compare them to the skills sets of working with laypersons engaged as medical tourism facilitators.

Chapter 12—"The Comprehensive Role and Functions of a Medical Tourism Facilitator," is structured for the benefit of a medical tourism facilitator who may have purchased this book inadvertently, but also to benefit the internal medical tourism facilitator at a hospital or clinic who has been assigned the task of logistical coordination but has not been thoroughly trained or briefed on the role and duties. It will also be helpful for managers who must hire for the role, human resources professionals who must recruit and determine professional development activities for this role, and to characterize the ideal candidate in job advertisements and descriptions.

Chapter 13—"Privacy and Data Security Concerns in Medical Tourism and Health Travel," covers Internet privacy and security. Privacy is a bit of an Internet buzzword these days. Just as not everyone wants others to see what they buy at the local bakery, healthcare providers and facilitators are supposed to use reasonable commercial efforts to ensure that the data they transfer across the Internet are as secure as they should be. If you solicit business from countries all over the world, you may be subject to those companies' marketing and security regulations over the Internet.

Chapter 14—"Implications of U.S. Medical Tourism Facilitator Bankruptcy," covers a sensitive topic that I have now witnessed twice. This short chapter may actually save you considerable headaches and preserve revenue if you take these points into consideration when contracting with facilitators you don't know and haven't critically assessed.

Chapter 15—"Considerations in Working with Hotels," visits the issues associated with collaborating with hotels to provide noninstitutional accommodations to your health travel patients and their travel companions. Medical tourism programs that don't have their own serviced apartment facilities will find that they must collaborate with hotels on hotel room rates, resort fee waivers, booking incentives, and overall negotiation.

Chapter 16—"Ultimate Customer Service: A Collaborative Effort," the longest chapter in the book, covers ultimate patient satisfaction. There's very little customer delight in medical tourism, and the index is likely very low in healthcare service delivery overall. Across different interaction types and different channels, very few hospitals in medical tourism regularly delight customers. If they did, there would be numerous published studies, the legitimate media (not press releases and social media blog posts) would be echoing the findings, and customers and employers would be clamoring for appointments instead of fearful and apprehensive about the health travel and destination medicine complexes.

Section III—Niche Market Opportunities

Chapter 17—"Medical Tourism Growth Potential for the United States," is a chapter written primarily for the U.S. audience and meant to coincide with President Barak Obama's Executive Order for the National Export Initiative. American healthcare providers really need to learn about these opportunities and determine how they can best add a small strategy to take advantage of this cash opportunity.

Chapter 18—"Medical Tourism Benefit Introduction for U.S. Health Insurance Plans," is written primarily for the reader from outside the United States who is unfamiliar with all the promises and hyperbole about pricing, third-party payer uptake, and why the system seems to be moving so slowly.

Chapter 19—"Medical Tourism for U.S. Employer-Sponsored Health Benefit ERISA Plans" is a technically complex chapter, even for most U.S. healthcare organizations to grasp, and just as daunting for insurance agents and brokers in the employer benefits markets. It is in this arena that I expect the market will be for the greatest growth in third-party reimbursement, employer benefit uptake, and where the competitive efforts of the healthcare delivery complex will be most appreciated if a layer of middlemen do not jump in and eliminate (or pocket) the savings and never allow the market to realize the benefits of true competitive behavior.

Chapter 20—"Health Travel Conceptual Challenges for ERISA Health Benefit Plan" addresses why employers resist and what it will take for them to be more receptive to health travel.

Chapter 21—"U.S. Retiree Health and the Challenges of GASB 45 Regulations," addresses another technical dilemma in American Healthcare for early retirees of state and municipal employers.

Section IV—Wellness and Medical Tourism

Chapter 22—"Wellness and Medical Tourism," acknowledges the wellness industry's role in medical tourism and health travel, as well as the idiomatic, cultural and historical differences in the approach to the word "wellness." I expect to see great things in true "medical tourism" industry growth for the wellness sector. I've also included a glossary of terms that has been helpful to our staff and also to the wellness providers who have experienced difficulty in translating the service and treatment descriptions.

PRODUCT DEFINITION, BUSINESS MODEL, AND STRATEGIC PLANNING

1

Chapter 1

Defining Medical Tourism and Its Stakeholders

Few terms in the English language (or several others for that matter) generate as many dumb-founded looks as the term "medical tourism" when uttered by a speaker to the average person or to a crowd of people outside this niche industry. Although the practice of traveling for healthcare, wellness, or specialty treatment available outside of one's hometown is not new at all, the term "medical tourism" is a *neologism* (a newly coined term, word or phrase, that may be in the process of entering common use, but has not yet been accepted into mainstream language).

Medical tourism (also called medical travel, health tourism, health travel, and global health-care, among other terms) is a term attributed to the popular news media, and some travel agencies that package wellness and medical spa vacations and holidays, primarily throughout Europe.

The term describes this rapidly growing practice of traveling away from one's hometown, where the de novo departure is often but not always across international borders, and made for the specific reason of obtaining necessary or elective health treatment, diagnosis, wellness services, medical spa services, participation in clinical drug therapy or treatment trials, avoiding long waits to access care or services in one's hometown, seeking care under cover of privacy and anonymity, and sometimes simply just a second opinion from key opinion leaders (KOLs) of world renown.

Medical tourism as a neologism is problematic because the standard definition of tourism in basic terms is generally interpreted as a collection of activities, services, and industries that deliver a travel experience comprising transportation, accommodation, eating and drinking establishments, retail shops, entertainment businesses, and other hospitality services provided for individuals or groups traveling away from home.

The first definition of tourism was made by Guyer Feuler in 1905 and although the practice of leaving home to obtain care or treatment or to visit a thermal water spa was not new then, I doubt he had this particular word pair in mind. Neither did the World Tourism Organization (UNWTO/OMT), a specialized agency of the United Nations and the leading international organization in the field of tourism. It serves as a global forum for tourism policy issues and a practical source of tourism know-how. and its membership includes 154 countries, 7 territories, and over

400 affiliate members representing the private sector, educational institutions, tourism associations, and local tourism authorities. The UNWTO defines tourism by three characteristics and states that not all travel is tourism. In order to prevent the discord in defining *tourism,* UNWTO defined it as: "Tourism comprises the activities of persons traveling to and staying in places outside their usual environment for not more than one consecutive year for leisure, business, and other purposes."

Tourism is different from travel. In order for tourism to happen, there must be a displacement: an individual has to travel, using any type of means of transportation (he might even travel on foot: nowadays, it is often the case for poorer societies, and happens even in more developed ones, and concerns pilgrims, hikers. and the like). But not all travel is tourism.

Three criteria are used simultaneously in order to characterize a trip as belonging to tourism. The displacement must be such that

- It involves a displacement outside the usual environment.
- Type of purpose: the travel must occur for any purpose different from being remunerated from within the place visited: the previous limits, where tourism was restricted to recreation and visiting family and friends are now expanded to include a vast array of purposes.
- Duration: only a maximal duration is mentioned, not a minimal. Tourism displacement can be with or without an overnight stay.

Medical tourists or travelers typically seek elective procedures as well as many complex specialized surgeries such as joint replacement, cardiac procedures, dental procedures, bariatric surgery, and cosmetic surgeries. Pretty much every type of healthcare including psychiatry, addiction, alternative medicine treatments, and even convalescent and suicide tourism services are also available. For example, if one is seeking to end long-term suffering one might travel to certain places in Europe that will provide assisted suicide services to the medical traveler who seeks dignity in death and may not be permitted to take action on such a decision legally in her own country. Assisted suicide for noncitizens, under certain conditions, is provided by Dignitas in Switzerland.[*]

In fact more than 50 countries have identified an interest or a commitment to medical tourism as a component of their national industry and export scheme. Their capabilities, quality, and service offerings vary greatly. Some destinations are advanced—with modern infrastructure, communications, and facilities—whereas others may lack decent roads to the facilities, modern treatment facilities, and may even be hazardous or dangerous for medical tourists considering them.

At the time of this writing, my company has been executing contracts with healthcare providers since 2003 for our Worldwide Wellness Adventure™ product (a medical checkup paired with adventure or leisure travel) in most of the countries listed in Table 1.1.

Although medical tourism may not be new in concept or practice, the industry as a whole and its medical providers as well as customers in recent years have faced much criticism, suspicion, and curiosity by the media, third-party insurance payers, the legal community, and even medical specialty trade associations who would seek to besmirch providers of their same specialty when located in another country.

---

[*] http://www.assistedsuicide.org/suicide_laws.html

Table 1.1 Countries with Worldwide Wellness Adventure™ Contracts

Africa and the Middle East		
Egypt	Kuwait	Tanzania
Israel	Mauritius	United Arab Emirates
Jordan	South Africa	
The Americas and Caribbean		
Argentina	Colombia	Mexico
Barbados	Costa Rica	Panama
Brazil	Cuba	Peru
Canada	Dominican Republic	United States
Chile	Jamaica	Uruguay
Asia/Pacific		
Australia	South Korea	Philippines
China	Malaysia	Singapore
Fiji	Maldives	Taiwan
Hong Kong	New Zealand	Thailand
India	Pakistan	Vietnam
Europe		
Belgium	Germany	Romania
Croatia	Hungary	Russia
Cyprus	Lithuania	Slovakia
Czech Republic	Netherlands	Sweden
Estonia	Norway	Turkey
Finland	Poland	
France	Romania	

Global Outsourcing of Medical Care Is and Has Been an Industry for Decades

Those who would describe it as "nascent" have some explaining to do if they use the word to describe an embryonic or start-up phase. Tell it to the ancient Romans who established Bath, England about 90 miles west of our London office. The city was first established as a spa resort with the Latin name, *Aquae Sulis* ("the waters of Sulis"), by the Romans in 43 A.D. although verbal tradition suggests that Bath was known before then. The Romans built baths and a temple on the surrounding hills of Bath in the valley of the River Avon around hot springs, which are the only ones naturally occurring in the United Kingdom. Much later, it became popular as a spa resort during the Georgian era and is currently a major center for tourism, with over 885,000 overnight guest visitors and 3.6 million day visitors to the city each year.* Similar statistical references can be argued for most cities with thermal waters present, and for developing nations where for decades, due to unavailable or inaccessible care for reasons of undeveloped infrastructure, local medical care has been sourced from other areas outside the patients' hometowns.

Even in the United States, health travel, not remotely associated with "tourism" whatsoever, has been ongoing for a number of years. Examples of this include patients who travel to specialty centers of world renown, such as Sloan-Kettering Institute for Cancer Research, M.D. Anderson Cancer Center, Cleveland Clinic, Mayo Clinic, and similar facilities. When a family member is ill or injured necessitating a trip to a specialty clinic of this nature, rarely are the family members in any frame of mind to go sightseeing, visit museums, amusement parks, or other attractions.

As a young travel counselor in the 1970s for the East Florida Division of the American Automobile Association at its Miami headquarters, I was requested to plan travel for road trips, flights, and rail trips involving the Auto Train, an 855-mile (1,376 km) long scheduled train service for passengers and their automobiles operated by Amtrak between Lorton, Virginia (near Washington, D.C.) and Sanford, Florida (near Orlando).

Requests would be fulfilled for itineraries to detail the routes for senior citizens in need of rapid denture repairs and denture appliances that could be prepared overnight in Florence, South Carolina. Routings would take families to the various aforementioned centers of excellence (COEs) to take a sick relative or child for evaluation and diagnosis, second opinions, or alternative treatment strategies from a far-away specialist who might bring hope, last chance therapies, clinical trials, and technology unavailable in the area in which they resided.

Medical tourism, or as I like to describe it, health travel, is still essentially a niche market. This means that there are subsets of individuals interested in, or with effective incentives to explore medical care abroad. Individuals with fewer jobs that offer healthcare benefits, companies downsizing and outsourcing to foreign lands, and more entrepreneurs with fledgling start-ups who have no money for expensive private health insurance policies, add to the population of seniors seeking affordable alternatives to services not covered under Medicare. The uninsured and underinsured seek care from outside their hometown for additional reasons that include affordability as well as the aforementioned, and also for privacy. Sometimes the privacy is for vanity reasons. ("My dear, you look so well rested after your vacation!") Sometimes it is for other privacy reasons (pregnancy outside of wedlock, weight-loss surgery, gender-reassignment surgery, etc.).

Health travel is an important option for both boundary (domestic and neighbor markets) as well as distant (farther away physically and culturally) patients. In the United States, the high quality of specialized medical care and the relatively rapid access to medical care may outweigh the cost obstacles and provide an important value proposition to inbound and cross-country/cross-market domestic health travel patients. In other markets, high quality may be paired with lower cost, and rapid access, and early adoption of certain technologies yet unavailable in the United States. According to a 2009 Gallup Poll report, up to 29% of Americans would consider traveling abroad for treatments including heart bypass surgery, hip or knee replacement, plastic surgery, cancer diagnosis and treatment, or alternative medical care.†

When coupled with the increasing uses of telemedicine, the growth of U.S. hospitals expanding into markets abroad, and the general increases in medical costs, there are opportunities for

---

* "Visit Bath." Statistics, *Value of Tourism*. Retrieved 31 December 2011.
† Gallup survey, reported May 18, 2009. "Americans Consider Crossing Borders for Medical Care" (www.gallup.com/poll/118423/Americans-Consider-Crossing-Borders-Medical-Care.aspx)

countries and hospitals worldwide to provide high-quality medical care at competitive costs. Indeed, medical tourism is advantageous to developing health markets in nations outside the United States and also to critical access hospitals in rural America, where educational standards and hometown culture and hospitals are high and labor costs are lower than big cities within the United States.

The same arguments can be made for other nations outside the United States. Adjacent neighbor markets across national borders as well as from other parts of the same country have a higher likelihood of generating volume and revenues for hospitals and other medical providers than distant target markets from the United States, Canada, and the United Kingdom, or from markets in the Middle East, where care is less accessible.

Although analysts and public health officials express concern that active promotion of medical tourism may pull resources from the public sector, facilities across the United States have little choice but to reassess market strategies to attract revenues from markets who can make good use of excess capacity at the local rural hospital and pay for that care, perhaps better than the public health reimbursement fee schedules, even if it means attracting that market share away from other competing rural access hospitals who haven't quite caught on to the concept of traveling for care.

Competing in the Global Marketplace, Even if It Is from the Rural United States

To compete in the global marketplace, hospitals everywhere seek and maintain accreditation from their regional and international accrediting bodies, they participate in international medical travel meetings, and continue to create awareness of their products through media opportunities, press releases, informative feature articles, and other marketing and promotional channels. The biggest mistakes that U.S. hospitals make in this niche market are

- Underestimating the market potential
- Undervaluation of their potential role in the national or global marketplace
- Ignoring educational opportunities to learn about market developments and new strategic ideas from thought leaders in the industry (from a false sense of security or overconfidence?)
- Hoping against hope that things will return to "business as usual"
- Thinking that healthcare reform will solve everyone's problems and Americans will once again regain the loyalty that they once demonstrated to the local town physician and his or her one and only hospital where she or he maintained staff privileges

From my vantage point as a healthcare executive working daily on issues surrounding the global marketplace, I also see similar mistakes being made by hospitals outside the United States, namely:

- Overestimating the market potential of the United States, Canada, and the United Kingdom
- Overestimation of the importance attributed to lower prices for care
- Failure to do due diligence on the actual prices being paid in the United States (where again, the popular media show ignorance in insight about paid versus billed charges) and failure to do due diligence on access cues and delays in the United Kingdom and Canada and Australia
- Also ignoring educational opportunities to learn about market developments and new strategic ideas from thought leaders in the industry

- Hoping against hope that everyone will realize their value without targeted and accurate, idiomatically correct messaging
- Believing that healthcare reform will create so many problems for access to care in the United States that Americans will come running to the less expensive, more accessible markets for care

Whatever the location or the provider orientation, successful promotion of health travel and medical tourism products, such as wellness travel and medical spa tourism, links a potentially strong market demand assessment to a value proposition that can be effectively promoted at the country as well as hospital-/physician-/spa-specific level.

Chapter 2

Defining Your Medical Tourism or Health Travel Business Model

This second chapter begins with a nod to the stakeholders in the medical tourism industry. Medical tourism is a service industry and our primary role is to be of service to the patients for whom care should be centered. The hospitals, physicians who admit patients to them and perform services through those hospitals and surgery centers, as well as dentists and alternative health providers, are all additional clinical stakeholders in the system and their role is to be of service.

The next chapter, and then all throughout the book, observations and comments are repeatedly touched on as well as some critical opinions surrounding the myths, realities, and values of some rating and accreditation bodies in healthcare, and the many options available from which to become accredited for patient quality and safety.

Later chapters integrate even more stakeholders and address the concerns of insurance providers and employers, who are just now beginning to examine the options and cost savings available for medical travel and are two subcategories of that group: self-employed individuals, who seek high value for their money as well as high-quality healthcare and wellness maintenance, so that they can continue to work as entrepreneurs rather than spend time in the health delivery system for the patient, and early retirees affected by regulation GASB-45.

It would be remiss to overlook the stakeholder roles of government ministries of public health, economy, tourism, and foreign export. These stakeholders need to be concerned with numerous health policy and sustainability implications in the local setting as well as infrastructure concerns. My colleague, Blair Gifford, PhD, at the University of Colorado, has conducted extensive sociological research on the impressions of physicians in for-profit, private, and teaching institution hospitals about medical tourism and its impact on local community resources, and "brain drain" (where physicians leave the public health system in favor of higher pay in the private sector, and the potential for world renown). There are tremendous implications for public health when a health travel patient with a communicable disease attempts to enter the country to receive elective treatment, for which policies have to be established for the safety of the local citizens.

As associate stakeholders in the industry, later in the book a discussion is woven in about underwriters, actuaries, brokers, and insurance agencies, as well as benefit design consultants whom I have had the pleasure of knowing, and to understand more about how they interpret this whole medical tourism health delivery system and how it will affect their calculations, estimations, client curiosity, and satisfaction. Also discussed are some of the concerns voiced by employer self-funded health benefit plan administrators who operate health benefit programs under the rules and regulations of the Employee Retirement Income Security Act of 1974 (ERISA).

But now, I want to jump a bit ahead. I don't want to belabor the stakeholder roster; it's a matter of including these key roles as internal and external customers in your business model and strategy. You are about to enter the planning stage to open your private cake bakery.

What kind of cake should you bake (cake flavor, texture, shape, type, and other characteristics)? What will your program offer to the marketplace? Let's hit the ground running with a high-level checklist to direct your thoughts more effectively. Start by completing the questions below.

Market Survey

Your Location: _____

1. Countries within three hours' commercial flight distance from your location (bakery options).
2. For each country listed above, identify at least three reasons (per country) why their citizens are currently "noncustomers" of your product. (What cakes are not being served at each bakery and why are they unavailable?)
3. Identify at least three similarities across the countries listed. (What's missing from all of them?)

Now let's refine the product a bit more by adding more knowledge about ingredients and how they work in cake-baking chemistry. Of the cakes previously identified as missing from the shelves, that you have decided are viable choices:

1. What technology, programs, etc. (ingredients) do you have ready and on hand?
2. What physicians, technicians, therapists, etc. (bakers) are available and idle, with excess capacity?
3. What is the cost of having idle excess capacity of the ingredients? (Drugs expire and have to be discarded, technology becomes outdated often before it is paid for, bored and underutilized physicians and therapists leave for busier more interesting places where the patients and cases are more available, etc.)
4. Which ingredients integrate easily with other ingredients?
5. Which ingredients are too different to pair up with others because their flavor is overpowering, their texture is a bad match, or their acidity or neutrality creates a negative synergy when paired with its partner ingredients?
6. Which types of these cakes take:
   - Too much investment to make or to buy
   - Too much time to create
   - Too much cost to learn the recipe and practice to perfection and market readiness
   - Too many expensive ingredients

Now fill in this blank:

To turn these non-cake purchasers into our cake customers, we should meet the following market deficiencies or needs:

_____

_____

_____

At this point, you should have a high-level idea of what it is you want to build from the available medical tourism product choices that the market is missing.

The key here is to begin thinking about continuity of care as you design this purpose-built business model. Health travel and medical tourism do not occur in a vacuum. In order to build a nationally or internationally integrated health delivery system, one has to address quality documentation and accreditation, and provider credentialing and privileging (which actually has its own chapter farther along in the book). I have also included chapters on the marketing of the network, service line development, and some of the revenue cycle implications with third-party reimbursement systems.

As you build your strategy and business models, don't forget the minutiae as they can make or break your success and your reputation with payers who can steer volumes to or away from you. In insurer and employer settings, it will be necessary to address and build policies and procedures to handle the international implications of preauthorization and precertification, billing, coding, claims submission, and follow-up for services rendered to insured patients whose plan includes a benefit design for healthcare accessed outside their home country. You will also need to address potential insurance claim denials and appeals, and the implications associated with attempting this tedious process across state and national borders. You'll need to address disparities in local standards of care that may be different from those where the patient resides. Also, you will need to have your talking points organized to address the issues and questions surrounding internationally accepted evidence-based medicine as it relates to procedures deemed investigational and experimental in one country, but which may be commonplace in another. Along that same line, be prepared to incorporate discussions about technology that may be new for some providers and commonplace for others, and the actuarial implications associated with payment for those services that an insurance plan may not have included in its risk assumptions for claims cost and benefit design.

As for revenue cycle implications, you will need to have a strategic plan to deal with either outsourcing or internally training revenue management staff and addressing billing software, forms management, and claims submission to distinctly different reimbursement systems found throughout the world.

This approach to the subject matter is not necessarily United States-centric, but instead global, thus it has a heavy emphasis on the complex and costly U.S. healthcare reimbursement system. However, make no mistake, the U.S. system is under tremendous overhaul. Mind you, I have zero confidence that it will become less problematic, therefore, it is by no means the sole focus for preparation by international hospitals endeavoring to develop a medical tourism program that is global in nature. As you target patient referrals from all over the world, keep this in mind; I am not basing everything on "how we do it in the United States."

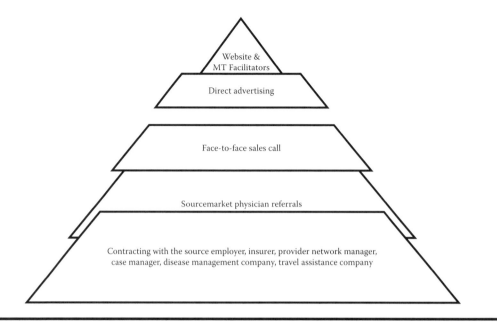

Figure 2.1   Referral steering options.

Additional Product Applications

In addition to health travel clients, there are a variety of others that are often "lumped" together as medical tourist statistics, which many believe should not be comingled statistically, including, but not limited to: retirees living outside a home country, travelers who are injured while abroad, employees from your country deployed internationally, expatriates from an employer in another country, immigrants who may return home for a visit and receive medical care in a familiar (and typically less expensive) environment, and even students or religious missionaries studying abroad. Assessing the market demand for one country over another takes many forms.

Which ones will you choose to target? Why? How will you let them know you are open to receive them? By what means will you influence steering to you? The most popular methods are shown in Figure 2.1 with their corresponding levels of influence.

Sources of Medical Tourism Referrals

The business of medical tourism referrals includes many stakeholders, namely:

■ Word of mouth from consumers
■ Physicians
■ Direct advertising efforts by the providers themselves
■ Web developers and Web-based directories
■ Medical tourism facilitator companies
■ Insurers, employers, case managers, and other provider network managers

Independent medical tourism facilitator performance varies widely. Because most of them rely upon their websites to attract clients, most have been ineffective in steering significant volumes. In face-to-face interviews with leading hospital executives throughout India, Malaysia, Thailand, Korea, Mexico,* and other popular and highly publicized destination markets, one resounding echo not seen in the popular press or trade association articles was the low success rate of their relationships with facilitators in realizing patient referrals. Most offered that their referrals from medical tourism facilitators were low (2–4 cases per month/per facilitator) and that the number of facilitators that actually referred successful conversions were fewer than five in all cases. In all cases, prior to asking these questions, we agreed that those classes of international patients listed previously would be eliminated from the mix, only taking into consideration those patients whose de novo departure was specifically to access healthcare on an elective, nonurgent, or emergent basis at their hospital from another community far enough away to require travel by car, plane, bus or other mode of transportation, for a travel duration of at least three hours.

My experience in hospital revenue cycle management and health administration led me to ask two other revealing questions about

1. Their average daily inpatient census (indicating excess capacity for sale to health travel patients)
2. Percentage of average daily net inpatient revenue from health travel patients

The first question enabled me to make educated assumptions as to how eager they might be to develop this market to fill gaps in capacity. Although a better indicator might have been to focus on particular service lines that the hospital has strategically chosen to develop and feature. That information would have been much harder to answer without deeper research on the executives' part. It is also extremely proprietary and could be considered particularly intrusive and sensitive, creating market vulnerabilities if the information landed in the wrong hands. Because our relationships were too new, and they had no compelling reason to trust me with such sensitive data, I dared not ask and run the risk of offending them in any way. I wish to acknowledge and thank them for their cooperation and candor.

The second question was one that I often use as a means to determine how strong their commitment might be to investing assets, resources, time, alternative billing and revenue cycle practices, and so on, in order to expand the business. Most attributed less than one-half of one percent (in many cases far less!) to medical travel revenue, based on the agreed-upon definition (de novo elective departure) described above. I view the gap between those two points as the entrepreneurial opportunity for the provider. The problem is, most of them seem to establish a "red ocean"† strategy of competing in the same service lines of bariatrics, cardiac care, orthopedics, cancer, and cosmetic surgery. I still shake my head as I reflect on their choices, given so many other viable and yet unexploited service line options.

As a healthcare executive whose business revolves around channeling larger books of business to select hospitals throughout the world, this important size-up question is important, because if there is no commitment to accommodate the billing format preferences of third-party payers, self-funded employer trust plans, and privately insured expatriates, I have a tough decision to make regarding their network participation. Do I accept them into the network and only steer a very low volume of consumer business to them and risk appearing no different from every other health travel facilitator, or do I accept them into the network and know in the back of my mind that we

---

* On site, telephonic, and Internet VOIP interviews (January 2011) ($n = 30$).
† A term used in the Blue Ocean strategy which refers to, among other features, competing in an existing market space.

will always have to commit our corporate resources and absorb the incremental direct costs of converting their bills, coding nomenclature, billing formats, and translated medical records supporting documentation into acceptable formats that our clients will accept and process for payment within the contractually stated timely payment terms?

The realities here are that the former reduces my leverage to request and receive preferential pricing terms and other accommodations. The latter puts the provider in a category that makes me less likely to refer him to our clients because my margins are thinner, my labor more intense and costly, and the likelihood of delays in payment, errors in processing, and other hassles that erode the relationship and reduce internal customer satisfaction for providers and payers (and our staff) increase significantly with higher volumes. Standing before that hospital executive as a peer or colleague, I cannot, with a straight face, expect any other response in requesting a commitment of more intense resources, advanced staff training, or new software applications when the incremental direct revenue from that particular line of business is so low.

On the other hand, if excess capacity exists and incremental revenue is low, and I can approach the executive with a direct request from an employer or insurer and state with firm commitment that the employer or insurer wants to buy 5,000 executive checkups over the next year at a price of "*x*," the executive is all ears and ready to deal. Are those executive checkups health travel clients? Yes, if they are derived from a source market that meets the criteria for health travel. Do they have any incremental value other than the revenue from the checkup? Absolutely! They have the ability to influence purchasing with their company for future services (steering potential) and they may choose to deal with any problematic findings or add additional services to their checkup package (colonoscopy, golf performance or other sports medicine clinic services, antiaging therapies, genetic and molecular biology/personalized medicine testing, etc.).

While in India, I was told by one marketing person from a large hospital that they only offer the checkup package as an up-sell to health travel companion travelers as "something to occupy their waiting time" because there is "so little revenue potential in it." How shortsighted! But…that's fine, that's their strategy. They are entitled to it, and I defend their right to maintain that strategy.

MBA School Mantra: It's Not the Results That Matter, It's the Interpretation of Those Results

Actually, that brings up a good point to raise here as we discuss building a strategy. When individuals and corporate decision makers are confronted with new experiences, they need to bring these experiences into line with their concept of self (identity). To do this, they might:

- Explore the new experience, categorize and accept it, and then relate it to their concept of self (accommodation).
- Ignore the new experience or part of it, because it may conflict with their concept of self (deletion, self-deception).
- Alter the new experience until it fits into their concept of self (assimilation, distortion, generalization).[*]

---

[*] Richard Bandler and John Grinder (1975): *The Structure of Magic 1. A Book About Language & Therapy*. Palo Alto, CA: Science and Behavior Books.

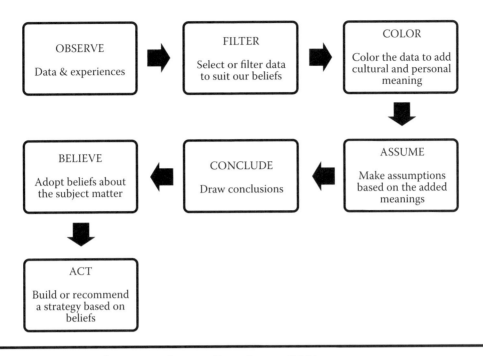

Figure 2.2 How we shape mental maps. (From Senge, 1994.)

These mechanisms of information processing (simplification, categorization, deletion, distortion, and generalization) can be observed on a day-to-day basis. "The map is not the reality." The famous quote of Alfred Korsybski is now supported by the results of neurobiological research on cognition and neuronal data processing. Peter Senge has described the "Ladder of Inference" which is based on the inner confidence that "Our map of the reality is the truth," and "The truth is obvious" as a sequence of cognitive steps:[*]

1. We receive data through our senses (observation).
2. We select data from what we observe (filter, subtraction).
3. We add meaning to the data (color, augmentation).
4. We draw assumptions on the basis of the selected data and the meaning we added.
5. We adopt beliefs (mental models) about the reality and continue to select data (as per step 2 that correspond to these beliefs.
6. We act upon our beliefs.

In the last 12 years, researchers have documented in detail how the processes of social influence shape our mental maps (see Figure 2.2).

> The impact of a message depends both on its content and style and on the individual motivations and characteristics of those exposed to it. Experimental studies have revealed, for example, that persuasive efforts that present thoughtful, detailed arguments can be very

---

[*] Peter Senge et. al. (1994), p. 243.

effective in changing people's attitudes but only if the audience has the knowledge and motivation to comprehend, scrutinize, and evaluate the message…. People consciously and unconsciously process their experiences in accord with pre-existing views (or filters) of reality. Because these views are unique to individual social histories, each person interprets reality in a distinct way and responds differently to events.[5]

How does this relate? Let's go back to the cake-baking analogy. I observe a durian fruit, with its thorny surface and its awful smell. I've never eaten a durian before, so I have no frame of reference by which to compare the taste. I do know that it smells like stinky feet. It looks like mush inside, and there are signs in many places in Asia that say "no durian" on the same sign that prohibits smoking, eating, drinking, or flammable goods (see Figure 2.3). Many others have heard the same message, and have never tasted the fruit. We all share a common bond of being inexperienced with the taste of durian but we have an opinion of it just the same; accurate or inaccurate, our beliefs are our realities.

You have decided that your market strategy is to fill an identified gap of durian fruit cakes that exists in the market. You create a message to describe how they taste, why we should buy them from you, and the compelling nutritional advantages of purchasing your freshly baked durian fruit cake.

I read your message, I filter the message, color it, and then make assumptions, regardless of accuracy. I draw my conclusions, adopt my beliefs about the value purchasing opportunity, including utility and cost, and then take action. The result is what is important here. Do I purchase your cake or not?

Now let's apply this to health travel. Assume that I have never had treatment in your country, at your hospital. Assume that I am like many other Americans in that I don't even have a valid passport, in fact, I've never had a passport. I don't speak other languages, have not traveled, and in fact, in my past (my reality) I've never even had surgery before. I also don't know anyone who has personally been to your country or required service from your hospital, so I have no way to receive recommendations from people whose opinions I trust. Regardless of what your social network comments, ratings, and other influencer scores might be, I'm not buying a book on Amazon.com; I am considering allowing someone to cut into my body, take parts out, and fix me. What strategy will you use to take me from being a noncustomer to a customer?

Figure 2.3 "No Durian" sign.

Many use accreditations, emblems, awards, certifications, designations, and other forms of external vetting as a part of that strategy, perhaps incorrectly assuming that it conveys a meaningful message to the receiver.

From my previous comments about some of the certifications, designations, and accreditations, you have probably surmised that I don't place much stock in them. Most hospital executives don't either. They know that these systems are simply emblems for which the market clamors, but only because certain louder voices either assume or have something to gain for advancing the market recognition of the emblem.

For instance, when I see a reference to the *MTQUA Top 10 World's Best Hospitals*™ or the golden lookalike to the JCI emblem of the Medical Tourism Association's logo, I am nonplussed. In the latter example, one pays a check to be a member and gets a license to use the logo. That's fine, there's nothing wrong with it, but what's the point of the message conveyed by the logo being posted on your branding and marketing materials? I don't see every doctor's office placing the AMA logo on their marketing materials, although most U.S. physicians are members. I don't see most hospitals placing the Healthcare Financial Management Association's (HFMA) logo on their materials, nor any of the other associations in which they hold active membership. Why do hospitals (mostly those outside the United States) post the MTA logo on their materials?

In the former, a self-declared "leading medical travel facilitator and health tourism expert" published a list of hospitals, and then upon being interviewed (challenged) by Ian Youngman of the *International Medical Travel Journal* (*IMTJ*) soon after publication, basically explained,

> We are not a research company so there was no thought of conducting a rigorous statistical review and comparing empirical data in determining the Top 10 World's Best Hospitals for medical tourists. We did not do a survey, nor are we pretending to have done one. Rather we focused on the surrounds that make up the elements of a successful medical journey in medical and personal terms for the traveling patient.

She went on to say that (at that time, 2010) "We considered probably most of the hospitals that are promoting themselves as destinations for medical tourists. How many were seriously considered? A much smaller number, about 40 to 50."

I can name over 50 countries, each with hospitals promoting medical tourism at that time, which tells me that she wasn't even truly aware of the depth and breadth of the market. Again, what she did was not illegal, immoral, or unethical. It was free enterprise at its finest. She published her opinion. Another example of the wild, wild west! Time will remedy this for our industry, but expect more of it in the near term.

Like it or not, in an unregulated market with a free informal but global press known as the Internet, she published her press release and let the readers come to their own conclusions. She may not have been forthcoming about her apparent lack of formal healthcare or travel industry expertise and experience, or professional training[*] (there is wide latitude in medical tourism facilitator expertise; I met one facilitator who had been a truck driver only six weeks prior who was seeking contracts with providers at an MTA event!) she possessed to make such proclamations, but she didn't really have any requirement to do so.

As for the hospitals that publish this designation or award on their website, they take the risk that the market might ignorantly translate that award and recognition as credible and valuable, or an even greater risk that the market might ridicule that hospital for including it in its

---

[*] LinkedIn profile, accessed May 31, 2011 (http://www.linkedin.com/in/juliemunro)

establishment of a reputation, or feel duped if they trust it at first and then find Ian's interview after they booked and paid for their package, having placed their trust in that *Top 10* designation. I would be outraged!

What other branding and designations will the developer of a medical tourism program earn, pay for, or otherwise acquire for display to establish trust and credibility? This chapter digs deeper into these certifications and asks the reader to consider some gut-wrenchingly brutal questions about strategic marketing, affiliations, branding, private inurement (as in *for the benefit of one or more persons with some significant relationship to*, or as I tend to paraphrase it, being known by the company one keeps). I would rather get to know the provider by its own brand, characteristics, and reputation, not affiliation logos, and I suspect that the marketplace would agree.

I continue with the development of the vision of your product, and I am reminded of Stephen Covey's *7 Habits of Highly Effective People* (2004, Free Press) and the lessons learned from that text, including one of the more intricate concepts that he advances, that of "begin with the end in mind." If you have not read that book, I suggest you take the time to do so. It is not a quick read or a skim. Much of what he wrote in that book is relevant: transitioning through paradigm shifts, which affects how one perceives and acts regarding productivity, profitability, time management, market realities, and positive thinking, developing proactive strategies, and acting with initiative rather than reacting. The chapters begin and end with tools and questionnaires, and wrap up with a lengthy worksheet to develop your business model, which is included as Appendix 1.

In most every hospital I have visited, in over 40 countries marketing medical tourism or health travel, fewer than 1% have answered this question. Most have not developed a strategy to this level. Instead, the majority have stopped at the point of saying,

> We have sun, we have a JCI accredited (now there are about 300 of them) hospital, we have world-class doctors and nurses (although I haven't seen that quantified or defined yet), we have an airport and hotels nearby, we know how to call a taxi for an arrival at the airport. We are cheaper than the United States, the United Kingdom, Australia, and other markets. We should put up a website, market our services to the medical tourism consumers, compare ourselves with other prices we've seen on the Internet, and we'll develop the actual price for their package when they call us. Until then, because there's no real compelling revenue that we've seen, just leave it at that and let's see what happens.

Would you care to venture a guess as to how effective that failed deployment of an incomplete strategy has been in attracting referrals?

So, in summary, your business model will describe your rationale of how your organization will create and deliver and communicate value to your consumers. The business model design process is part of your medical tourism or health travel strategy. This business model will include, but not be limited to

- Purpose
- Offerings
- Strategies
- Infrastructure
- Organizational structures
- Trading practices and business rules for contracting
- Operational processes and policies

- Standard operating procedures, safety guidelines
- Quality and outcome measurement methods

The business model you develop will describe your organization design, product design, and describe the architecture or hierarchy of your value creation and care delivery methods, and it will capture steering mechanisms put into play by your organization.

This business model will be used as a vision-sharing tool to communicate to department managers, physicians, nurses, and other staff members and to explore possibilities for future development. It can also operate as a baking recipe for creative managers. It can be used to define the manner by which the business enterprise delivers value to present and future customers, converts them from noncustomers to customers, and converts their payments into profit margins. It is used to define and embody the hospital executive's educated assumptions about what customers want, how they wish to purchase it, and how your organization will meet those needs, derive revenue from doing so, and make a profit.

An Assortment of Business Models for Medical Tourism and Health Travel

A few examples I have encountered in my travels include the following.

Collective business models (medical tourism clusters): A business organization or association typically composed of relatively large numbers of businesses or healthcare professionals that pools resources, shares information, or provides other benefits for their members.

Cutting out the middleman model: The removal of intermediaries in a supply chain. Eliminates the medical tourism facilitator in favor of handling referrals directly (e.g., Bumrungrad).

Direct sales model: Direct selling is marketing and selling products directly to consumers. The direct personal presentation, demonstration, and sale of products and services to consumers, usually in their homes or through their employers. (Tourism Authority of Thailand, KHIDI, and India market representatives have done this and held consumer shows in what they believed to be potent source markets.) I have no idea of the success or outcome of these efforts, but having attended them, I assume the results were less than optimal.

Franchise: Franchising is the practice of using another firm's successful business model. For the franchisor, the franchise is an alternative to building "chain stores" to distribute goods and avoids investment in and liability of a chain. The franchisor's success is the success of the franchisees. The franchisee is said to have a greater incentive than a direct employee because he or she has a direct stake in the business (Harvard International, John's Hopkins International, and others).

Industrialization of services business model: A business model used in strategic management and services marketing that treats service provision as an industrial process, subject to industrial optimization procedures (widely seen in various stages throughout the medical tourism sector).

Auction business model: Attempted by one medical tourism facilitator of Indian descent located in the northeast United States around 2008. Each month, they supposedly auctioned off a surgery. Website currently returns "Error 404" (Not found).

All-in-one business model: A hospital contracts with nearby hotels that return commissions to the hospital, as do other suppliers in the supply chain. The hospital sells the package only if you use their complete package, whether or not the hotel level of service is to one's preference. (Seen in Monterrey, Mexico, Costa Rica, and other markets, primarily in Latin America).

Low-cost option business model: Seen in India, although many providers in India seem to be increasing their costs depending on who the customer is. I call it the "we see you coming" rate. The WSYC rate seems to be spreading to other markets as well, throughout Europe, in particular.

Loyalty business models: Used in strategic management in which company resources are employed so as to increase the loyalty of customers and other stakeholders in the expectation that corporate objectives will be met or surpassed. (Think frequent flyer and hotel guest loyalty programs in the travel industry.) A typical example of this type of model is: quality of product or service leads to customer satisfaction, which leads to customer loyalty, which leads to profitability. The strength of this business model is generally determined by the level of satisfaction with recent experience, overall perceptions of quality, customer commitment to the relationship, and bonds between the parties. (I've read and heard a lot of pitches that assert this, but have not seen real "loyalty"-driven volume through other than physician-to-physician referrals back to a mentor or teacher.)

Monopolistic business model: Business model whereby the hospital controls how cases are distributed to the independent medical staff. The hospital sets a price for a surgery and negotiates independently with each physician who will be invited to participate in the program. Regardless of the competitive price accepted by the independent physician, the hospital neutralizes all competition by naked price fixing* and then retaining the margin difference for the hospital. (Because this is illegal in most Organisation for Economic Cooperation and Development [OECD] countries that have published collaborative antitrust policies and regulations, I do not name names of those hospitals where I have witnessed these practices. They know who they are. They also have a tendency to refuse to allow the doctors into Admissions and surgical blocks for cases the doctors have independently contracted, thus further insulting the spirit of competition with restraint of trade barriers.)

Monopsonistic business model: A model where the market may only buy through one single entity's control over a market to purchase a good or service. One member of our consulting team, a former medical travel facilitator, experienced this firsthand, after paying several thousand dollars to fly to the hospital, pay for accommodations, driver, and travel expenses, only to be told that as a nonmember of the seemingly monopsonistic trade association, a contract would not be offered. Too bad she wasn't advised of those conditions before she incurred the expenses to travel there. We have no choice but to assume the hospitals that have adopted this business model find more value in the referrals, relationship, and other perceived value sourced from the trade association than from the potential revenues from the free market.

Network effect model: Network effects become significant after a certain subscription percentage has been achieved, called critical mass. At the critical mass point, the value obtained from the good or service is greater than or equal to the price paid for the good or service. As the value of the good is determined by the user base, this implies that after a certain number of people have subscribed to the service or purchased the good, additional people will subscribe to the service or purchase the good due to the positive utility to price ratio. PPOs and insurers tend to use this model to some extent. Many network effects are often mistaken for economies of scale, which result from business size rather than interoperability. The best

---

* An organization that acts as a meeting ground for 30 countries which believe strongly in the free market system, The OECD provides a forum for discussing issues and reaching agreements, some of which are legally binding.

possible scenario is when a network organizer amasses the critical mass of a variety of purchasers in need of the product of the providers, and where the critical mass will be steered to providers in a wide network. A key success or failure determinant is how the organizer preserves the competition between the members of the network (instead of price fixing or leveling) allowing for broad consumer choice. Through interoperability the network organizer produces economies of scale beneficial to both the supply side and the demand side, such as credentialing, inspections, contracting, case management, logistical management, destination management, quality measurement and reporting, and handling contracting details and ongoing contractual relationship demands with purchasers. (Mercury Healthcare's trademarked globally integrated health delivery system® is an example of this.)

Premium business model: The premium business model is the concept of offering high-end products and services appealing to discriminating consumers. Brand image is an important factor in the premium business model, as quality is often a subjective matter. This business model seeks a higher profit margin on a lower sales volume.

It is my hope that the expansion of these definitions will prove convenient for you as you evaluate your options for a viable business model. The list above is not exhaustive, but it represents a large percentage of the models we've seen in the marketplace.

Also included, in Appendix 1, is a business model development tool that we routinely use with our consulting clients to help them refine the business model for their program from a 30,000-foot level of random thoughts to a more detailed description at a more focused level. We hope including it in this book helps you realize your model more easily.

Chapter 3

Succeeding with Bundled Pricing for Medical Tourism

Spiraling cost increases, coupled with lagging quality outcomes and a chronic lack of transparency, have garnered the attention of payers, patients, and policymakers, not just in the United States but in several international markets where employers contribute to the cost of healthcare benefits as a supplement to national health program coverage. Healthcare organizations face growing pressure to address these issues: one promising way to cut costs is through bundled pricing, an innovation that market leaders are employing.

Comes now the medical tourism niche market, where facilitators who know very little about price bundling have a website to post confidential bundled rates to attract would-be medical tourists and potential local competitors who can spin a counteroffer to their advantage in hindsight. This could obviously create an advantage if they do it correctly, or a public relations and patient financial services disaster if the necessary disclaimers are omitted or not clearly disclosed to these medical tourists. Nonetheless, it is not the facilitator's job to know what to post and how.

In its most basic form, bundled pricing offers a fixed price for a defined set of services. Although it sounds simple, this radically different approach to pricing and risk brings its own challenges. The key to success with bundled pricing is to define clearly the beginning and ending of an episode of care.

The first step in your accountability once your bundled price for the episode of care is constructed is to ensure it is marketed properly, and even go so far as to require right of first review and right to object and correct the marketing message so that it remains brand consistent prior to the facilitator's inclusion in her marketing materials and website. After all, it is your organization that has the duty of the deliverable.

Lessons learned from those who have tried it (my first book addressed this in 1996) and failed include admonitions from administrators of healthcare delivery organizations who failed to evaluate carefully whether their organizations were prepared for implementation. Those who failed report organizational and financial setbacks and uncontrolled financial risk that might have caused them to be classified as "insurers."

Readiness for Bundled Pricing

To implement bundled pricing, healthcare administrators and clinicians must come together to examine their internal capabilities and resources—technical, managerial, and organizational—to take on this analysis and strategy. You'll need at least an accepted guideline from published evidence-based care paths to use as a punch list of services, drugs, supplies, and technologies to consider for inclusion. From there, call in the finance people to perform economic analyses and reporting benchmarks, variance management tools, and to help the clinical team to develop the economic- and clinical-value case.

Bundled pricing entails a level of collaboration between managers and clinicians that is rare for the U.S. healthcare market. In other markets, specifically in Asia and Europe, hospital administrators are often also clinicians or "paper doctors." This term means that they went to medical school, and learned the anatomy, physiology, pharmacology, microbiology, and other sciences and completed residencies and internships in direct patient care. They can walk the walk and talk the talk with the medicos and the nurses; they simply did not go on to practice medicine, but instead chose the health administration path. The term is not meant to be pejorative in any way. In fact, I was first introduced to it by university professors from top-notch European universities at a conference on health quality and hospital management. Success with bundled pricing requires managers to be involved in clinical decision-making, a skills set that in the U.S. healthcare market has traditionally been missing. An assessment of your organization's readiness for bundled pricing must start with a clear-eyed evaluation of the relationship between managers and physicians. The ray of hope here is that a record number of physicians have been enrolling in MBA courses, and you might find a hybrid or two among the medical staff who will be keen to assist.

Administrators have been reluctant to intrude on clinical decision making because of concerns that doing so would drive community physicians to competitors. In the future, it will be a key to survival! Even with the growth in physician employment in the United States, this remains a sensitive area. Again, physician integration and employment are commonplace in many medical tourism markets, so the United States could learn from a visit to their developing nation counterparts in this respect.

Two contributing factors that are critical for bundled price success include: compliance with treatment guidelines and clearly stating the episode of care and the inclusions and exclusions bundled into the case rate.

Experience has taught me that if you hand the doctors a reputable clinical guidelines book and tell them to practice medicine according to the guidelines, consider the book as a new doorstop. These healthcare professionals will play according to playground rules if they have a hand in refining the rules a bit. Otherwise, the administrators will always have to play referee and line judge. Nobody has any fun on the playground that way and eventually, they take their ball and go play someplace else.

If you fail to establish the episode of care limitations, everything becomes part of the episode. Just ask a payer! They will be the first ones to point to the contract and its silence as to any limitation. It doesn't matter here if the payer is a consumer or an employer or a health plan. The reaction will be the same. If you raise the consumers' ire, and they report you to the insurance commissioner, a cursory examination of the offer could cause you serious fines for failing to follow regulations as a limited risk healthcare organization, an insurer designation in states such as California, Colorado, and elsewhere. All it takes is a telephone call.

Here is how you overcome this hurdle. Control that which you can. Fee schedule any remaining charges on a fallback transparent rate such as a percentage of billed charges. For example, the quote becomes much simpler to create by framing it the way a restaurant places a multicourse meal on special:

> This bundled rate includes salad, two side dishes, an entree, and iced tea. Salad consists of iceberg lettuce, five slices of tomato, carrot shreds, croutons, and two ounces of salad dressing in the following flavors, side dishes include a choice of 1/2 cup of corn, peas, summer squash, or lentils; and the entree includes a choice of three ounces of wild salmon, three ounces of chicken breast, or six ounces of tofu. Dessert, additional side dishes, other flavors of salad dressing, and beverages other than iced black tea are subject to an additional charge of x. No substitutions are permitted without the advance written consent of the management.

You can go on to list some of the prices of the extras which evidence and sales history indicate are either popular, often requested, or necessary in a high number of cases because of comorbidities such as diabetes, anticoagulant therapy, obesity, chronic asthma, or hemophilia.

The Next Hurdle Has to Do with the Mechanics of Billing

Medical tourism hospitals need to assess their relationships not only with consumers and independent facilitators, but also third-party providers who will provide services under a bundled price. Laboratory technicians, pathologists, and outside specialists who typically bill patients separately will need to bill the hospital so a single bill can be provided at the promised price to patients and payers. If the price is not comprehensive, it's not really a bundled price.

The need to restructure these billing arrangements raises other questions. Part of this stems from the fact that medical tourism cases may not follow the traditional revenue cycle flow, at least in the United States. In other countries, where cash is the norm, it is not an issue. The final bill is tendered *at discharge* from hospital (not 60- to 90-days later, as is customary in the United States, by comparison), and the transparent price is quoted *at the time of admission*.

How is the risk of variance in utilization allocated among outside providers? How will expected costs for outside providers be factored into a fixed price when those costs are not part of the charge database of the hospital and, therefore, not visible? Those matters are easily dealt with similarly to the case of IPA and PHO participation agreements of the 1990s. I've dealt with thousands of them in my career.

The one recurring concern I've had has been with anesthesiologists, and rightfully so. If they offer a flat fee price and then pull duty with a slow surgeon, their revenue per hour suffers. The one who is lucky enough to be assigned to the room with "Speedy Gonzalez, MD" makes quite a bit more per hour, as the case throughput is faster. One way I have remedied this disparity was to create an hourly rate per surgeon. The rate goes into the database, the hospital quotes the price based on the surgeon (although it has proven to result in only minor variances in the grand scheme of things) and quotes the case on an average timeframe. Time outside the stated episode of care timeframe is subject to a fee at x per hour, or absorbed if it only happens occasionally.

If you have a specific physician group who seems ready for this, sometimes the level of collaboration will be especially good in a particular service line or with a specific physician group. If so, these collaborations would be a good way to approach bundled pricing. Competent managers who are engaged in a good working relationship with involved clinicians are necessary for successful implementation of bundled pricing. Attempting to implement this approach without some reasonable level of trust and collaboration likely will be futile. However, don't wait until everybody is ready. Go with what you have initially and the rest will follow, if for no other reason but out of curiosity. It is much like the first couple on the dance floor. You always have a few couples that came to dance the night away and are confident on the dance floor and not the least bit shy to go first. Eventually, the rest follow when they hear a tune they like.

A few consultants generate lots of hourly fees for meeting facilitation between physicians in order to establish consensus among clinicians regarding the way they treat patients with a specified condition. They would have you believe that developing care paths is difficult and controversial. If you cap their fees and require a firm fixed cost proposal, you'll notice a curious change in the methodology proposed to guide you to this point. Hmm.

Having been involved in these exercises for the better part of my career, I've found a tried and true method of doing this without a consultant to hold your hand. Here's how to avoid the experience of the many organizations that have developed care paths that ended up being nothing more than a stack of paper collecting dust on a shelf: assign every team member a procedure. Start with the top 5–15 cases for which you intend to create package prices. Their homework is to research the evidence-based guidelines, apply their insight of resources in technology at the hospital, surgical skills, and so on, and then prepare a model draft of the case rate and its episode of care and criteria for eligibility. When the team reconvenes, each surgeon presents his proposal and the floor is opened for discussion. A recorder takes notes and publishes the draft in final form for pricing research and final approval. Done! Effective and quicker than the consultant method I've seen so often. You can slate each package price for review periodically depending on volumes.

Research Is Crucial

It is important to understand that some of the grunt work involves research. The problem is that most hospital revenue cycle and decision-support systems have this information in several silos, making it nearly impossible to find the needed data to create a financial model easily. If this is the case, attempt fewer cases to create packages at first, until you learn which silo owns which piece of the needed data. The datasets include, at a minimum,

- Analysis of historic resource costs and charges and surgeon and anesthesia start and end times
- Modeling of expected costs, time, and revenue (throughput is a critical variance)
- Cost and quality reporting to enable variance management

You'll need to undertake an analysis of historic resource costs and charges. The chargemaster (or "list") prices for services provided in hospitals reflect many factors, but usually not direct costs. Consultants who are stuck on the judgment of the Centers for Medicare and Medicaid Services as to what the underlying resource costs *should* be (as reflected in what it will pay) often deal in "fantasyland" statistics.

For medical tourism, deal in reality, not CMS-math, CMS-accounting, and CMS-statistics. The population alone could skew your datasets as CMS-covered individuals are often older or sicker than the average medical tourism patient. For medical tourism, CMS data may be tainted by the amount other institutions in the market area are charging, what various private payers will allow, and, more generally, not enough about what the market will bear.

In most organizations, cost-based accounting, which associates the labor and capital costs of each input to a service, is no longer an idea or future-world fantasy, it is a necessity to price services and supplies and technology consumption accurately.

What is typically available in the healthcare delivery setting is a historical database of charges and collections at the patient level. These data are of minimal value other than to analyze who bought what and how much of it.

If your research is for the purpose of setting a cash price for medical tourism packages, you won't need analysis of what the market around you will bear, as these health travel patients will be coming from other places. What you will need are some cost estimates of interpreters if necessary, accommodations for companion travelers and meals, if they remain by the bedside, or hotel costs and airport transportation to and from your location if they plan to stay nearby. Don't add the costs to the package unless you intend to convert some surplus space into accommodation the way that hospitals in Turkey, Thailand, and even here in the United States (Cancer Treatment Centers of America is one example I can think of) have done.

If you are doing this packaging for consumer-driven healthcare programs (most of those may be domestic medical tourism as well), and cash or what is known as defined benefit account (limited expense, reimbursement-only) programs where the prudent shopping consumer pays cash up front and then obtains a limited benefit reimbursement amount from her employer. Examples of these cases include bariatrics, cardiac cases, joint replacement, spine surgery, minimally invasive procedures, organ transplant, in vitro fertilization (IVF), and annual checkups. On the purely elective side, the entire realm of cosmetic procedures is able to be packaged up competitively.

If you plan to do this for accountable care organization (ACO) contracting, you will need data related to payer pricing, and commercial or CMS rules, information on the average charges and collections characteristic of a particular diagnosis or procedure by payer and by their individual product lines, and even for workers' compensation cases according to a state-mandated fee schedule.

As you progress beyond the basic price bundle, you will need to determine if the bundled price covers just the acute care episode or will it include such postacute care as rehabilitation or home health? My experience has taught me not to do this for a number of reasons, the first being the patient's condition after surgery, their motivation to get better, and their independence or dependence and assistance at home, and learned helplessness.

You could get creative and include preacute care components such as weight-loss programs or physical conditioning, or follow-up saline adjustment fills for gastric banding patients, for example. If your package covers more than acute care (and eventually it will), determine whether you have access to accurate and recent data to enable you to price these services, and a means to handle variances if services, supplies, or labor costs vary from the fixed price. The trick here for beginners is to start with less-complicated, straightforward procedures, and carve out as many variances without disassembling the bundle. Avoid including other than what the data show are the historic costs that one can assume about the costs of treatment for expected comorbidities. Will these be included in the bundled price, or billed separately? If they are to be billed separately, how will they be identified and handled in the billing process? I believe that these issues can be addressed as I described earlier with a fallback rate for services rendered outside the package price.

Forward-thinking strategists will address cost and quality reporting formats on the front end to facilitate variance management. With bundled pricing, hospital administrators and clinicians must manage utilization and outcomes to prove value. These results will vary from clinical and administrative decision making, by diagnosis and by physician. The finance department must be able to generate a variety of cost analysis reports that are intelligible and credible. Design the reports at the beginning and tweak and refine as necessary, rather than skip this process until it is too late. Clinical outcomes likewise must be reported regularly in ways that clinicians can understand, so they can discuss variances from financial and clinical targets. Otherwise these data will be stuffed into the drawer with the other stack of evidence-based cookbook medicine protocols mentioned earlier.

An ad hoc task force should be assembled for at least 12 months to review reports, make program modifications, and to seek to manage cost and document quality and outcomes effectively. Part of the professional development and leadership training of midlevel managers—department heads and clinical chairs—should focus on how to initiate difficult conversations with clinicians about the impact of their clinical choices on cost and quality. Care must be taken not to dictate the practice of medicine, but rather to look for solutions with the political, if not real, acknowledgment that patients and practice patterns are different. Roles need to be redefined, and new accountabilities and capabilities need to be originated and consensus developed on those accountabilities and authorities.

For patients, bundled pricing provides more transparency and certainty in the cost of treatment and the services included. For payers, bundled pricing is a reduction in the risk of cost outliers and, more important, the assumption by providers of "skin in the game" for managing utilization, but that's really antithetical because of the reasons I reviewed earlier regarding insurance risk. The only other way to play hardball on bundled rates is to do so under contact capitation, a payment methodology that for the most part failed miserably in the 1990s and contributed to many provider bankruptcies.

Providers have an incentive to adopt this approach soon, because it entails a significant development curve, and cautious and careful first movers can gain competitive advantage and a premium for their efforts. Over the long term, however, some argue that bundled pricing brings a significant strategic threat, commoditization, arguing that bundled pricing will reach a point in its development where one brand has no features that differentiate it from other brands, and consumers buy on price alone. For those pundits, I recommend they read the *Blue Ocean Strategy* (Kim and Mauborgne 2005). They clearly don't get it. People don't buy healthcare on the basis of price alone. On the other hand, health plans often do. Therefore, part of the art of bundled pricing is determining the profile of your customer.

These same critics argue that competitive pricing for specific bundled-price procedures will steer toward equivalence. Hogwash! Competitive pricing for specific bundled-price procedures will steer toward value-based purchasing (i.e., how much service or utility can I buy for this much money?). That's where the economic- and clinical-value case becomes critical, and why providers need to turn their attention to developing and proving theirs sooner, rather than later.

The economic- and clinical-value case study is the narrative, backed up by data, that explains how a provider institution provides superior clinical value (according to various measures of clinical success), and economic value (as measured by factors such as recovery time, returns for unanticipated complications, and return to work). Many providers settle for mortality and morbidity statistics. These two statistics have different meanings for clinicians than for the public, especially a qualitative metric such as morbidity. Given the public's vocal dissatisfaction with quality and growing consumer sentiment, undertaking bundled pricing without a plan for creating an economic- and clinical-value case is a setup for future financial and public relations problems.

Select cases where the savings you can generate range in the $6,000–$15,000 range from target market competitors, and $2,500–$6,000 for those from a driving distance away from you. Don't go overboard at first. Start slowly, test, monitor, and measure, Have a list of cases you want to bundle, grab low-hanging fruit first, and pace yourself.

Chapter 4

Integrated Health Delivery Systems

In building successful healthcare provider alliances, a variety of terms can be used to describe the corporate form of the entity.

In 1997, I authored a book titled *IPA, PHO, MSO Development Strategies, Building Successful Provider Alliances* (1997, Chicago: McGraw-Hill and the Healthcare Financial Management Association). Once I recover from these two medical tourism books, a revision to that title will be undertaken, and retitled, *Physician Integration: Refocusing the Lens* (2012, New York: Productivity Press).

Managed care, which is not by any means unique to the United States, long ago shifted the delivery of healthcare away from inpatient hospital stays toward networks of primary and out-patient care. Anyone who has studied microbiology and understands the transmission of nosocomial (hospital-acquired) infections (HAIs) knows that it is actually often safer for the patient to be out of the hospital as soon as medically appropriate.

In the United States, the Centers for Disease Control and Prevention estimate that roughly 1.7 million hospital-associated infections, from all types of micro-organisms, including bacteria, combined, cause or contribute to 99,000 deaths each year. In Europe, where hospital surveys have been conducted, the category of Gram-negative infections is estimated to account for two-thirds of the 25,000 deaths each year. Nosocomial infections can cause severe pneumonia and infections of the urinary tract, bloodstream, and other parts of the body. Many types are difficult to attack with antibiotics, and antibiotic resistance is spreading to Gram-negative bacteria that can infect people outside the hospital.[*]

Perhaps someone should share those tidbits of information with the medical tourism marketing representative from a huge Indian hospital chain who told me that "We don't *throw* people out of the hospital so fast, and we are *cheaper* than American hospitals." The key consideration of length of stay is to keep the patient safe from harm and all decisions must be made along those lines, not cheap or affordable, or discharged too soon or not soon enough. I found some hospitals I have visited

---

[*] Pollack, Andrew. "Rising Threat of Infections Unfazed by Antibiotics" *The New York Times*, Feb. 27, 2010.

throughout the world so dirty (with photographs for documentation) or unsafe (as in my introduction example) that I would want to be transferred out immediately if only to a safer or cleaner hospital.

So this concept of managed care and the objective of reducing inpatient utilization is not always so "evil." Many managed care initiatives are undertaken by physicians, hospitals, and insurers in order to devise a coordinated, integrated health delivery option that will allow them to lower costs and simultaneously improve direct patient care and ultimately improve satisfaction and clinical outcomes associated with the episode of care. I will relentlessly argue that this single concept will transcend any and all healthcare reform efforts no matter by which nationality or special interest group, and any group of providers and administrators integrated for this purpose that can deliver these goals will thrive regardless of regulations promulgated by any authority or national healthcare reform initiative. The simultaneous achievement of reducing unnecessary healthcare costs, increasing appropriate access to the correct treatment, and coordinating care, if necessary, through a globally integrated effort will be a winner.

Healthcare currently seems to function in a silo, worldwide. For those readers who are not native speakers of idiomatic English, by this term, I refer to an expression that is typically applied to management systems where the focus is inward and information communication is vertical. In a silo, managers or information owners serve as information gatekeepers, making timely coordination and communication among departments difficult to achieve, and seamless interoperability with external parties impractical. Silos tend to limit productivity in practically all organizations and are pervasive in healthcare organizational cultures which in turn provide greater opportunity for security lapses and privacy breaches, and frustrate consumers, who increasingly expect information to be immediately available and complete. The silo in my example is the antonym of clinical and provider integration.

In the integration models of the 1990s in the United States, we created four widely used acronyms, IPAs (independent practice associations), PHOs (physician hospital organizations), and MSOs (management services organizations), along with a fourth that came from California, the CWOW or Clinic Without Walls. I was recently (April 2011) amused when I met with a group of physicians in Barcelona who told me that they had come up with a fantastic idea with their consultants to integrate these independent physicians into a new corporate entity that would consult and treat patients in a number of hospitals. Hmm, "I-P-A," as but for the activities through the collective, they each retained their business autonomy. I was even more amused when their consulting firm spokesperson began to tell me how they were replicating this amazing *new* business concept not only in Spain but across Europe and countries in South America. Yup, pretty amazing! Actually, I wish them well, for this movement toward physician and health delivery integration, if done correctly, will be successful.

In the 1990s, I lectured extensively on this topic, consulted on about 150 projects, and published many white papers on various aspects of the organization and operation of these entities, served as executive director of a few, and even testified in court on some cases where consultants were being sued for damages because of alleged incompetence and for providing advice that when followed, proved fatal to the organization.

In addition to having the ingredients of inpatient and outpatient treatment facilities and an associated medical staff in the right balance to be profitable, globally integrated health delivery requires deep insight to a number of subspecialty business routines, including, but not limited to

■ Business services integration
  – Development of standards and procedures for provider credentials vetting
  – Development of standards to benchmark facility site inspections

- Brokering and negotiating payer contracts for network providers
- Medical claims submission and revenue cycle management functions to ensure timely and accurate payment to the providers
- Pricing of medical services
- Facilitating electronic claims submission and payment transactions
  - Performing medical records and bill translation
- Co-ordination of medical services via the Internet or telecommunication networks
- Establishment of internal credentials and privileging standards
- Development and implementation and monitoring of healthcare quality and patient safety standards
- Creation of a database to maintain and monitor publishable statistics on health care quality and outcomes
- Collaborative marketing
- Development of customer service operations and management
- Facilitation of medical tourism / health travel services, namely, to
  - Coordinate medical destination reception services
  - Coordinate predeparture case management
  - Coordinate surgery bookings for the medical traveler to the service destination in order to obtain health care
  - Coordinate aftercare
  - Establish a means to implement case management and outcomes monitoring
- Acquiring and deploying technology that will manage and store
  - Electronic health records to maintain clinical recordkeeping
  - Claims submissions
  - Automated payment processing records
  - And monitor and manage healthcare cost containment

In addition to the above, if the network will then work with external facilitators in addition to professionally certified nurse case managers and social workers, the network then has to determine the role and scope of the facilitator, and contract for those services. The contract has to be developed, negotiated, and executed, and some remuneration must be decided upon, in the form and amount appropriate to the task to be performed. In a setting such as ours at Mercury Healthcare, we perform those facilitation services, but we don't hire "facilitators" with their own websites and provider relationships because we realize that their business operation is so small that we can only assume as former hospital executives that there would be no compelling reason to give them rates discounted below the published public rates, inasmuch as there is little if any quid pro quo in exchange for doing so. We also have no knowledge of how they vetted provider and facility credentials, and granted privileges to perform treatments and surgery on clients. The minute one of them begins to explain that all their hospitals "are accredited by the JCI" as a vetting reference, my most polite response is usually, "How wonderful!"

If your provider network intends to negotiate with third-party payers, depending on where the payer is located and its customers (individual consumers, unions, health trusts, employers, etc.), they may be seeking to contract with "ready-made" networks of preferred providers whose credentials have been vetted and the network developed and designed in accordance with accreditation standards that they must uphold. In the United States, these standards are set forth for health plans by the National Committee for Quality Assurance (NCQA).

For those readers who are not native speakers of idiomatic English, we use the term "health plans" in the United States as an entity that is different from an traditional indemnity "insurer." In the United States, historically, HMOs tended to use the term "health plan," and commercial insurance companies used the term "health insurance." Unlike traditional indemnity insurance, which indemnifies (makes the claimant "whole") the claimant for the risk of the cost of the claim as long as it is a covered item under the policy, an HMO covers only care rendered by those doctors and other professionals who have agreed to treat patients in accordance with the HMO's guidelines and be vetted and privileged into the HMO's impaneled network and abide by restrictions and limitations in coverage and reimbursement in exchange for a steady stream of customers. HMOs are regulated under a different set of laws than insurers in each state.

Here is where some of the confusion for providers outside the United States arises. To have a contract with one insurance company or health plan (in some cases, the corporation operates both with separate and distinct rules, networks, coverage products, and objectives) in say, Arizona, does not mean that you also have a contract that makes you accessible to patients with the same logo on their subscriber identification card in the adjacent states of Colorado, Nevada, New Mexico, California, or Utah. That goes for Blue Cross and Blue Shield, United Healthcare, Cigna, Anthem, Aetna, and others. The administrative cost redundancies of operating each of these health plans or an insurance company takes so much out of the premium dollar paid as each one must develop or contract with a ready-made network. Each must perform credential vetting, provider contracting, grant privileging to each physician, receive, adjudicate, and pay claims, handle cost containment activities, including preauthorization, precertification, disease management, case management, grievance committee, peer review, and a host of other costly activities. Then, each must appoint or employ a cadre of brokers, agents, and salespeople to sell policies, underwriters to evaluate claims risk exposures, actuaries to model and predict risk, and skilled staff to prepare annual and quarterly reports to the state that report metrics and statistics of claims payments, timeliness, accuracy, compliance, and so on. To appreciate the depth of these reports an interesting report and summary was published by Lord and Benoit, on their website, www.Section404.org.[*]

In addition, each plan state-by-state then must go through the accreditation survey process by the National Committee for Quality Assurance (www.ncqa.org) which has no specific requirement about hospitals in the network in its standards, or the hospitals' accreditation type or brand. Employers seek out health plans with this NCQA accreditation over other competitors.

NCQA began accrediting managed care organizations (MCOs) in 1991, in response to a demand for standardized objective information about performance, and now evaluates all types of health plans including MCOs, preferred provider organizations (PPOs), and other types of networks such as IPAs, PHOs, and credentialing verification organizations (CVOs), using a common set of standards.

Today, more than 100 million Americans (70.5% of all health plan members) are covered by an NCQA-accredited health plan. In 1991, I worked for a health plan and was a provider relations coordinator and very involved in the preparation for the health plan's accreditation, for which we ultimately spent $10,000 as the base fee, plus $0.10 per member (we had 290,000 members) plus the cost of the preparation, and the expenses of the surveyors to travel to Denver and perform the survey. We had to submit to repeat surveys every two years. This money, in today's dollars equates to roughly $62,000 for the accreditation survey fees. The prices have escalated since 1991, no doubt.

---

[*] http://www.section404.org/UserFiles/File/Lord%20%20Benoit%20Report%20NAIC%20Model%20Regulation.pdf accessed June 1, 2011.

So, for example, when a medical tourism provider contracts with Companion Global Healthcare, Inc. (CGC) in Columbia, South Carolina, they are not executing a contract that gives the entire Blue Cross Blue Shield family of companies' subscribers across the United States access to that provider, but instead, they are contracted with CGC which happens to be located in South Carolina. The same applies to contracts with UnitedHealthcare (U.S.A.) and the others in the various states. The companies in India, China, or elsewhere, are also not the same company as for example, UnitedHealthcare in New York which is yet again different from UnitedHealthcare in Minnesota where the corporate headquarters happens to be located. Likewise, if someone tells you that their employment history is with one of these companies in one state, that does not imply that they are or were ever remotely connected to the corporate headquarters. These organizational charts are daunting to keep up with, and the situation becomes more complex with each and every merger.

PPOs are a completely different type of organization and in most cases, neither fit the description of an indemnity insurance company or a health plan. Indemnity insurance plans and health plans assume financial risk for the cost of claims. PPOs do not. PPOs are simply a network of providers wishing to provide access to subscribers of the network and offer a discount in exchange for "steering." In these agreements, a PPO is typically seeking a 15–30% discount from usual and customary quoted charges in exchange for placing a hospital in its preferred network. The preference comes from nothing more than the discount. Unless the PPO offers enrollees a specific incentive (e.g., a lower copay or deductible or competitive rate transparency) to select an in-network provider, there is no real steering of volume, and thus no reason for the hospital to offer a discount. A "true" PPO will not have a problem agreeing to contract language to that effect, and in those cases the hospital is making a reasonable trade. In addition, there should not be a problem with contractual assurances that patients will identify themselves as a member of that PPO at the time of admission through identification on their insurance cards.

In the United States, PPOs tend to have smaller insurance companies and self-funded employer-sponsored benefit programs operated under yet a different regulation known as ERISA (Employee Retirement and Income Security Act of 1974) which I describe in greater detail in later chapters. The smaller insurance companies have no choice but to contract with a network of prenegotiated discounted providers, as they cannot afford the overhead to create their own network of providers. Labor union health and welfare benefit plans also contract through PPOs quite often, but tend not to want to outsource healthcare to providers outside the United States for various reasons, the main one being that health benefits are negotiated as part of a contract, and to extend the network beyond American shores is considered unpopular due to their fierce sense of loyalty to the American marketplace, even if it saves money.

Throughout my travels I have encountered PPO models in Malaysia, China, India, England, and a few other localities; I have not been able to locate much in the way of additional information about them, but if and when I do, I will post it on the medicaltourismhandbooks.com website designated as the official compendium site for this book and *The Medical Tourism Facilitator Handbook*.

As I tour hospitals and meet with physicians and hospital and clinic administrators throughout the world, I have to mind my behavior and my bemused facial expressions as I listen to some of the stories and promises that have been made by several U.S. facilitation firms who clearly don't know much about these organizations but have led these unwitting hospital administrators to sign contracts with them in anticipation of receiving hundreds of patients in the near future from insurance plans and employers in the United States. When you see me in a crowded room and I hear things like that and smile with a twinkle in my eye and just say, "How wonderful," you'll know what I am thinking. Shh! Don't tell! Let them dream!

Chapter 5

Measuring the ROI of JCI Accreditation

Return on Investment (ROI) means that there is a financial return. If no traceable revenue was generated as a result of the marketing effort, there is no ROI.

Introduction

This chapter is not meant to be a criticism of JCI in particular, but is intended instead as a thought-provoking critical evaluation tool.

At the time of this writing, our firm has seven professional healthcare operational, nursing, and medical staff, credentialing and privileging physician and administrative experts located strategically throughout the world, who have a 100% success rate on every accreditation preparation client engagement in five countries. I am proud to be one of them.

As a healthcare professional, I personally have had more than 15 years' experience in accreditation preparation of hospitals and healthcare organizations, and more than 20 years' experience and familiarity with health plan and HMO/PPO plan accreditation. Our consulting team that specializes in accreditation preparation has over 200 years combined in healthcare experience, and has been assisting hospitals and healthcare organizations through ISO, Joint Commission (U.S.A.), Joint Commission International, Malaysian Society for Quality in Health (MSQH), Hospital Accreditation of Thailand (HAT), and others for more than 15 years, each. As a result of this combined and personal experience, unlike many new medical tourism facilitators who have never purchased or read the current or past standards, my team and I have done both. We know what they review and measure, and what they don't.

In addition, I have independently funded primary research on consumer perspectives on branded accreditation recognition, and found that a very high percentage of consumers have no brand name recognition of any particular brand of accreditation.

Please don't misunderstand; as a business owner who offers accreditation preparation as a service, I am grateful to the Joint Commission International. Preparing hospitals and healthcare organizations for international accreditation or specialty-specific accreditation has generated excellent income to our firm. Just like its sibling, International Society of Quality (ISQua), it serves the valuable purpose of external review and validation of policies compared to practices, the greatest of these being the tracer methodology, which follows cases from start to finish to demonstrate that what was published was more than a paper policy.

JCI was never meant to be a hallmark of medical tourism readiness. I argue that it isn't. It is my strong opinion that the promotional misunderstanding and misapplication by many newcomer commercial facilitators with little to no clinical knowledge or health administration background have increased hospital budgets by many millions of dollars spent on a coveted medallion that is construed by many to be something that it is not.

It is said that having JCI accreditation is a strong positive when a facility is attempting to promote itself as a medical tourism destination. However, I cannot determine, nor has it been measureable to others, just how much of a strong positive it is. I believe this is the result of two main reasons: marketing by the JCI and the echoes of syndicated columnists and media outlets who perhaps did not do all the necessary due diligence prior to publication, and a further misinterpretation by the many budding medical tourism facilitators who are not adequately qualified to critically sort out the claims of the media and marketing hype of the JCI.

In a 2011 five-part blog post, I published my opinion on this and have included excerpts from those posts below.

Let's First Address the Due Diligence

Due diligence is a term used for a number of concepts involving either the performance of an investigation of a topic or fact prior to the signing of a contract or publishing something, or the performance of an act with a certain standard of care.

Much of the medical tourism business these days involves start-up facilitators who are not medically trained or personally familiar with the accreditation process associated with JCI or other ISQua-accredited schemes. As such, these start-up facilitators who don't have the core knowledge of medicine, healthcare administration, life safety code, healthcare delivery, quality management in healthcare, patient safety, medical records, physician credentialing and privileging, infection control, and the vast array of surgical and medical procedures, would likely be confused by the standards, their terminology, or the rationale behind them. If it were so easy that one who is literate could easily read them, why would most hospitals require an external consultant to assist in preparing them? Therefore, simply to read them might not help the situation.

The Difficulty Associated with Performing Due Diligence on International Hospital Accreditation through JCI

For one thing, JCI does not make the standards easy to obtain. They have a high price tag that many facilitators (or journalists) are not prepared to pay. Second, to order them is not easy. You have to answer questions about what you need them for, if you are a hospital, how you will use them, and so on. By comparison, many of the other systems that are also accredited by ISQua are readily available, online, open source, or available for purchase upon payment of a nominal fee.

It is my opinion that this was done for three reasons: (1) to rightfully protect the marketing and intellectual property investment, (2) to source and vet potential leads, and (3) to possibly limit access to the standards by consultants who are not employed by JCI who might steal potential market share from the JCI commercial consulting arm. The latter is just my impression, because I have experienced it firsthand. I may also have certain sensitivities because of the questions that were asked when I admitted that we are a firm with such a consultancy, and it took nearly three months to obtain a standards set once the order was placed. We were given many excuses as to why the order had not gone out. What it boils down to is that if your selected consultant has no up-to-date work tools, it is a bit difficult to accept the consulting engagement, but oh well, that's another blog post.

Call it a minimal barrier to entry, but it also impedes access to the standards by dedicated and inquisitive facilitators who might want to review the standards as part of their due diligence. Who wants to jump through all those hoops to buy a book? Thanks to Amazon.com, everyone is now accustomed to the simplicity of the customary procedure of an online order. When one encounters resistance or difficulty with the purchase, the "shopping cart" is abandoned and the sale pended to another day and time when one is up for navigating the obstacles, if really so inclined.

Perhaps that is also perverse. Is ignorance really bliss? Perhaps it is for one who may not really want the masses to know what the standards are, and what they aren't. I have no proof that there is any conspiracy here, just similar notes from casual conversations with other colleagues who have also independently consulted in JCI accreditation preparation over the last three years.

Next, I want to address the media hyperbole and promotional success that forms the basis of these claims that having JCI accreditation is a strong positive when a facility is attempting to promote itself as a medical tourism destination.

I am not sure that there are any available data to suggest how the claim is substantiated, or just how much of a strong positive it is from a revenue or volume standpoint. The repeated statements of the uninformed media, enhanced by Deloitte's 2008 published, redacted, and restated statistics of how large the market is and what it wants to buy and from where, creates a troublesome or intractable situation. Industry analysts, investors, and start-ups echo these statements in their business plans, websites, and syndicated columns. Reading the claim that JCI accreditation is a strong positive when a facility is attempting to promote itself as a medical tourism destination doesn't automatically make it so; repeating it doesn't necessarily make it any truer. Show me the numbers that prove this return on investment for medical tourism. In the case of rumors about insurers that "require" JCI specifically in order for hospitals to receive reimbursement for medical tourism services, show me "insurers" who pay for "medical tourism," and furthermore, show me 20 examples of the specific contract language that contains this requirement. That shouldn't be difficult given there were 5,293 insurance companies operating in 50 states in the United States in 2010.

Who Are the Facilitators and What Are Their Domain Competencies?

More often than not, medical tourism facilitators are budding entrepreneurs with a BlackBerry, a computer, an Internet connection, a website, not a lot of money, and lots of hope. Just regular people trying to make a living doing something for their clients to the best of their ability, with the resources they have. Some have had one personal, life-changing encounter with a foreign health system, but lack medical training or significant road warrior travel background or travel agency operations training, but they want a piece of the billion or more dollars out there to be had. Often, the sort of creative person who generates innovative ideas such as building a business-to-consumer medical tourism business rarely has the skills to turn the ideas into reality. Medical tourism business is a great idea, however, turning it into a product or service is a complex process that few ideas complete.

There is a great deal of skill competency and domain knowledge between "medical tourism facilitators." So much so that medically trained, competent, health travel professionals with core competencies in nursing, medicine, dentistry, and healthcare business administration find it difficult to be described in the same batch as those who obtained a certification from some association or private vocational training program offered by other entrepreneurs.

Reportedly, many medical tourism facilitators don't personally inspect their chosen hospitals but instead rely upon this arbitrary benchmark as a perceived prestige factor, that the hospital is JCI accredited. Having been a patient in a JCI-accredited hospital, I can tell you the difference between being on a premium service level floor and being on the floor where the regular patients go. Although the published standard for the hospital may be hospitalwide, the delivery of the care within the same hospital is extremely different.

Those knowledgeable about healthcare, nursing, quality, and safety who have activated a medical tourism business don't have any preconceived notions about one accreditation scheme or another. They assume the accreditation is merely a baseline and conduct their own inspections and grade the findings on meaningful observations, interpretations, and rigors. Personally, given the opportunity to choose, I would ultimately prefer to give my business and entrust my well-being to a facilitator who has this background over any facilitator who does not have a medical background supported by travel professionals, and who has performed a deep inspection of the facility, rather than, if anything, a 45-minute mega-familiarization tour meet and greet and video of the hospitals' smiling faces, over a facilitator who simply advertises that all their hospitals are JCI accredited.

In this next section, I share my concerns arising from the misconception that JCI accreditation is intended for use as an indicator of readiness for medical tourism on the part of any facility.

Who Is JCI and What Is So Special about Their System over All Others?

JCI is a private U.S.-based accreditation group that fulfills the requirements of an independent international body for healthcare standards accreditation. JCI is accredited by ISQua, an accreditor of accrediting bodies. It was in early 2008 that JCI was recognized by ISQua. It is not the same organization that accredits U.S. hospitals, known as the Joint Commission, also located in the same office park in a suburb of the Chicago metro area, nor does it utilize the same standards of accreditation across the two systems. This subtlety escapes many journalists, facilitators, and others.

One has standards geared toward healthcare in America, the most expensive system in the world, laden with problems of economic and quality accountability, redundancy, disconnected silos, and fragmented delivery. In the United States, there are several qualified accreditation schemes for healthcare facilities, including: DNV, Joint Commission, AOA, AAAHC, NY, Medicare, and others. Each year, quality lapses in healthcare delivery exact a staggering financial and human toll. Inefficiency and mistakes cost each American around $1,200 to $2,500 every year and prescription errors—a preventable lapse in quality control—cause 25,000 deaths annually. Most of these hospitals are accredited by one accrediting body or another.

Apart from JCI, at least 16 other accreditation bodies are approved by ISQua. This international standardization body conveys the following message. "Any hospital that is accredited by an ISQua approved accreditation body will be assured of the same patient safety and procedures of any hospital in the developed world." The different accreditation schemes vary in approach, quality, size, intent, and the skill of their marketing. They also vary in terms of costs incurred by hospitals and healthcare institutions. No one has shown me sound statistical evidence to prove that one system creates sustainable competitive advantages in medical tourism over another.

I also have some concerns regarding the standards associated with the accreditation process and additional concerns regarding interrater reliability between surveyors. To a trained observer who is knowledgeable about healthcare delivery, quality assurance, and the accreditation survey process, it is clear that there are a few misconceptions about the accreditation survey value and the process that leads to accreditation.

Accreditation preparation takes hundreds of hours and thousands of dollars in internal overhead costs for each hospital and its department heads, nurses, and administrators to plan, implement, and maintain a safe and high-quality patient care environment. That is true in all cases. If they hire a consultant to guide the process, there are additional costs to compensate the consultant for time, insight, experience, and advice, plus the expense to travel to the facility. The reason hospitals commit to this endeavor has absolutely nothing to do with medical tourism, and it is offensive to those both at the facility and the surveyors who are involved in the accreditation survey itself to suggest so.

The "What" and "How" of International Hospital Accreditation Surveys

As I mentioned previously, the Joint Commission International (JCI) and the Joint Commission (TJC) formerly known as JCAHO are two different organizations that happen to be headquartered in the same office park in suburban Chicago. Surveyors from the Joint Commission International and the Joint Commission are not interchangeable. If they were, it would mean that there would be no need for two systems. The reason for the differences are the very core of the difference between the survey standards.

Accreditation Canada International, Trent, Hospital Accreditation of Thailand, ICONTEC, MSQH, Trent Accreditation Scheme, and many others each focus in improving patient safety. Like JCI, Accreditation Canada recognizes that one standard approach does not work for everyone; it customizes its accreditation program to meet the client's needs. I thought "standard" meant "a basis for comparison; a reference point against which other things can be evaluated." Therefore customization of a standard is essentially conjoining contradictory terms, which is by definition an oxymoron.

Therein lies the paradox. If Joint Commission International and others customize accreditation surveys and allow for local norms, medical standards of care of the community, cultural differences, and the like, then to assume a standard can be used to imply a basis of comparison for applicability to medical tourism or other competitive advantages is simply wrong. One does not endeavor to seek accreditation by any accrediting body for medical tourism or for prestige. One endeavors accreditation to have the benefit of a critical external observer verify that what was published by that organization as its proprietary adopted standard to be practiced as a routine, and not simply a paper policy and procedure. No more, no less.

Next, I continue to question the matter of interrater reliability. If one truly understands this process and what it means, then one cannot avoid this question. For those who are not familiar with this term, it is a statistics term that means the raters agree on the official rating of a performance, agree with each other, and would have the same or very similar findings if raters were "swapped" randomly. With so many facilities electing JCI accreditation, and the rules for JCI accreditation requiring that surveyors come from a different country, I question the training and observation skills development of a surveyor.

When comparing them, if the critical observers do not come up with the same findings and therefore do not rate the same findings consistently between raters because the findings are essentially different, and accommodated to meet the client's local norms, and so on, then how does interrater reliability occur? Furthermore, in recent years, the number of JCI-accredited public and private hospitals around the world has increased by nearly 1,000%. As these hospitals must be reaccredited every few years, how many surveyors does it take to keep the system on this trajectory? Where are they trained, and what are they being trained to survey? This is not something that can be trained in mass production, nor can the rate of production be increased similar to the *I Love Lucy* episode in the chocolate factory.* With all due respect to the dedicated men and women who are the surveyors, I just wonder how fast the conveyor belt can be sped up before the system deteriorates?

Again, I must stress "what" is being surveyed. International hospital accreditation surveys allow for local norms, local medical standards of care of the community, and cultural differences, and so on, not a basis of comparison for applicability to medical tourism or other competitive advantages. The critical external observer(s) verifies(verify) that what was published by that organization as its proprietary adopted standard to be practiced is a routine, and not simply a paper policy and procedure. No more, no less.

Although I agree that a commitment to patient safety and continuous vigilance and process improvement for high-quality and safe patient care is paramount, I do not agree that one accreditation brand is a strong positive over another when a facility is attempting to promote itself as a medical tourism destination. I am all for JCI accreditation, or any other accreditation for the right reasons. I don't believe that using JCI as a hallmark of medical tourism readiness is appropriate or indicative of that status. My attitude is, "Show me your accreditation standards and survey results, and then show me your market readiness for medical tourism patients."

Evaluating the ROI of JCI Branded Accreditation

Consider this for a moment: If you submitted your organization for an accreditation survey under any ISQua-accredited program or Planetree designation or similar, can you pinpoint the exact revenue gained because of it?

What if you chose a different one?
What if you had none?
Have you surveyed the patients to ask them why they chose your hospital without prompting them for any response whatsoever? No checklists, no tick boxes, no guiding rails to suggest one reason over any other as to why they chose you, just an open-ended option for them to fill in a blank?

---

* http://youtu.be/GLp7Y4TxXSA.

Many medical tourism destination hospital administrators I chat with tell me that they have been told that in order to be eligible to contract with U.S. insurance plans and employer-sponsored health plans, that JCI accreditation is "required" as threshold criteria.

Who told you that and which contracts can they produce as evidence to back up their assertion? Can they show you 50 contracts that require this? It is important that you evaluate what you hear on this topic by applying some critical thinking. I have a copy of thousands of managed care agreements from U.S. health plans. I have them because I have negotiated them on behalf of hospitals and physicians nationwide over the last 25 years. I haven't found one that requires JCI or even Joint Commission, per se. I challenge you to prove me wrong with examples of at least 50 contracts. That will equate to perhaps .0005% of the contracts on the street.

Cross-border healthcare has been ongoing for more than 10 years in Southern California with health plans that specifically include and require care to be delivered in Mexico. JCI is not a requirement of these plans, nor was it ever. The payers include Blue Shield, HealthNet, and more recently Aetna and CIGNA. The former two report that statistically, quality is not an issue nor is patient satisfaction; in fact, patient satisfaction is higher than in their stateside plans.

When a Hospital Advertises That It Is JCI Accredited, What Does That Mean to the Recipient of the Marketing Message, Really?

For the most part, nothing. In order to register with the recipient of the message one has to consider the following:

1. If they were not listening carefully for it, it may not register.
2. If they don't know what JCI is, it is a meaningless reference.
3. If they have never read an article referencing JCI, they have no clue what it stands for.

Are You Using "JCI" as a Shorthand Reference to Imply You Render High-Quality and Safe Care?

Why lose the opportunity to say what you mean and associate your true qualities with your own brand? (See Figure 5.1.) Instead of propping up someone else's brand by using their name, why not share a message that says you deliver high-quality, safe patient care? Associate those words with your own brand!

Have you ever read someone else's notes when they wrote in conventional shorthand or their own note hand? Unless you have been trained to understand the symbolism it is meaningless scribble. Just look at computer code for CSS or XHTML for a reality check. Hand the code to someone who knows as much about computer programming as the average patient knows about hospital quality and safety. Enough said!

Does Your Audience Understand the Meaning of JCI or Another National or International Hospital Accreditation, What It Is and What It Isn't?

Most entry-level and even many experienced medical tourism facilitators don't understand this themselves. Instead, they echo what others say, like a parrot, and many even associate attributes

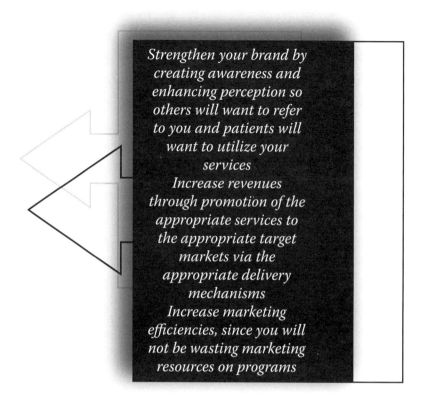

Strengthen your brand by creating awareness and enhancing perception so others will want to refer to you and patients will want to utilize your services

Increase revenues through promotion of the appropriate services to the appropriate target markets via the appropriate delivery mechanisms

Increase marketing efficiencies, since you will not be wasting marketing resources on programs

Figure 5.1 Marketing strategies for brand awareness and revenue boosting.

to accreditation that do not exist. Most have never read the accreditation standards for themselves and assume it has some correlation to readiness for medical tourism client reception. That could not be further from the truth!

Consider this: if the facilitators who represent your brand do not understand international hospital accreditation, they could be misrepresenting your brand. This can cause serious brand damage by setting clients up for unreasonable and unrealistic expectations, ultimately leading to brand damage, for which they may or may not have insurance to cover in the event that they damage your brand. Have you checked to determine if they are insured for their actions if they significantly damage your brand enough to warrant legal action to restore you and make you whole?

It is absolutely essential that you determine and put in place the tracking system and metrics, including key performance indicators, in advance of the marketing effort. Any preparation for JCI or other hospital accreditation is going to have significant cost tags associated with the training, filing fees, consultation, and staff readiness. Make sure that before you choose any accreditation survey program, you are (1) doing it for the right reasons (quality assurance, quality improvement, and patient safety) and (2) if you are doing it for the sake of marketing, that you can make quantifiable measurements to enable a true ROI analysis.

As a trained observer and one who is professionally qualified to guide a hospital through the accreditation preparation process, I commend any hospital who seeks any international hospital accreditation program that has been accredited by ISQua. I view such accreditation as a minimum standard that our own proprietary and well-developed network participation standards mirror and exceed. However, it is by that measure beyond the minimum standards of accreditation that hospitals and other healthcare providers differentiate themselves in the consumer-driven market of medical tourism, not the brand of accreditation framed on the wall.

Chapter 6

Shaping and Managing Your Medical Tourism/Health Travel Product Offering

As you begin development of your medical tourism and hospital's general marketing plan, you need to design an offering that meets your target customers' needs or wants. These customers are going to judge your offering by looking at four basic elements: the included features of the package price, the quality of your service as the patient perceives it, the services mix that you offer, and the price you charge.

Marketing medical tourism and other healthcare services is somewhat different than offering retail products that are often considered tangible goods. In the most general sense, a product is anything that can be offered to the market to satisfy a patient's need or want. As such, this can include physical goods, such as walkers, wheelchairs, canes, crutches, braces, stem cells, organ transplants, pharmaceutical drugs, and supplies. It can also include services such as surgery, executive check-up, golf swing analysis, diagnostic tests, or even a consultation. For a medical tourism facilitator, a product could be defined as a wellness checkup combined with a cruise, winery tour, amusement park, cooking class, or any other combination experience that can be paired with a medical service such as a massage or spa visit. It could also be interpreted to mean something like a hen night mammography group experience, where a group of women get together, have their mammograms, and then go out for a spa getaway, a night on the town, a weekend away, or some other experience that they share together. In medical tourism, many times we see this type of activity when a group of executive women get together and decide to go off to an exotic place to have a Botox® weekend.

Your Medical Tourism Product

In order to appeal to customers whether they are consumers, health insurance plans, employers, or some other type of end user, your hospital or medical group needs to address five different product

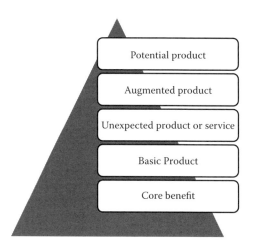

Figure 6.1 Healthcare products.

levels. The most basic level is the *core benefit* that the customer is really seeking. For example, a patient with knee pain visiting the hospital or physician simply wants to get rid of the pain and also to make sure that whatever intervention they elect is going to mitigate further pain, debilitation, and perhaps joint degradation. The core benefit sought is pain relief. As the hospital markets its services, it needs to see itself as a benefit provider. See Figure 6.1.

Working from the bottom up, the second level is where the provider must convert the core benefit into a *basic product*. For example, the core benefit of pain relief is translated into the basic product of a therapeutic or analgesic injection, or surgery.

The next level up is where the facility or medical group develops an *unexpected product*, such as a set of attributes or conditions that buyers normally expect when they purchase your product. As a U.S. patient, no matter in what country I'm admitted to a hospital, it's not unreasonable that I would expect that if the hospital planned for my arrival and my admission, when I turn on the television I should expect to find English-language programming. After all, what else am I supposed to do while I'm sitting in a hospital bed? I should also expect a clean fresh hospital gown or pajamas daily, I should expect to be fed nutritious food that tastes good, and if there are no dietary restrictions to the contrary, I should expect to be able to have a cup of coffee whenever I want to, and I should expect the nurse to be able to communicate with me in English.

If the medical tourism program developers thought through the entire episode of care, in order to sell its expected product and anticipate a high level of patient satisfaction, and if the hospital was expecting significant volume from patients from the United States, they should ensure that the hospital staff on the floor where the patients are treated have adequate English language fluency, signage, and other amenities to meet or exceed those expectations. In order to do this, the hospital might commission some research to be carried out, to find out exactly what those expectations might be, before marketing the product to the purchasers and referring facilitators.

Continuing along this chain, the facility might also offer an *augmented product,* one that exceeds customer expectations with perhaps additional amenities such as a VIP suite, an extended menu from the dietary department, concierge service level, and other amenities available at an upgraded price. For hospitals in developed nations, these amenities are often included in the basic service level at which the hospital competes. In other nations the competition occurs mainly at the expected product level.

Your medical tourism product differentiation takes place mainly at the level of product augmentation and leads the facilities to look at the patient's total consumption system the way that the patient performs tasks of getting and using products and related services. This means that the hospital needs to research who is buying their medical tourism services, by what means they are locating the provider, and by what benchmarks they evaluate the provider's perceived quality, value, and price. The research alone adds cost to the augmentation level, as does each of the amenities. If the amenity is not communicated clearly to the purchaser, it may not be considered in the value proposition. Hospitals outside the United States that are not used to presenting marketing and promotional copy in their hospital brochures and other marketing materials without appropriate idiomatic translation for an American, British, or other reader, may clearly include all of the amenities but fail to bring them to the forefront. This could lead to the provider being passed over in favor of a facility or medical provider of lesser technical quality that simply does a better job of telling the story of its benefits.

Another concern that facilities and physicians need to be mindful of, is that as these amenities soon become expected and necessary competitive points-of-parity, providers will have to continue to add to those amenities in order to remain competitive. Because adding amenities adds to the cost structure, at what point do the amenities become excessive? Furthermore, how much value will the patient place on certain amenities over other amenities? And what happens to the provider who selects the wrong amenities to offer, or places the wrong emphasis on an amenity that the patient neither expects nor values? What happens if the purchaser fails to learn about the values that align with the core benefit sought but didn't notice them due to space, promotional copy and message limitations, or idiomatic translation errors? Finally, medical tourism providers need to be mindful of the fact that as they raise their price for the amenity-based package, their competitor will likely offer a stripped-down version of the core service at a lower price to attract the price-conscious purchaser.

The highest level of the product, the *potential product*, encompasses all of the possible augmentations and transformations of the product or offering that it might undergo in the future. For example, at the basic level, a provider may offer an executive physical that is appealing to accounting, architectural, and law firms as well as other high net worth individuals. The potential product might also include a spa relaxation massage, and for those executives who make real business deals on the golf course, a golf swing analysis designed to identify swing anomalies caused by pain, muscle contracture, weakness, or some other reason such as vision anomalies, inability to concentrate, or poor training and lack of practice. At this level, the provider seeks a different way to distinguish its offering to the medical traveler.

Product Mix

A medical tourism hospital in Korea might offer a cancer service line consisting of diagnostic imaging and lab services, chemotherapy, radiation therapy, patient and family counseling, and a variety of therapeutic interventions that might include organ transplant, excisional resection, or grafting procedures. The product mix which that hospital offers to patients might include a variety of service lines and other independent standalone services.

In healthcare administration we learn that hospitals use product line management to offer a comprehensive range of clinical services. These providers set their priorities to feature specific clinical specialties. As I tour most medical tourism hospitals, it seems they always include the "big three": cancer care, orthopedics, cardiac services, and often a fourth, bariatrics. Many times these are labeled as the hospital's "Centers of Excellence." In the United States the term *center of excellence* has specific meaning, determined by quality outcomes, and adherence to other evidence-based medicine guidelines. In other nations, the term "center of excellence" is more loosely defined by the user who simply states it is so.

In health administration master's programs, students are taught that a hospital's product mix has width, length, depth, and consistency. The *width* of a product mix refers to how many different product lines the hospital or clinic carries. For example, a large teaching hospital is going to have a stated product mix with many service lines such as cancer, children's services, cardiac, emergency services, orthopedics, and diagnostic imaging services. By comparison, an ambulatory surgery center may only include outpatient surgery, and pain management services. The width of the outpatient surgery offering may be further restricted if the ambulatory surgery center is not licensed to accommodate overnight patients.

The *length* of the product mix refers to the total number of items in the mix. Health services product mix length assessments are complex, as there can be many hundreds of items with many overlaps per item. For example, the children's services product line may be drawn from a mixture of all of the services offered by the Department of Pediatrics, its clinical programs if it is a teaching hospital, surgical services, neonatal intensive care services, primary pediatric care, and satellite specialty clinics within the community or extended as outreach in other nearby communities.

The *depth* of a product mix refers to how many variants of each product in the line are offered; for example, cancer care could be subdivided into three layers of depth if the cancer care can be distinctly managed for adults, children, and perhaps da Vinci minimally invasive robotic prostate surgery for men.

Last, the *consistency* of the product mix refers to how closely related the variety of services is in such features as how the patient uses them, how the service line is developed, or how it might be sold or promoted to medical tourism patients.

The way in which a medical tourism hospital organizes its product mix allows the hospital or ambulatory surgery center to expand its medical tourism business in several different ways: first, it can add new product lines and widen the product mix. Second, it can extend the length of each product line to include many items that overlap in its service offerings. Third, it can add more varieties to each product or pursue more consistency, such as adding additional services that are easy for medical tourism facilitators to sell.

Managing Medical Tourism Service Lines

As a hospital administrator in a medical tourism facility, the administrator needs to know the purpose of the sales and profits of each item in the medical tourism service line in order to strategize which services to expand, maintain, eliminate, or exchange with another. The administrator also needs to understand how each service line is sold, and develop a market profile.

The first step in developing a market profile is to establish the purpose of the service; although some service lines may be offered at a profit, others may be simply introduced as part of the organization's mission and community benefit contribution. In fact, there may be no profitability at all, and the service may be a loss leader, a charity service, or a gesture of goodwill. The administrator and her department managers really need to understand the service line and its purpose before jumping to conclusions on sales and profits.

Once the purpose is understood, the next order of business is to develop a profitability report that services a dashboard for sales by service line. Often, as I walk a hospital to perform an on-site inspection I ask about a profitability report. Rarely do I receive meaningful answers about volumes of procedures, or contribution margins for one service over another that might be featured by a medical tourism facilitator, or about planned expansions for the service line. It frustrates me that the typical person assigned to conduct the tour of the hospital is not knowledgeable about this. It is essential for anyone who will represent your hospital and refer patients to you on an official basis to know these things, much the same as the chef in the kitchen of a restaurant tells the waitstaff what to push and which items to refrain from offering with regard to suggestive sells for special promotions.

The simplest profit and sales report need only include the number of sales, the revenue, and profit margin for each service in the line. When I examine a hospital, I often measure this in average revenue-per-encounter terms. In an ambulatory surgery center, if the facility is capable of offering a five-product service line such as orthopedics, otorhinolaryngology, eye surgery, pain management, and hernia repairs, if orthopedics accounts for 30% of total sales and 70% of total profits, an astute administrator will seek to add more orthopedic surgery times, more sets of orthopedic instrumentation, and will likely seek to keep the orthopedic surgeons who bring cases they're very happy. By the same token if the hernia repairs take the same amount of time as a diagnostic arthroscopy, but only bring one-fifth of the revenue, the same administrator might not make as many slots available for those minor cases that displace higher-paying cases and frustrate the orthopedic surgeons due to lack of available rooms, instrumentation, or light sources for the operating scope, because it is in use by the general surgeon performing the hernia repair by laparoscopic means. In some cases the marketing manager for the hospital may consider dropping a particular service unless it has strong growth potential or is a necessary part of some other profitable medical tourism package.

Currently, there's so much marketing hype regarding the da Vinci minimally invasive surgical approach that many hospitals considering medical tourism as a service line addition to its product mix feel pressured to purchase at least one, and ensure that the surgeons are ready, able, and willing to use it. At the same time, hospitals and other countries that have had the da Vinci equipment for several years have put it through its paces as an offering, and in some cases have decided against pushing minimally invasive surgery by the da Vinci robot because of the amount of time that it takes to carry out the procedure. Those hospitals have found the throughput of a higher volume of cases is more profitable than attracting one da Vinci case which occupies an operating room for 10 to 12 hours.

When considering service line growth, one little element that many administrators and marketing managers fail to remember is that women make most of the healthcare purchasing decisions in the United States. They not only make them for themselves but for their entire family. They often opine on extended family member medical decisions. Therefore, in determining a marketing strategy keep in mind that if there is any way to create a female satisfied customer or companion of a customer, the result of that patient or companion satisfaction could be that they refer additional patients to the provider and also seek further services from that provider for themselves.

In developing a market profile for a particular service line item, an analysis of competitors is needed. For this, the marketing manager or medical tourism service line strategist can use product mapping to compare competitive offerings between nearby competitors or particular country competitors in the medical tourism marketplace. To do this, individual products are plotted using a graph with *A/B* and *X/Y* axes that represent the product attributes most important for buyers. These axes may be depicted as: more painful, less painful; inpatient, outpatient; conservative, radical; open, laparoscopic; and the like. By plotting these on a graph, one can then start to assess price differentiation, amenities, potential up-sell opportunities for expanded service such as in the case of the executive physical and its companion golf swing analysis, and so on. The product map can also be used to reveal new service locations, expanded products, and also identify and forecast unmet demand. Another use for the map would be to produce and price a service at a low cost, or to consider adding a new service line altogether. One final capability with the map is a hospital or facility administrator or an entrepreneurial physician considering adding new technology or a new procedure can also identify new or additional medical tourism market segments.

Product Line Analyses

When a hospital or clinic decides it wants to add a new service line or invest resources to increase market share for a new piece of technology or new procedure, the product line analysis must be conducted. This includes the calculation of costs, revenues, and margin by diagnostic related group or some other taxonomic classification. In the United States, DRGs or MS DRGs are related groups of diagnoses assigned to a specific category for which payers pay the hospital a fixed amount. Under the DRG system, hospitals may lose money or make margin depending upon their costs. Globally, there are least 18 DRG systems in use. Not all pay the same as the Medicare system in the United States. Some use DRG systems to be able to categorically classify outcomes, length of stay, and other characteristics of inpatient admissions. In any event, the purpose of the analysis is to measure margins and examine product lines by these diagnostic related groups. I don't know of any hospital chief financial officer who is unaware of which services or products have negative margins and which have positive ones. The product line analysis needs to be considered in the context of the hospital's strategic plan and budget for technology, new services, staffing, marketing, and in cases where they actually hire physicians as direct employees, to determine how many physicians are needed to operate a hospital. This product line analysis always needs to be considered in the context of expected reimbursement, fluctuations in the source of the reimbursement, and changes in the payer mix. Administrators can also use this tool in order to find surplus revenue, and focus process improvements such as LEAN, and Six Sigma activities. They can also use this tool in order to determine which procedures, services, and technology will be expanded or abandoned.

Next, the hospital needs to determine market share, and does so by benchmarking statistics on admissions and discharges by particular service line for the relevant market. This may be able to be done for the hospital overall; in 2010, in most markets, however, it's probably premature to expect to produce statistically relevant data to benchmark medical tourism admissions and discharges to this extent.

Calculate the Costs of Increasing Market Share

Following that, the next order of business is to calculate the costs of increasing market share. Hospital managers and clinic administrators must calculate and estimate the fixed and variable costs to add new market share. Only then, after the results are quantified, can new service investments and projected rates of return on invested capital be forecast. Without that, it's simply a crapshoot, and you probably have better odds in Las Vegas or Monte Carlo. This has happened to many hospitals who have undertaken the cost and labor to prepare for and undergo Joint Commission International accreditation only to find afterwards that there was no correlation between JCI and medical tourism program readiness. The hospital was simply internationally accredited; in many cases, this comes at a price of more than USD $250,000 once the costs of preparation, staff resource commitment, consulting, and the fees and travel expenses of the surveyors is taken into account for a large hospital.

This same procedure needs to be replicated for other products and services: for each service line regular profitability updates, market share analyses, and other datasets such as a detailed analysis of where one might acquire more patients. This information can then be used for strategic planning, marketing budgets, and promotional activities aimed at targeting specific new groups of medical tourism patients.

ROI Analysis

Finally, the old saying, "You can't manage what you can't measure," applies here. In order to determine if the marketing results were what they should have been it's always necessary to calculate return on investment (ROI).

Back to Basics

As hospitals seek to develop new business, the first need is to define their own perspective, as many often consider health services marketing fundamentally different from product marketing. Still there's a camp that believes they're essentially the same in approach. I, for one, believe that retail and even knowledge-based product marketing still conform essentially to the 4Ps of price, product, place, and promotion.

I also believe that healthcare marketing is set into a different set of four letters, namely: service, access, quality, and price. I've long been an advocate that *access* places first and foremost. I believe this because if one cannot access the services, price and quality and the level of service will never be realized. Access refers to location, availability of appointments for care, and so on. The second of the four is *price*, for if one can access the services, then they need to be able to pay for the services if there's no insurance available for reimbursement. If they can't pay for the services or if they can't access the services because of payment hurdles, the patient will never have the opportunity to experience the service level or the quality and outcomes. Third, once access and price have been reconciled, the level of *service* is the next marketing element. I believe this because most patients, who are not clinically trained, evaluate the value for the price paid prior to the treatment by the level of service or apparent service promised in the promotion from which they purchased the package. This includes things such as the decor of the hospital, English language fluency, if the facility is fancy or drab, and so on.

Finally, only after the service has been rendered and the pain has been abated, functionality has been restored, or whatever that basic core benefit was to begin with, only then will the patient or his family indicate their impression of perceived *quality* or value. It is only at this level that patients will choose to refer others for services similar to the ones that they received, or caution against receiving services from the provider that they chose.

Conclusion

As you seek to develop or expand your medical tourism program service lines, and build strategy, I hope this section will have helped to at least develop a very high-level checklist of things to be considered in order to market medical tourism services or expand your current offerings. Please

Healthcare Marketing...

P-P-P-P vs. A-P-S-Q

Which one applies?

Figure 6.2 Healthcare marketing.

see Figure 6.2. It's also important in the consideration of budget development for new technology, drugs, and supplies, that part of the calculation prior to purchasing the fancy gadget is that you figure out how to pay for it rather than buy it and hope for the best. It's also necessary that your expectations of volume and revenue for medical tourism services are realistic and not overinflated and baseless. For if they are, no medical tourism facilitator will ever be able to satisfy you, and your frustration level with medical tourism business development as a whole will increase to an untenable level. Keep in mind that the facilitator must have a product to sell at an affordable price, where he can stake his name and reputation on the value proposition you offer for medical tourism services.

Chapter 7

Planning and Conducting Familiarization Tours

As a medical tourism facility, you will likely have many opportunities to show interested visitors your hospital. One thing I have learned after touring countless hospitals in the United States and abroad is that not all familiarization (fam) tours should be conducted the same way, or even by the same person. This chapter discusses the planning and hosting of tours for medical tourism facilitators that a hospital should strategically be prepared to conduct and who should be involved and provide guidance as to the level of detail that should be provided. Failure to do this wastes everyone's time, which is counterproductive and can be frustrating for both the guest and the hospital.

For one thing, if the information sought by the one taking the tour is not available, incorrect, or if the guide is unprepared, the guest leaves with a less than favorable impression of the level of preparedness of the hospital or clinic. If the tour highlights parts of the hospital in which the guest is not interested or is not likely to use (e.g., maternity services and medical tourism are not usually a match) that time is probably taken away from parts of the hospital for which there may be greater interest.

Because medical tourism is new for many hospitals, I always provide a checklist of questions, concerns, and statistics I would like to know in advance of my arrival. Because of my professional background and experience, I have a completely different orientation to a hospital tour than an inexperienced but enthusiastic facilitator.

As the CEO of a globally integrated health delivery system another dimension to my curiosity and inspection detail exists, as I am there as the eyes and ears of the international health insurance plans and employers who are my clients. Although it is nice to know about the upscale VIP rooms, and I certainly want to see them, if only briefly, I know that my health plan clients and insurers are probably only going to consider coverage for a private or semiprivate regular room in the event a plan subscriber takes ill or is injured while in their area.

For our medical tourism service lines, I certainly need to know about the amenities and basic products for medical tourists who choose to travel to the hotel and may select one hospital over another for myriad personal reasons. For that, my facilitation and case management staff needs to be fluent about the hospital but at a completely different level than that which meets my needs at the network level, and about different things. If I am accompanying an insurance executive or a human resources benefits buyer for a self-insured, employer-sponsored health plan, the tour agenda and information highlighted will be completely different from either of the two previously mentioned visitors.

So, let's start at the beginning. The first order of business is to determine the type of visitor you will host. In this chapter, we focus on planning the fam tour for the typical medical tourism facilitator. Out of respect to those facilitators who may possess medical or healthcare administration knowledge, I recognize that their interest may include information that is of a more technical and advanced nature, but even they will agree with me that this is the exception rather than the rule. The majority of today's facilitators do not possess a formal educational background and experience in hospital or healthcare administration or direct patient care. They are interested in what they can sell, how much it costs, value for the price paid, and know their typical client profile (assuming they have had more than one or two in the life of their business). They are also interested in the financial relationship and how much income they will generate if they feature and steer heavily to your hospital or clinic over another. They will also be interested in making a face-to-face connection with the person who will likely take their calls and answer their e-mails to arrange a patient interview, prepare a price quotation, and handle monetary transactions related to additional expense beyond the package, and who will interact with the patient at checkout time.

The typical medical tourism facilitator may have no clear understanding about international hospital accreditation beyond the fact that many articles state that a hospital should have a certain "brand" of international accreditation over another. They may not have a grasp of exactly what is surveyed during the biennial inspection survey. They may also have no background in statistics and thus have no ability to critically evaluate the data included in clinical outcomes which may be presented in a manner in which doctors, hospital quality personnel, and healthcare executives are accustomed to conversing. If they have no understanding about hospital provider credentialing, life safety code compliance, or quality and infection control metrics, now is not the time, nor is it your responsibility to teach it to them. It may simply be over their heads. It may suffice to tell them simply that your facility is or is not accredited and by whom, and where you are in the accreditation process if you are not, and when the next inspection is scheduled if you are.

He or she may or may not understand the medical technology, may have little to no anatomy and physiology or medical terminology vocabulary, and may have never seen the inside of the hospital beyond the emergency room, front lobby, newborn nursery from a window, or labor and delivery. It might be that they had their own surgery or accompanied a loved one or friend through an episode of care. If that is the case, they may have a distorted recollection of what was happening around them, perhaps because of perioperative medications, stress, or preoccupation from the medical event, as opposed to having a clear head and thinking through a checklist of things they need to note.

As facilitators they should be interested in talking with the arrival coordinator for the hospital, and to learn where their client will initially be received and by whom. They may also wish to see the car or mode of transportation that will be used to collect the patient on arrival at the airport and to understand what happens to their client from the moment he steps off the aircraft onto the jet bridge (assuming there is one). They will want to assess the English (or other) language fluency of the medical tourism department staff, the nursing staff, the physicians who will treat their clients, and the administrative staff responsible for checkout, medical records, diet, and so on. Their job is to prepare their client for what to expect through the entire episode of care. This in turn contributes to higher patient satisfaction scores when outcomes are measured.

One way the hospital can help with this is to structure the tour so that they not only experience the on-site arrival process, but also experience a typical patient meal, view the patient menu selections, review the availability of television station options, Internet connectivity, and expected behavior or rules that the patient must follow during his confinement. For example, are the patients permitted to go to the gift shop or food establishments in the hospital lobby if their conditions permit? What if they would like to purchase stationery, postage stamps, a magazine, or shampoo? If there is a telephone in the room, is the patient permitted (and is the telephone enabled) to call mobile phones and landlines alike? In many countries, calls to mobile phones incur a surcharge. Are their clients able to leave a credit card deposit for such incidentals? Is it included in the room rate? Or is it simply unavailable. Where will their luggage be stored while they are confined in the hospital? Can they smoke in their rooms? Are they permitted to request a snack from the dietary department any time of the day or night? What about a cup of coffee or tea?

If their client has a question or concern while confined in the hospital, who will be her advocate? How will the advocate be summoned to the bedside? If there is a problem with an Internet connection in the room, who will troubleshoot it? Will the Internet connection have enough bandwidth to use VOIP connections such as Skype or Google Chat? Is the connection wireless or LAN?

The facilitator should also be interested in bilingual signage and patient information resources. Are the exit maps in each room in more than one language? What about telephone dialing directions? Patient instructions? One suggestion: in every hotel in the world, there exists a guest services directory. It lists information about guest mail, laundry and dry cleaning, automated teller machine (ATM) availability to access cash for incidentals, Internet service, spa menus, room service and restaurant options, gift shop hours, telephone surcharges and dialing instructions, and so on. It might also list things like a Fahrenheit to Celsius conversion table to help the client set an individually controlled thermostat in the room. It might also describe a programming list for the television stations and give a sample of what types of familiar programs may be broadcast and at which times.

Finally, they should be interested in the discharge process that their client will experience.

- How will coordination back to the airport be handled and by whom?
- Will a hospital-employed driver take her to the airport or a taxi?
- If she recently had surgery, who will assist her with her luggage?
- Is she expected to tip? If so, how much?
- Will someone accompany her to the gate?
- Will a wheelchair or other assistance be provided?
- What if the clients have pain after discharge?
- Will they be discharged with adequate pain medication for the journey home?
- How and when will patients receive a copy of their medical records?
- Will the records be translated to the language they need to share the records with their aftercare provider?
- What about X-rays, MRIs, and other diagnostic imaging reports?
- Are they supplied on a CD, DVD, or USB drive?
- Will they be transmitted directly to the aftercare physician or to the facilitator? When will they be available?

Because this is a medical "tourism" facilitator, he will likely be interested in what is nearby to the facility. Hotels, tourist activities, safety concerns, approved tour guides, historic and cultural sites, restaurants, and other travel and hospitality topics should be discussed. It is helpful to have brochures and a contact list handy for the facilitator and to note whether the hospital will be involved in any of those relationships or if the information is supplied simply as a courtesy. There should be transparency with regard to any commissionable relationships already established between the hospital and those other companies or providers, so that there are no misunderstandings or stepped-on toes.

Some of the more established medical tourism facilitators will likely carry professional liability insurance for their own actions. A knowledgeable representative from the hospital should be prepared to discuss matters surrounding a negative turn of events, including patient falls and other injuries, iatrogenic injuries, anaphylactic reactions, and things for which there may be professional liability on the part of the hospital or physician or nurse. What happens if awareness of the matter occurs after discharge and after the patient returns home? An open and honest discussion of these topics should be part of any tour, but especially for the facilitator who is giving his personal recommendation of the provider. Another related matter that should be discussed is what to expect if the client unexpectedly dies during the episode of care.

If the facilitator is based in the United States, he or she will be subject to certain federal regulatory compliance, including the Health Insurance Portability and Accountability Act (HIPAA) of 1996 (P.L.104-191), and Health Information Technology for Economic and Clinical Health Act (HITECH), the Privacy Act of 1974, among others. As such, he will be interested in how the hospital, physician, and others will assist him in maintaining compliance with these regulations. There are similar regulatory compliance concerns in other countries. Regardless of where the facilitator is located, the hospital, its employees, subcontractors, and attending physicians will be expected to maintain seamless compliance with any of these as a vendor to the facilitator. From a marketing and sales perspective, what should you share with the facilitator who will be your extended sales agent? Of course, pricing and service lines or products are key. But what about recent or differentiating services, innovations, packages, amenities, and the like? Upcoming additions to the service lines, new technology and what it does (in lay terms), new physicians of regional or international renown, physicians who have recently been recognized or published for using a certain technique or a discovery or an advancement (again, translated into lay terms). Just as when you are seated in a restaurant and the server proffers the menu, she also directs the customer's attention to any special promotions, and often suggests certain items that may have a short perishability or variability because they are dependent on who provides them and when and where they will be provided. You may wish to share with him the products or services that the hospital wishes to launch, push, or feature. In the same regard, the hospital may wish to downplay certain services it will soon abandon, has determined to be unprofitable, inappropriate for high-satisfaction medical travel outcomes from both a clinical or patient satisfaction perspective, or the hospital will soon lose the key physician due to retirement or job change. Does the hospital or physician provide a confidential newsletter update especially for facilitators to apprise them of special promotions, events, or featured new services since their fam tour? If so, provide back issues to them.

So now I have highlighted for you some of the things to consider when designing the tour and preparing for the medical tourism facilitator. The next consideration is how to structure the agenda of the tour itself. Upon arrival, the guests should be taken to a reception area and offered bottled water, a coffee, or tea. On the way to the reception area, it is always nice to pass by the wall of honor that displays the hospital's accreditation and other meritorious recognitions. In many hospitals, there is usually a bust or statue of the founder. It is nice to review the contributions of that benefactor and a short concise history of the hospital.

As far as introductions go, it is nice to have the hospital administrator, managing director, or executive welcome the facilitator, deliver a short welcome statement, and introduce the staff and key personnel. Business cards should be provided as each one introduces herself so that name and role associations may be made one by one. Next, the facilitator should be permitted to make his own introduction and express his delight and appreciation for the hospital's willingness to receive him and take time to show him the hospital. You should expect that the facilitator will want to tell you a little about his business, its history, and its background in the industry. If necessary, plan to have an interpreter on hand.

At a teaching hospital, often the attending physicians who will treat patients are on campus and may wish to say hello. At a private hospital, the physicians may not be available to take the time to do more than say hello and often may be where they should be, in clinic or in the operating room. If that is the case, have their CVs and a brief introduction about their cases, special interests, and their photographs available. One thing that we can arrange for a private hospital is a video brochure compilation of the featured medical tourism specialists, each with a 20-second video to enable the facilitator to assess language fluency, accent, and a glimpse of their personality and special interests. Often, the private physicians are willing to contribute to the cost of this video and it can be added to any video production that the hospital will undertake, for very little additional cost.

Next, take time to introduce the staff who will interact with the facilitator, from the person who answers the e-mails all the way up to the executive in charge of the department. Offer a one-page directory of names, addresses, telephone, fax, and e-mail addresses with a departmental hierarchy tree. This is helpful if the facilitator needs to climb up the chain of command to resolve a serious issue.

If a video about the hospital is to be shown, it should include some brief footage about the history of the hospital, whether it is related to a larger corporation or has multiple noteworthy benefactors, and if it has received honors in the healthcare quality area, community recognition, and recognition from the Ministry of Health or Ministry of Tourism. A bullet point list of the currently available technology, the number of beds, nursing ratios, medical staff, medical records details, and the like, should be shown along with any notes about upcoming additions to the hospital's technology portfolio. These should be up to date. A video postproduction editor can slip in recent updates to technology without having to reshoot the entire video and simply resave the edited update onto new media. The video should not have a runtime of more than 8–10 minutes. Don't forget to show a short clip of the mode of transportation to get the client to and from the airport, whether it is a nice clean taxi, light rail, limousine, shuttle bus, or something else, and discuss driver credentialing and insurance in the case of an accident on the way to or from the hospital.

The facilitator should be advised to bring a USB drive that contains a short presentation of 8–10 minutes duration about her business, client profiles, and current business model and future plans. This is your opportunity to vet their ability to properly and appropriately represent your hospital or clinic and be entrusted with responsibility to maintain your brand integrity. A brief questionnaire should also be sent in advance of arrival that can tell you specifically in which parts of the hospital they are most interested. You should also leave room for and encourage them to add any additional questions for which research will have to be done to have answers ready. Although it is never necessary or expected, if you plan to give the facilitator a token gift as a memento of her visit to the hospital, allow the facilitator the opportunity to know who will be present at the meeting by name and title in case she wishes to reciprocate. I have often felt embarrassed because

I was not prepared for the gift exchange and brought an inadequate supply of token gifts with me, having left the needed supply in my hotel room.

After both presentations, another 5–10 minutes should be allowed in which to ask any questions of one another that may have arisen as a result of watching the video or facilitator's presentation. At that point, the hospital executives and physicians may leave to go about their business. Once this initial session is completed, offer a bio (bathroom) break before continuing on with the walking tour. Make sure the toilet area is clean! Although no one will tell you, this is the one thing on which most facilitators will judge the hospital or clinic. Make sure that there are adequate hand-washing supplies, a way to dry hands, tissue paper, adequate lighting to check makeup, and so on. This is important because there will undoubtedly be photo opportunities and most women will want to check lipstick, hair, and other details because the photos will likely go on their website, to show they were there and also to make it easy to associate names and faces after the tour. Men will want to check their hair and their neckties, and so on.

Start the tour where the client will arrive and describe the arrival and admitting process. Next, proceed to the patient care areas and pay special attention to amenities and patient conveniences. Show them where companion travelers may be accommodated, and let them try the bed mattresses and any convertible sofas or other bedding that the companion traveler may utilize. Describe where luggage will be stored during the confinement. Show them the quality of the television reception on all channels, good or bad.

While passing through the hospital, whether it is the custom and culture of the local area, if the facilitators are from the United States, brief the staff to look up, make eye contact, and smile. A smile and direct eye contact go a long way to break down language barriers. In some cultures, eye contact is considered rude, whereas in others not to make eye contact is considered unfriendly, dishonest, or standoffish. One way to handle this is to prepare a visitor name tag with a small flag emblem on it. This can cue the staff as to how to act upon encountering your visitors.

As you pass the patient care areas, the typical medical tourism facilitator is not likely to be impressed or grasp the value of technology such as electronic medical records, computerized physician order entry, and the like, so unless it has been marked on the prearrival questionnaire, acknowledge that you have it and move on to things he can appreciate.

Contrary to popular belief, not all facilitators want to go into your surgical suite. Some get queasy at the sight of blood and body parts, and others may not have the training to understand what they are looking at or how to behave in that area. Include a question in the prearrival questionnaire to determine the level of interest in visiting the operating room. If they are interested, explain that they will have to don appropriate attire and explain what that is so that they may opt to dress for the visit in clothing that is easy to change in and out of. Then, provide a locker room for changing with a way to lock up purses, briefcases, and so on, and brief them on what is and is not appropriate to photograph.

Chances are the medical tourist will not likely need to experience the emergency room, or labor and delivery. The medical tourism facilitator will not usually be able to appreciate the technical aspects of the laboratory and pathology department, or the radiology imaging suite. Therefore, the facilitator will most likely be interested in extra-wide/extra-weight-bearing bariatric accommodations, orthopedics, physical therapy, cardiology and cardiac rehabilitation, outpatient department, and outpatient recovery accommodations for same-day surgery. If the hospital features any unique services such as stem cell research, transplant, robotics or other Centers of Excellence, or has within it a medical spa or dental facility, be sure to show those to the facilitators if you want them to feature this to their clients.

Time to Say "Goodbye"

Once the tour is concluded, return to the briefing or reception room for follow-up questions and answers. Executives and department heads may or may not wish to be on hand to answer any questions that the tour guides are unable to address. If a contract or letter of intent is to be offered, this is the perfect time to take care of business. Have a photographer on hand for the contract signing ceremony. Make the photographs available to them via direct transfer to their laptops from the digital camera used by the photographer or send them as an e-mail attachment upon their return home.

This meeting would also be a great opportunity to present the facilitator with a CD that has the physician credentials, all the marketing collateral, and sample package prices that the facilitator will need to promote the hospital and copies of the video and information shown earlier, all on the same CD or DVD. I cannot tell you how difficult it is to carry home all the extra added weight of paper brochures, notebooks, folders, and so on, on international flights. If token gifts are to be exchanged, it is better to do this at the conclusion of the tour rather than at the beginning on arrival and have to carry them throughout the hospital on the tour. If it is time for a meal, instead of a fancy special meal, have the dietary department bring an assortment of the daily menu offerings that patients will receive, so that the facilitator may attest to the taste and varieties of the food personally to their clients. Better yet, prior to leaving for the walking tour have the facilitator select what she would like to eat from the patient menu selection, if one is offered, so that it can be prepared and delivered to the meeting room upon return.

How to Sell Your Product to Insurers and Employers

Next, let's redirect our focus to conducting fam tours for insurance companies and employer-sponsored health plan representatives. Most salespeople miss the point. When talking to clients and potential clients, they focus on their products or services, on what they offer, or on themselves. But the customer doesn't care. At least, not until you answer the one question that matters: so what?

In his book *So What? How to Communicate What Really Matters to Your Audience* (FT Press, 2009), Mark Magnacca, president of Insight Development Group in East Sandwich, MA, shows how to use a "so what" mindset to become a more effective salesperson. A former road warrior who still appreciates the value of a travel agent, Magnacca suggests that travel sellers who focus on price don't get it. "The idea that fare is the only variable that matters when traveling speaks to a lack of salesmanship." The same is true in health travel and medical tourism. If you sell on price and accreditation, you just plunged yourself into the bloody red sea of undifferentiated competition.

When selling employers and insurers on the advantages of a health travel benefit, especially to larger groups, the greatest disservice one can do to the product is to think in terms of "what's in it for me" (WIIFM). If you change the question you ask yourself, you change the way you think, and if you change the way you think, you can understand what matters to potential clients. It's thinking about what's important to the client and thinking about that first. So for medical tourism and hospital marketers, to the extent you communicate the benefit of going to an international hospital instead of receiving treatment locally, you break through the clutter and get their attention, rather than telling them the hospital has world-class doctors and state-of-the-art technology, or JCI accreditation. But for the last qualifier on that list, they all do these days and the list keeps getting longer.

What's the Game Changer Here for Sales Professionals?

The big idea is that following a process changes everything. Winging it, which is what a lot of sales representatives and marketing reps do, makes everything harder. The "so what" matrix uses three simple questions:

- For What?
- So What?
- Now What?

Before you get on the phone, send an e-mail, or request a connection on Skype, the first question is: "For what reason are you having this conversation?" The second is: "So what? Why does the other person care?" And the third is: "Now what? "

I have had instances recently where the person on the other end of the Skype conversation tells me the reason for the call. When I say nothing and wait for the next phase, which is the anticipation of being told why I should care, the conversation goes dead. In fact, three times this week, it was followed by, "Hello, can you hear me?" I said, "Yes, but you haven't said anything that warrants a response, so I have nothing to say."

What Habits Do Sales and Marketing Representatives Need to Adopt?

One is the ability to do some research on your prospect, spending a few minutes to learn about the person you're calling and the opportunity he represents to you and the opportunity you represent to him. This is another entirely unbaked cake being served before it is fully ready to be presented to the market. When you've thought about what's important to your target audience, it's so much easier to be confident because you know they're engaged. On the other hand, calling without the proper game plan is a tremendous demonstration of lack of respect for the other person's time.

Today, in medical tourism the marketing and business development role is a more consultative role than ever. Part of being a consultant is being able to ask better, deeper, probing questions. That's the thing a website can't do. The site can have a list (for consumers) to fill in. But to truly understand what you're trying to accomplish, that's where a talented human being provides huge value. In fact, for American hospitals that wish to get in on medical tourism and health travel opportunities, it is far more consultative and complicated than contracting with third-party payers, and the due diligence vetting process is entirely different.

To find the value proposition to sell, think about what you actually do and how it connects to your target audience. For example, at Mercury, our clients tell us they can pick up the phone and call hospitals anywhere in the world and say, "We have cases that we need done and we want to buy them from you." They don't *really* need us for that. Our value proposition is that we coordinate the logistics for their employees and insureds, and that we have vetted the hospitals by deep inspection, credentialing, and privileging reviews to the standards they use themselves here in the States.

A second value proposition is that we have the staff to translate claims to English, translate medical records to English, convert claims with foreign currencies and procedure and billing taxonomy to U.S. standards, and have staff located worldwide to accommodate time zones that are unavailable during our clients' normal business hours. These things are frequently the bane of their dealings with foreign providers. We solve their problems faster than they can. In fact, we solve their problems in advance, so that they never become their problems.

A third value proposition is that our network is huge, with over 6,000 hospitals and over 600,000 physicians to choose from in the United States and throughout the world. We offer our clients choices in places where they are now, where they will expand, and near places that are remote where there are no choices. In exchange for a nominal network access fee, they adopt our network as their own and don't have to build one from scratch. We have the pricing all under contract, in a nice, neat database. They can request a price for any procedure from any provider in our network, and we can quote it with confidence and transparency.

Finally, as far as technique, we use the power of a personal biography. Because we've traveled to the hospitals and interviewed the staff and the physicians and even observed surgery as former surgical nurses, surgeons, and physicians, we are able to package what makes working with us unique. We communicate our competence, our character, and our standards, which we know meet or exceed theirs as well as our common ground (which allows us to shift gears quickly to what matters to our client). We've also worked on the insurance plan side (a prerequisite for our provider relations staff (clinical training or hospital leadership work experience combined with health plan experience). In cake-baking parlance, we baked and tasted the cakes, and lived to tell about it. We know which bakers excel at which recipes, which bakeries to avoid, which bakers don't meet our performance standards, quality standards, and operating standards, and we know the price of every cake on the shelf and the ones in the ovens.

Your sales and marketing teams have to do the same. They have to find the common ground. They cannot simply read the slide deck. In order to help you connect, I've included the list of frequently asked questions we receive from employers and insurers below.

It is possible, and actually highly likely, that you will receive requests and solicit opportunities to show your hospital, clinic, or healthcare organization to an employer or insurer, or a combination (self-funded/self-insured employer). It is in the latter space that Mercury Healthcare actually does a good majority of its business, and therefore I can speak from experience on the questions I receive and our brokers receive from potential health travel benefit designers, both employers and insurers.

I am going to list them in random order, and where it makes sense to do so, I give further details on the nature and orientation of the question.

- How long has the hospital been in business?
- How many rooms do they have?
- What is their average daily inpatient census?
- What is average daily outpatient census?
- What insurance plans do they contract with now?
- Have you (meaning Mercury Healthcare, or me personally sometimes) inspected the hospital?
- Have you (meaning Mercury Healthcare) reviewed the credentials of the physicians to the same level that our current health plan has done for providers here in our country?
- How do their infection rates and complication rates compare with Johns Hopkins in Baltimore, or Cleveland Clinic in Ohio?
- What advanced technology do they have in the hospital?
- What is the nursing ratio on a regular floor?
- Are the rooms private or semiprivate? What's the average room rate?
- Do the nurses speak English? All nurses? All shifts?

- What is their billing format?
- Which DRG system do they use?
- Are they on ICD-10 or ICD-9?
- Do they bill in their own currency or U.S. dollars?
- Are the medical records electronic?
- Are they on a PACS for imaging?
- Will they release medical records with bills?
- Will they send digitized images with bills?
- Are the medical records maintained in English?
- Does their country have some regulation in place that is similar to HIPAA?
- How quickly do we have to pay them?
- Can we audit the bills with the medical records?
- Can we object to a billed charge we don't want to cover?
- We heard about fraudulent billing practices in some countries and "bill padding" (extra unsubstantiated or medically unnecessary charges) in others. How can we guard against that?
- Do they bill us by line items or by a package price?
- What about extra items or services not included in the package?
- For how long are the prices you negotiated in effect?
- Are the prices discounted from their usual and customary charges?
- How long does it take to get an appointment?
- Will the doctor speak English?
- Will they co-operate with our credentialing and privileging procedures?
- Will they share the credentialing and privileging procedures that they currently use?
- Where were the doctors trained?
- Are they board certified? By which boards?
- Have the doctors published peer-reviewed papers on these special techniques?
- How many cases do they have to perform before they are allowed to use things like a robot or other advanced technology?
- Have you observed them during surgery? (Usually directed to me or our medical director)
- Will our insured/plan participant be treated by the specialist? Or his or her residents?
- Can our plan medical director and plan administrator visit the hospital and observe in surgery?
- Will they cover our travel expenses to visit them?
- Will you (usually meaning me or our medical director, or both) accompany them on the trip?
- Can we see more than one hospital in the local area?
- How close is this hospital to its nearest competitor in price and customer service?
- Can we pick and choose certain doctors and avoid others?
- Can we pick and choose some hospitals for certain procedures and limit what they do for us?
- What happens if there is a complication that was the fault of the doctor or hospital?
- Will they indemnify us if we get sued in the United States because of a negative outcome because we included them in our approved network? (Ostensible agency liability)
- What happens if there is a death of our insured? What is the procedure they follow?
- Will the discharge planners at the hospital work with our case managers for continuity of care?
- Who does the admission co-ordination?
- If we add a health travel benefit, who will meet the plan participant at the airport?
- Where will the companion traveler stay while the plan participant is in the hospital?
- We don't want to pay for VIP rooms, we just want a regular private or semiprivate room. Is that available? How much is it? Is it in the same ward as the local patients are admitted?

- What is the food like?
- Is there Wi-Fi in the rooms? LAN?
- How clean is the hospital?
- How safe is the neighborhood where the hospital is located?
- If they need physical therapy, do the therapists speak English?

With this line of questioning, one can easily see that the fam tour, if they choose to visit, will be distinctively different in emphasis and interests than the concerns of a business-to-consumer (B2C) facilitator.

If you want to look like a superstar, have the majority of these questions answered in a brochure that can be sent in advance of the visit as a .PDF document. Limit gifts and things to carry such as bags and brochures to something that can be tucked away as a memento of their visit. Make sure you allow time for photo opportunities, and review Fred Lee's book, *If Disney Ran Your Hospital* (2004). The hospital hallways become the public face of the hospital. Lights, tidy up, smiles and places everyone. Action!

Chapter 8

Quality and Safety Transparency

This chapter contains the opinions, analysis, and statements of the author. It is the responsibility of every reader to evaluate the accuracy, completeness, or usefulness of any information, opinion, advice, or other content contained in this chapter.

Lisa Beichl, Transparent Borders LLC
Consulting Affiliate, Mercury Healthcare Advisory Group, Inc.

Successful business enterprises typically provide smart solutions to fill a market demand. Sustainable solutions not only meet market demand, but also provide high perceived quality. In healthcare, quality focused and patient safety practices yielding positive medical outcomes have become the hallmark of successful hospital strategies. As hospitals consider expanding into the medical tourism market, transitioning from a traditional domestic strategy to global outreach requires a fundamental shift from a focus on purely domestic quality agendas to expanding and including strategies that proactively address cultural bias, social/psychological preferences, travel constraints, and effective transitions of care to the locally based provider.

Medical tourism is a nascent industry. In this chapter we review quality program development. In summary we aim to

1. Define the different medical tourism groupings and general patient flow.
2. Identify resulting medical tourism risks (that quality programs seek to manage).
3. Highlight the importance of transparency to manage risks.
4. Outline system-level quality and propose tools to support quality initiatives.
5. Suggest medical tourism quality outcomes measures (medical, functional, patient satisfaction) as well as patient preference groupings.

To put quality initiatives in context, Figure 8.1 summarizes the general strategic development of a medical tourism strategy.

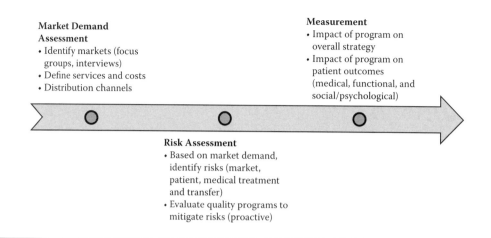

Figure 8.1   Main steps in developing a medical tourism strategy.

This chapter does not define market demand assessment, but does outline the two general demand groupings (general and selective medical tourists) and two general venues (domestic and international). It also provides important ideas regarding risk assessment for these groupings and venues, how quality initiatives can mitigate these risks, and the measurement of outcomes (medical, functional, social/psychological). At the end of the chapter are recommended metrics for the industry to begin assessing medical and social outcomes of medical tourism.

Two General Types of Medical Tourism Groups and Venues That Shape Quality Initiatives

Medical Tourism Groups

Medical tourism has existed for a long time. In the United States, there are Centers of Excellence[*] attracting patients with unusual or complicated medical histories seeking specific treatments. Studies show that there is a relation between select medical specialties and quality outcomes: trained specialists performing a consistent volume of a service yield better quality outcomes than generalists.[†] In addition, higher surgeon and hospital volumes are often associated with improved clinical outcomes, in particular for less common and more complex operations.[‡]

In the United States, hospitals including the Mayo Clinic and Johns Hopkins have international departments designed to manage the medical tourism patient segment. In some markets such as Nigeria, a lack of availability of some specialized healthcare treatments means that patients must travel to neighboring countries for those services. In both of these instances, medical tourism

---

[*] A hospital that provides specialty services typically associated with high volume and positive medical outcomes. Although the U.S. government has criteria for the term, some hospitals and insurers have created their own criteria for defining a Center of Excellence.

[†] "Relation between hospital orthopaedic specialization and outcomes in patients aged 65 and older: Retrospective analysis of U.S. Medicare data," *BMJ* 2010; 340 doi 10.1136/bmj.c165 (Published 11 February 2010).

[‡] "Provider volume and clinical outcomes in surgery: Issues and implications," Lee, Clara N., MD, MPP, Daly, John M., MD, FACS: June 2002, *Bulletin of the American College of Surgeons.*

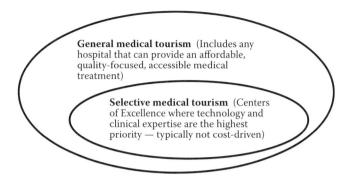

Figure 8.2   Diagram of the relationship between selective and general medical tourism.

occurs as an "exception," and is termed *selective* medical tourism. Selective medical tourism is driven by specialization, typically at important institutions (Centers of Excellence) with proven medical quality outcomes.

The concept of medical care outsourcing for complex cases or selective treatments is not a new idea; however, the expansion of the concept to attract patients in the general population (*general medical tourism*) requires a shift in focus. *General* medical tourism defines those cases where an individual selects an alternative (not home-based) venue to receive medical treatment. The general medical tourist typically seeks treatment for a straightforward intervention, including elective and cosmetic treatments, at a reasonable cost. The medical treatment may take place in a hospital that is not considered a Center of Excellence. Competition for these services is growing; therefore cost (rather than specialization) is often an important criterion. Selective medical tourism is a subset of general medical tourism. See Figure 8.2.

Medical Tourism Venues

The two venues where medical tourism can take place are *domestic* and *international*. Domestic medical tourism refers to medical treatment where travel for care occurs within the boundaries of a state or region. International medical tourism refers to movement for healthcare beyond the national border. Both domestic and international medical tourism are similar and involve travel to another locale for medical treatment, however, international medical tourism is complicated by involving a foreign marketplace with different regulations, quality standards, culture, communication styles, and so forth.

General Medical Tourism Flow (Domestic and International)

Figure 8.3 depicts a simple medical tourism event.* The internal circle generally depicts a traditional inpatient admission (gray hatch indicates the actions that would happen in the local context). Taken together, the two concentric circles illustrate the patient flow both in the home and medical tourism environments. The dotted edge surrounding the home environment points to the fact that the market in which the medical tourism care is received is expected to be different. Closer inspection of the external circle reveals the two aspects of a medical tourism event:

---

* The framework is drawn from the Health Climate Calculator™, from Transparent Borders™ LLC (2010).

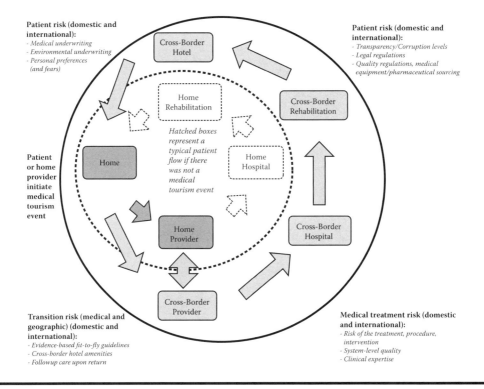

Figure 8.3 General relationship between the home and medical tourism.

- Medical treatment/intervention
- Travel, transition of care (medical transition, getting to and from the destination and follow-up care)

Successful management of these aspects increases the likelihood of a positive medical outcome. These two aspects of a medical tourism event are susceptible to four distinct risks[*]: *market* risk, *transition* risk, *medical* treatment risk, and *patient* risk. Effective identification and management of these risks increases likelihood of a quality medical outcome.

In a domestic medical tourism event, the market in which the care is received is similar to the home environment so there are limited compatibility risks. However, when the event is international, there is not only market risk, but the market characteristics influence the other risk groups.

Risk Assessments[†] within the Medical Tourism Flow Identify Quality Gaps

Before embarking on a medical tourism strategy, hospitals typically coordinate a thorough demand assessment. Creating quality programs for target markets requires risk assessments of the following categories.

---

[*] Risk groupings taken from the Health Climate Calculator™, from Transparent Borders™ LLC (2010).
[†] The Risk Assessment methodology is drawn from the Health Climate Calculator™, from Transparent Borders™ LLC (2010).

Market risk assessment requires a solid understanding of the market elements that could affect a safe patient journey. These include regulations regarding medical device and pharmaceutical importing, the level of healthcare innovation, as well as the importance of efficiency and effectiveness. For example, if a patient elects to undergo knee replacement surgery in an international market, matching the device regulations to the home market is critical both for follow-up care (a home doctor may refuse to manage a complication on a device that is not accepted in the home market) as well as for a positive medical outcome (if the inserted device fails in a shorter period of time than other options). Another example is Singapore, which has a strong medical quality history including superior blood management and supply protocols. However, the donor population could potentially be infected with dengue,* adding a patient safety issue that might be important to an individual (who may prefer to bring his own blood). Finally, matching legal liability differences may also be important to identify, particularly if a patient is receiving care in a market with substantially different malpractice regulations. Market risk affects all other risks (transition, medical treatment, and patient).

Transition risk refers to both the administrative management of the travel itself, as well as the clinical components of ensuring fitness to fly/travel and coordinating medical follow-up when the patient returns home. For example, a patient seeking bariatric banding may determine that the procedure does not require any follow-up at home. However, both in terms of clinical outcomes and creating transparency, all treatments are ideally discussed with the home provider to ensure a complete patient history.

An important development in reducing transition risk of a medical tourism event is the advancement of telemedicine. Telemedicine is defined as "the use of medical information exchanged from one site to another via electronic communications for the health and education of the patient or healthcare provider and for the purpose of improving patient care. Telemedicine includes consultative, diagnostic, and treatment services."† Advancing telemedicine techniques will support the globalization of healthcare by enabling the distant medical provider to follow up with the patient directly rather than solely depending on the home provider.

Medical treatment risk identifies the potential hazards that arise from the treatment and include a clinical and facility components. Here are four types of risk typically identified.

- *System* risk: The chance that a bottleneck in the hospital system will negatively affect patient safety (e.g., patient discharge was delayed due to the attending physician being on vacation, ensuring equipment use is understood and practiced regularly, use of checklists, practices to manage similar sounding drug names)
- *Medical* risk: The hazard of the medical treatment itself (e.g., the chance of a poor medical outcome, impact of comorbid conditions, new and available technology)
- *Human management* risk: the risk that the clinical expertise or sufficient patient care is not available (e.g., the chance that the attending physician is not apprised of best practices for a new surgery or medical technology)
- *Infrastructure* risk: the chance that something will go wrong due to poor infrastructure management (e.g., the patient had an adverse outcome because of the lack of necessary equipment such as an MRI machine needed to diagnose a head injury and necessary treatment)

---

* Merriam Webster, www.merriam-webster.com/dictionary/dengue, an acute infectious disease caused by a flavivirus (species *Dengue virus* of the genus *Flavivirus*), transmitted by aedes mosquitoes, and characterized by headache, severe joint pain and a rash—called also *breakbone fever, dengue fever.*
† Medicine.net website: http://www.medterms.com/script/main/art.asp?articlekey=33620 extracted November 2010.

Patient risk for medical tourism treatments includes not only basic medical underwriting (e.g., assessing the individual risk of the treatment due to high body mass index (BMI), smoking history, chronic diseases, etc.), but also environmental underwriting (e.g., risks associated with the home or medical tourism venue that could complicate a positive medical outcome including pollution levels, infectious diseases, and food-borne illnesses), and personal preferences (e.g., if the patient feels strongly about the country having a positive human rights track record, or if the person is afraid of being away from family and friends for a long period of time). All of these issues affect a patient outcome. With these risks effectively identified, the development of quality and safety transparency begins.

Importance of Transparency in Managing Risks

Merriam Webster defines something transparent as being free from deceit or pretense, easily detected or seen through, readily understood, characterized by visibility or accessibility of information especially concerning business practices.[*] The presence of transparency enables a full assessment of issues in the open, so that both problems and successes can be identified and studied. In the medical tourism context, transparency is important at the market level (where the medical tourism event occurs) as well as at the patient level (what and how medical treatments and processes occur).

Importance of Market Transparency in International Medical Tourism

Market transparency in an international context refers to the extent of corruption or the existence of gray markets[†] in a country. Transparency International (www.transparency.org) publishes an annual *Corruptions Perception Index* providing insight into perceived corruption based on analysis of myriad international data sources and opinion surveys from credible country experts and business leaders.[‡] Empirical work to quantify the economic extent of corruption in a market has been limited; however, studies show that the more market corruption, the less investment and economic growth in a country.[§] This suggests that innovation and quality standards are less likely to be present because there is reduced investment initiative. Translated, if healthcare quality is driven by innovation and competition, a corrupt market could have a more difficult time achieving a sustainable medical tourism strategy. However, there are examples of very successful (quality-focused) medical tourism hospitals operating in corrupt markets. Market transparency, therefore can be managed. Finally, without a reliable regulatory environment that can be trusted to manage basic services, the quality of infrastructure and services in corrupt markets requires additional verification.

Attracting patients from markets with high corruption levels, or seeking medical care in markets with a different corruption level is ripe for conflict. A critical component of a risk analysis

---

[*] Merriam Webster dictionary, extracted 15 Nov 2010 www.merriam-webster.com/dictionary/transparent.

[†] A gray market exists when solutions are created through unofficial means.

[‡] Corruptions Perceptions Index 2010, "Short methodological note" http://www.transparency.org/policy_research/surveys_indices/cpi/2010/in_detail#4 (November 18, 2010).

[§] Mauro, Paolo, "Why Worry About Corruption," *International Monetary Fund*, Economic Issues (6), 1997.

Table 8.1   Market Transparency and Effect on International Medical Tourism Risk

Risk Category	*Some Market Transparency Matching Tasks*
Patient	Identify the difference between the home and medical tourism destination corruption levels for possible communication or behavior concerns
Medical treatment	Identify differences in hospital and healthcare regulations between the home and medical tourism destination and how market transparency could affect (e.g., counterfeit medicines, using a medical device that is not supported by evidence-based medicine, etc.) Map the likelihood of an adverse event based on the identified market differences
Transition (medical and geographic)	Create a process to identify the impact of corruption on the transition of care including evidence of home provider's willingness to take care of the patient upon return home.

includes understanding the difference between the patient market and the target medical tourism market so that gaps are identified and addressed. Table 8.1 identifies some important issues to consider.

Quality and Safety Transparency

With a solid understanding of the market demand and associated risks, hospitals can develop quality-focused medical tourism programs. In healthcare, quality is often the umbrella term for superior outcomes, but the Institute of Medicine (*Crossing the Quality Chasm: A New Health System for the 21st Century*) expanded the idea by expressing the quality as the "degree to which health services for individuals and populations increase the likelihood of desired health outcomes and are consistent with current professional knowledge."[*]

As a starting point in the quality discussion, a standard model of healthcare quality developed by Avedia Donabedian focuses on structure, process, and outcomes. Specifically, effective structures and processes support positive medical outcomes.[†] This approach also states that the ultimate medical outcome reflects all influences (even external) on the patient journey.

When adapting this concept to the medical tourism market, medical outcome evaluation will have to address specific quality components in transitions of care. This theoretically includes patient fitness to fly/travel as well as ensuring that the home physician is willing to provide follow-up care and ways to measure the effectiveness of the process. A positive medical outcome that is compromised through a poor transition plan will emerge as a poor medical outcome in spite of the effective on-site medical treatment. Knowing specifically where the problem occurred (and why) increases the likelihood of resolution. Furthermore, follow-up of a medical tourism quality program typically includes a longer tail than typically practiced, specifically up to 36 months post discharge.

---

[*] Institute of Medicine, *Crossing the Quality Chasm: A New Health System for the 21st Century*, National Academies Press; 1 edition (July 18, 2001).

[†] Donabedian, A., 1988, "The quality of care: How can it be assessed" *JAMA* 260, (12); 1743–1748.

Accreditation

Hospital accreditation seeks to improve healthcare delivery and quality of care. The concept is broadly accepted by the international community including the World Health Organization (WHO) which views accreditation as an important component of healthcare quality.[*]

Internationally, there are many hospital credentialing groups including: Trent Accreditation Scheme (United Kingdom–Europe), Joint Commission International (JCI; United States), Australian Council for Healthcare Standards International (ACHSI), and the Canadian Council on Health Services (CCHSA). If your hospital strategy is focused on targeting one specific country, consider the accreditation most closely associated with it. Additional domestic and international safety standards include ISQUA (International Society for Quality HealthCare). In 1999 it launched the International Accreditation Programme (IAP), designed to "Accredit the Accreditors."[†]

Patient Safety

Patient safety focuses on prevention of errors leading to adverse events. This can include physical patient safety (avoiding slips and falls) and negative medical outcomes such as postsurgical infections. Safety includes continuous identification of potentially harmful issues and methods to measure and manage them.

Along with the vast quality credentialing and safety approaches, there are growing information resources on the Internet that offer information on safety issues that potential patients can access. These information sources may create both real and imagined quality obstacles that hospitals should be able to address. Consider the availability of instant online information in the form of "Google Alerts" and as well as the impact of country geography (tsunamis, pandemics, etc.). Proactively identify, address, and communicate safety issues that may be present in your environment. Both hospital and patient safety initiatives primarily work to reduce medical treatment risk.

Quality Tools to Promote Transparency

There are international quality tools that support hospital quality and patient safety initiatives. These generally focus on error prevention. Consider two general types of errors:[‡]

■ *Errors of ignorance:* Mistakes occurring because there is insufficient knowledge
■ *Errors of ineptitude:* Mistakes occurring due to inadequate use of available knowledge

Errors of ignorance can be reduced by research, knowledge sharing, and incentives to use best international evidence-based medicine when treating a patient. Evidence-based medicine development includes identifying clinical information needs, searching published objective literature for findings, and application to a clinical pathway.[§]

---

[*] http://www.emro.who.int/mei/HA.htm

[†] ISQua website: http://www.isqua.org/accreditations.htm. Extracted 21 November 2010.

[‡] Gawande, A., *The Checklist Manifesto*. Metropolitan Books; 1st edition (December 22, 2009).

[§] Sackett, D.L.; Rosenberg, W.M.; Gray, J.A.; Haynes, R.B.; and Richardson, W.S. (1996). Evidence based medicine: What it is and what it isn't. *British Medical Journal* 312(7023):71–72.

Errors of ineptitude can be reduced by adopting best practices through the use of checklists. Checklists, or lists of items that need to be completed before completing a procedure, treatment, or surgery, are a growing source of discussion in the medical field.* Sample surgical checklists (aimed at transparency) collect information confirming patient status, specific steps required in the briefing process, contingency plans with defined action items listed, as well as a debriefing of the episode postsurgery including counting instruments. The World Health Organization offers a surgical safety checklist and documentation in concert with the Institute for Healthcare Improvement (www.ihi.org).† In both instances, transparency in information (defining the particular best practice), and use of checklists (to identify action items) emerge as consistent with a best medical practice.

Risks and Rewards of Medical Tourism

Although most agree that quality and safety transparency are critical components of a medical tourism journey, being transparent has benefits as well as drawbacks. Before the medical tourism community commits to providing data on medical outcomes in both the short- and the long-term, a first step is to accept relatively basic quality and safety approaches. Returning to the four identified risk groupings that *quality initiatives* can control, here are some practical recommendations.

- ■ Market Risk
  - – Depending on your strategy (general or selective medical tourism; domestic or international patients) identify potential risks, and proactively manage.
- ■ Transition Risk
  - – Access evidence-based guidelines on fitness to fly or travel for medical care.
  - – Ensure appropriate accommodations including culture-specific issues (local language television) as well as physical site issues (telephone in the bathroom, wheelchair accommodation).
  - – Identify potential transition risks including: pharmaceutical management (pre- and posttreatment), local regulations regarding durable medical equipment or medical device sourcing.
  - – Create a standard process to communicate and confirm follow-up treatment with the local provider, including follow-up assessments up to 36 months post discharge
  - – Create measurements to identify (internally) management of the transition risks (both clinical and geographic).
- ■ Medical Treatment Risk
  - – If checklists are part of the surgical process, document which were included and affect patient safety, evaluate impact of use on patient outcome.
  - – Identify best practices for the procedure, treatment, or intervention and the general clinical pathway.
  - – Create a case management protocol for internal use to identify clinical and social issues potentially impeding a positive medical outcome.
- ■ Patient Risk
  - – Identify medical, environmental, and personal preference risks specific to your hospital strategy.

---

* Gawande, A.l, *The Checklist Manifesto,* Metropolitan Books; First Edition (December 22, 2009). New York, NY.
† WHO Surgical Safety Checklist: http://www.ihi.org/IHI/Programs/ImprovementMap/WHOSurgicalSafetyChecklist.htm (extracted 22 November 2010)

With these four risk groupings evaluated and proactively managed prior to the medical treatment, assess medical outcomes posttreatment.

Measuring Outcomes

Medical approaches are affected by culture. From the practice of alternative treatments in China, to the aggressive medical treatments in the United States,* understanding the medical approach (and managing patient expectations) is important to a long-term positive outcome. Although it is difficult to separate the physician from the culture, the impact on outcomes is even less obvious. For this reason, the mapping of both clinical as well as patient satisfaction rates is critical to the growth of the industry.

Overall health outcome measures refer to the impact of the treatment on the patient (all things being equal). For medical tourism treatments for the general population, collect data on three aspects of medical tourism: (1) medical outcomes, (2) patient improvement and functional health, and (3) patient satisfaction.

Each hospital may collect outcome data on specific issues; however, for potential comparison purposes in the medical tourism arena, the following medical outcome data are suggested:

- ◾ Surgical site infection rates: Postoperative infection is a major cause of patient injury, mortality and healthcare cost. Specifically, in the United States:[†]
  - – An estimated 2.6% of 30 million operations are complicated by surgical site infections (SSIs) annually.
  - – Infection rates up to 11% are reported for certain types of operations.
  - – Each infection is estimated to increase a hospital stay by an average of 7 days and add over $3,000 in charges (1992 data).
  - – Appropriate preoperative administration of antibiotics is effective in preventing infection.
- ◾ Readmission rates within seven and 30 days (both for initial diagnosis as well as any other diagnosis): Readmissions are an important quality metric pointing to potential quality issues in the initial patient stay. Categorizing the type of readmission (related and nonrelated to the initial admission) is important to capture, as it provides insight into both quality and population characteristics. As an example, the Mayo Clinic defines a hospital readmission as a patient admitted to a hospital within seven days after being discharged from an earlier hospital stay. The standard benchmark used by the Centers for Medicare and Medicaid (CMS) is the seven-day readmission rate. Rates at the 75th percentile or lower are considered optimal by CMS.[‡]
- ◾ Mortality rates and discharge status: to capture patients discharged to home, or to hotel or a long-term care facility. Basic discharge status options: discharged to home, discharged to hotel, discharged to rehabilitation, and death.

There are challenges collecting these data,[§] particularly if hospitals are not required to provide them to a regulatory body. If the results are not audited, assessing validity and reliability can be

---

* Payer, L.. *Medicine and Culture*, New York: Holt Paperbacks (November 15, 1996).
† Institute for Healthcare Improvement: http://www.ihi.org/IHI/Topics/PatientSafety/SurgicalSiteInfections/ (extracted 22 November 2010).
‡ Mayo Clinic website: http://www.mayoclinic.org/quality/readmission-rates.html (extracted 24 November 2010).
§ Any analysis of medical outcomes requires a robust assessment of demographics and diagnoses to ensure case mix adjustments accurately reflect population differences.

problematic, particularly in corrupt markets. This could discourage sharing outcome data publicly. One alternative is to give an international governing group the authority to verify the veracity of results, so that there is a perceived fair environment. Alternatively, objective and licensed third-party administrators or licensed insurers could also fulfill this role.

Assess patient satisfaction and functional status. For patient improvement and functional status, consider using the Short Form 36 (SF 36) questionnaire (developed by RAND) at both pre- and posttreatments. The SF 36 surveys patient health and is used in economic studies as a variable in the calculation of a Quality Adjusted Life Year (QALY). QALYs are used in studies to measure the cost-effectiveness of procedures or treatments.

The original SF 36 was constructed by the RAND Corporation (http://rand.org) and is a multipurpose survey profiling both functional health and well-being. It is a generic measure rather than disease- or age-specific. The questionnaire has been translated in more than 50 countries as part of the International Quality of Life Assessment (IQOLA) Project.[*]

The SF survey evaluates patient health from the following perspectives: health perception (and change over time), physical limitations and impact on personal life, personal mental health (feelings of negativity or uselessness), and the individual's perspective on physical impairments. A critical advantage of the SF approach is that the survey has been tested in multiple languages. This enables the beginning of documentation regarding health improvement (or deterioration) upon completing a medical tourism treatment. This approach, therefore, includes a cultural sensitivity that may be lacking in other methodologies.

Patient satisfaction surveys should be designed to address the specific medical tourism grouping (general or selective) as well as venue (domestic or international). Surveys should include satisfaction with the medical treatment, the medical outcome, the provider's capabilities and communication, the hotel or rehabilitation accommodations (functional, social, and longevity), and the ease of transitioning back home to receive follow-up care.

Although follow-ups after 7 days and 30 days after discharge occur, for the medical tourism patient, perform overall follow-ups for up to 36 months posthospital discharge to ensure solid understanding of issues in health, transitioning care, follow-up treatment, and any personal behavioral changes as a result of the experience.

An additional aspect to medical outcomes analysis particular to medical tourism is to profile the demographics of your patient base. This information enables retrospective review of market characteristics, which can be linked to patient outcomes. Specifically, track the following demographic data:

- *Reasons for medical tourism event:* where the medical tourist emerged and reason he or she sought medical tourism
- *Insurances*: insurances held (or not; including travel insurance)
- *Travel history*: passports held, languages spoken, last time on a flight, frequent flyer status, general use of Internet to book travel, and so forth
- *Preferences and fears:* country requirements (e.g., human rights or personal safety), personal concerns/fears. Fears are important to identify as they may impede an otherwise healthy medical outcome and include issues such as, "I am worried I will not understand my doctor, fearful of the long flight, and missing my family and friends."

With these cumulative data, hospitals can identify quality gaps and opportunities to proactively address patient concerns and preferences.

---

[*] SF-36.org, http://www.sf-36.org/tools/sf36.shtml extracted November 15, 2010.

Movement to Standard Best Practices

As the medical tourism market expands from selective to general medical tourism, hospitals have the opportunity to develop targeted strategies aimed at increasing consumer awareness of both the risks and rewards involved. Proactive development of quality-focused, patient-centered, and transparent processes and results will enforce the importance of quality medical, transition, and social outcomes as well as elevated professionalism of top-tier hospital participants.

Chapter 9

Risk Management and Liability Mitigation in the Medical Travel Industry

This chapter contains the opinions, analysis, and statements of the author. It is the responsibility of every reader to evaluate the accuracy, completeness, or usefulness of any information, opinion, advice, or other content contained in this chapter.

Tracy H. Simons
President, Custom Assurance Placements, Ltd.

How does the liability exposure of the medical travel industry affect you? The question that seems to be on everyone's mind is, "What if something goes wrong for a medical traveler?"

Stakeholders have done a good job in setting standards of care for the medical travel industry. There is an AMA recommendation on the topic of medical tourism. In addition there are many other studies and scholars who have explored and published findings about the criteria for setting benchmarks for quality care in the medical travel industry. Stakeholders are using provider credentialing tools, developing procedures for medical records, hiring medical professionals to advise patients, implementing privacy protections, and introducing many other services to provide high-quality care and service to medical travelers. However, the industry is still in the developmental stages of setting self-regulating guidelines to determine what the quality and safety requirements should include and where the liability for administrators, facilitators, hospitals, employers, and individuals begins and ends.

It has taken several years to develop insurance solutions that provide coverage for all the aspects of liability for all the stakeholders involved. The products are continuously changing as claim exposure is realized through loss experience and exposures are assessed and understood in international settings. What are the known exposures?

■ The Individual Medical Traveler
  – Unforeseen expenses from a medical complication
    • Immediate and long-term expenses
  – Additional expenses of unforeseen emergent care or corrective care once the patient returns home
  – A medical malpractice occurrence
  – An accident that occurs in the course of travel to and from a medical destination
■ Facilitators, Receiving Hospitals and Employers
  – Both direct and indirect or vicarious liability associated with a mishap from implementing a medical travel benefit or managing a person's healthcare

The individual will look to a "professional advisor" (i.e., facilitator), receiving hospital, or employer to solve unforeseen problems during the course of travel or while under care. He or she will have an expectation of knowledge that is assumed from verbal and published descriptions of service, from descriptions of high-quality medical care, and from any other direct, implied, or assumed level of expertise that is expected by the client. This exposure is called "managed healthcare liability."

Managed healthcare liability, broadly defined, includes services and activities performed whether by the organization itself or performed by others on the organization's behalf (vicarious liability) and it includes these activities whether they are provided on paper, in person, electronically, or in any other form.

Services and activities include all of the following:

■ Provider selection
■ Utilization review
■ Care coordination
■ Advertising, marketing, selling, or enrollment for sponsored benefit plans
■ Claim services
■ Establishing provider networks
■ Reviewing the quality of medical services or providing quality assurance; design or implementation of financial incentive plans
■ Wellness or health promotion education
■ Development or implementation of clinical guidelines, practice parameters, or protocols
■ Approval of payment for covered medical services or directives on what services would be allowable
■ Services or activities performed in the selection, administration, servicing, or management of, including but not limited to, handling records in conjunction with such plans, or affecting enrollment, termination, or cancelation of coverage for participants under such plans.

In the medical travel arena, this can be broadened to include other aspects of the services provided by a medical travel service stakeholder, and then adding the exposure of an international setting.

Risk management provides a solution, and a venue to stand out from the competition. There are two lines of defense, liability insurance and accident insurance. Insurance has helped industries be on the developing edge of emerging markets by allowing those at risk to transfer it to an insurer. This is evidenced from the first ship that was insured from a coffee house in London, which later became known as Lloyd's of London.

- Liability Insurance
  - Managed healthcare liability
    - Includes vicarious liability—the liability associated with the act of another party.
    - Includes defense costs.
    - Includes damages and settlements.
    - Is available from a few carriers in the United States.
    - You will need a local representative to purchase this type of coverage in your home country.
- Accident Insurance
  - First-party coverage
    - These types of policies do not require one to recover from an at-fault party. The claimant is also the insured.
    - Claim payments are intended to make the injured party whole and mitigate the need for a lawsuit against an at-fault party.

Accident insurance has long been used as a risk mitigation tool. Your everyday and common liability policies include a no-fault accident benefit for the purpose of mitigating a liability claim proceeding.

Note: Be careful when assuming that a regular travel accident policy will meet the needs of a medical traveler. There are specific exclusions on travel accident policies for persons traveling for the purpose of receiving medical care. There is also no coverage for complications on these policies. Furthermore, specially designed medical travel accident policies vary greatly in what they will cover. Make sure that you explore and compare the policies and know the strengths and weaknesses of each.

Here are some types of coverage typically on a medical travel accident policy.

- Additional medical or surgical treatment as the result of a complication
- Accidental death and dismemberment
- Disability
- Repatriation of mortal remains
- Family coordination
- Household modification
- Loss of reproductive function
- 24/7 International assistance service

Coverage can also include an accidental injury not associated with the procedure: that is, the taxi accident or trip and fall that could be blamed on the result of traveling for a medical procedure.
Who is buying this coverage?

- Individuals: alone or through medical travel facilitators, appointed agents or directly online
- Groups
  - Employers are providing this for all employees when they utilize the medical travel benefit on their group plan
  - Hospitals/facilitators are including the coverage on every patient to mitigate liability exposure

In summary, insurers can help you transfer your business risk and exposure by providing defense costs coverage when the recourse in the international setting is tested. Insurance provides the deep pockets and keeps the hands out of your pocket. Insurers can work with attorneys to determine the legal system that will preside at their expense and not yours. Insurers can provide the settlements to make an injured party whole again. Lastly, insurers create standards for care by underwriting an exposure, because they will not insure an exposure that they feel has not taken a professional and educated approach to their business model or management.

Tracy H. Simons, President
Custom Assurance Placements, Ltd.
A Specialty Lines Insurance Broker
Columbia, SC 29250-5736
Phone: (803) 799-1770, Fax: (803) 799-1817
www.globalprotectivesolutions.com
for the medical travel industry

Chapter 10

Introduce Your Program to the Media

Let's agree on a few realities.

1. Medical tourism has generated a tremendous amount of media attention.
2. Ruben Toral was extremely clever when it came to his efforts in 2005–2007 at Bumrungrad, for his efforts placed that hospital underneath a giant pushpin on the map of the medical tourism world. The brilliance that man has is demonstrated by making what he did there look easy.

As the Internet has made communicating with reporters and editors extremely easy, breaking through using the online methods everyone else uses has become increasingly difficult. These days, all you need is a Twitter account and the name of the target editor, reporter, or journalist. There are also commercial services that sell subscriptions to their databases of thousands of journalists, or you can simply search using a search engine.

Unfortunately, there is also a glut of people holding themselves out to be public relations (PR) people, spamming journalists with unsolicited and unrelenting commercial messages in the form of "news releases" and untargeted broadcast "pitches."

One lesson my mother, a descendant of Spanish nobility, always told me, "Maria, don't be common." Is your PR person making your organization appear the same as every other spammer out there? Have they been shotgun blasting the media with the same messages as every other medical tourism hospital and physician or the facilitators that have also been doing this?

Do your news releases contain these words?

- World class
- Leading

When I searched "medical tourism" and "world class," using Google, the search yielded 3,450,000 results. A search of world class + medical resulted in 6,650,000,000 results. A search of world class + hospital resulted in 60,100,000 results.

To make it more interesting, I used one of Google's search tools to look up "world class fully equipped modern hospital" (musing as I read what I wrote, and the opposite of that would be?). There were 1,190,000 results, and I then requested the statistics of translated pages and was unprepared for what I saw:

French	700,000
Spanish	392,000
Italian	81,400
German	8,610
Russian	818,000
Croatian	13,000
Slovak	2,300
Thai	43
Albanian	566
Turkish	143,000
Lithuanian	4,410
Korean	345,000
Vietnamese	2,650,000
Polish	133,000
Hungarian	7,840
Norwegian	18,000
Icelandic	79
Swahili	581
Japanese	83,700
Portuguese	110,000

Who uses this language in common speech? How did all those pages get on the Internet in all those languages when there aren't anywhere near that number of Hungarian hospitals, Icelandic hospitals, and Vietnamese hospitals?

As I've said before, I get hundreds of news releases, pitches, and announcements from PR agency staffers, hospital marketing staffers, facilitators, and other corporate communications people every day. My e-mail address is available in many places: in the articles I write, on my blogs, in my books, and at the *eContent* magazine website where I am a contributing columnist. That easy availability means that my address has also been added to various databases and lists of journalists. Unfortunately, my e-mail address also gets added without my permission to many press lists that PR agencies and companies compile and maintain; so whenever they have a new announcement, no matter what the subject, I am a part of that broadcast message. Then there are the headhunter (executive search) firm messages. I am harassed with messages from people wanting me to quit my job to work for someone else! I receive broadcast messages with openings that don't even relate to healthcare. I receive solicitations of candidates that I don't need, didn't ask for, and who aren't qualified to work for us. The spam approach doesn't work. It brands your organization as one of the "bad guys" that (a) doesn't care, (b) hasn't researched our needs, (c) hasn't figured out the "so what," and (d) has way too much time on his hands to be sending this many broadcast spam messages.

Ok, so that's the bad news. The good news is that reporters are always looking for subject matter that is unique, leading edge, special interest, human interest, and so on. They want to find you and if you have great content on your website and your online media room, reporters will find you via search engines. The key is that you have to find a way to reach the journalists who aren't just one-way spam. Pay attention to what they write about by reading their stories. Comment on them, but don't just use the comment field as a way to post a link-back. That's gauche!

Start a real relationship with reporters by commenting personally, outside the public eye, or by sending them information that is not a blatant pitch for your company. Become a part of their network of editorial resources. Don't forget to pitch bloggers. Not only does a blog mention your buyers, reporters, and editors, it reaches theirs.

Here are a few pointers for you:

1. Avoid nontargeted pitches and news releases that are irrelevant to what the reporter covers; they are spam.
2. Make sure reporters can find you on Google, Technorati, and other channels.
3. If you blog about something specific and useful, reporters will find you.
4. Pitch bloggers because being covered in important blogs means the media will find you.
5. Make sure your organization appears "busy," not noisy!
6. Journalists want a great online media room full of content that they can review at their leisure. It becomes their watering hole if your content is of high quality.
7. Some but not all reporters use RSS feeds, so add them to your blogs and white papers.
8. Personal relationships with editors and journalists are important.
9. Don't tell what your product does, tell what specific problem it solves.
10. Comment on reporters' blogs.
11. Know the publication or media channel you are pitching to (e.g., don't sell liberal ideas and products for certain listeners to an ultraconservative talk show!).
12. Once you know what a reporter is interested in, send her an individualized pitch crafted especially for her. Take care to be accurate on idiomatic translation lest you lose the message on the errors and the journalist decides you are an amateur and not to be taken seriously.

For a medical tourism product that sells into a niche, you'll likely never get noticed by editors at major publications like *The Wall Street Journal*, *USA Today*, and *Financial Times*, but you will get noticed by niche bloggers and they will be interested in you. There are several in medical tourism and more emerging in importance and popularity each week.

COLLABORATION WITH OTHER PARTS OF THE MEDICAL TOURISM/HEALTH TRAVEL SUPPLY CHAIN

This next section discusses the topic of working with facilitators, case managers, and other referral sources. Here I discuss relationship arrangements and compensation issues associated with fee-for-service and commission-based arrangements. Keep in mind that the relationship with the facilitator, hotels, and destination managers can make or break a medical tourism provider's reputation, brand image, and can carry serious consequences and implications for patient satisfaction and clinical outcomes measured over the entire episode of care. This chapter also discusses a little bit about how to vet the credentials and experience and professional liability implications that stem from working with medical tourism facilitators.

It has been my experience as I speak with hospital administrators and physicians worldwide, that they receive tens if not hundreds of requests per week by well-intentioned, hopeful, new medical tourism facilitation business owners who may be inexperienced, undercapitalized, untrained, and totally unfamiliar with healthcare administration, statistical outcomes analysis, marketing and branding, and other core competencies such as medical terminology, anatomy, and physiology, and a knowledge of the cases and procedures to which they will direct medical tourism clients.

Chapter 11

Working with Case Managers

This chapter, albeit brief, reviews some of the case management issues that arise in medical tourism and health travel care coordination. For the majority of readers of this book, you are very familiar with the traditional roles of case managers in the hospital or managed care organization setting. Therefore, I do not draw this out, nor do I start with a deep introduction to medical case management.

The concept of case management for vulnerable persons who need complex management of an episode of care is an important part of the solution to the problem of fragmented and hard-to-access service. Given the story I shared at the beginning of this book, it is easy to see how anyone, even someone with all my training, experience, and familiarity with the operations of health delivery systems, can be deemed vulnerable.

Case management is the organizational glue that binds together a coordinated plan of treatment, rehabilitation, and support services for patients. Case management is often seen as a solution for preventing medical or psychiatric rehospitalization, enhancing access to needed services across different delivery systems, and promoting improved patient functioning and quality of life. The role is far beyond the scope of the traditional medical tourism facilitator and is often practiced by a registered or advanced practice nurse who has passed a certification examination.

Conventional case management programs usually address five core functions:

- Needs assessment
- Treatment planning
- Linkage
- Monitoring
- Advocacy

A variety of case management models exists, from generalist models, in which managers work with large caseloads and broker services from external providers and agencies, to clinical models, in which managers work with smaller caseloads and provide some mental health and care coordination across a continuum or rehabilitative services.

Models also differ in how the case manager works: alone or as part of a team, with funds authorized to purchase services, or with control over access to clinical services such as admission privileges for inpatient care or to order and organize a medical evacuation.

Within the private sector, case management is often used as a mechanism of utilization review, aimed at reducing or limiting access to some questionable or medically unnecessary services in order to reduce costs. Under managed care, changes in the delivery of mental and medical health services have occurred and will continue, and case managers strive to reconcile these opposing perspectives.

Throughout the patient care process, a medical case manager consistently monitors and reviews the services of each resource, ensuring that progress is made in an effective and timely manner. The impressions formed during the monitoring and review activities are influenced by their practical direct patient care experience, continuing education, and the study that led to licensure as nurses. This is not appropriately compared with a medical tourism facilitator with little or no comparable training in either healthcare or travel logistics.

The important duties of a case manager are

1. Initial intake to ensure eligibility and medical appropriateness
2. Medical director review prior to contact with the destination physician, if unsure of appropriateness
3. Advance, in-depth assessment of service needs, companion availability, and aftercare recuperative settings
4. Development of a comprehensive individualized plan of care covering the entire episode of care to the extent that it can be assessed (barring any complications)
5. Coordination of services required to coordinate all logistics
6. Full-time client care and rehabilitation monitoring
7. Periodic reevaluation and adaptation of the plan as necessary over the life of the client

In our company, we take it one step further. The case manager remains in contact with the patient through the entire outcomes measurement period, which can last up to 36 months. During the outcomes interviews, a proprietary tool is used that is similar to the SF-36® (Rand Corporation) that measures and remeasures responses from the patient on various recovery status questions. Applying their medical knowledge of anatomy, physiology, as well as other sciences, the nurses are trained to question further if they suspect a need for deeper investigation. If they feel it is warranted, they have full access to the medical director, and the treating surgeon or other provider, and also to the aftercare provider. The doctors seem to be more comfortable speaking with a registered nurse than with a medical tourism facilitator without comparable training, education, and experience.

Chapter 12

The Comprehensive Role and Functions of a Medical Tourism Facilitator

Medical tourism facilitator roles and responsibilities will vary according to the type of organization, the population served, the client mix, a medical tourism facilitator's education and training, and the type of facilitation offered. In today's medical tourism arena, facilitation is offered by a variety of organizations in a variety of ways, and each job carries with it its own set of priorities and variations to the role, including, but not limited to those shown in Figure 12.1.

For example, a concierge who performs a meet-and-greet service and destination management service may be completely different from the facilitator who actually books cases using the Internet and other marketing channels, and different again from the role of the facilitator located inside a hospital or medical clinic who coordinates cases with the external facilitator. A facilitator assigned to an insurer or an independent case manager may have yet a different role.

Consequently, roles and responsibilities vary because virtually every category of client served will have its own needs, and these needs will dictate the scope and depth of the facilitation required.

The facilitation model may be hospital driven, or primary service driven in mental health, and a generalist approach offered to a specific group of clients, (e.g., transplant cases or others with a specific disease). However, most of the same essential components remain. The common and essential components are processes for the following:

- Identification of appropriate clients
- Assessment of clients for the services they require
- Coordination, planning, and identification of the level of care, and then the level of services and scope of resources required to meet patient care needs
- Implementation, coordination, and linkage of clients expeditiously to the sources they require
- Direction, oversight, and monitoring of the distribution of services clients require and ensuring that appropriate and effective services have been established as clients move through the episode of care

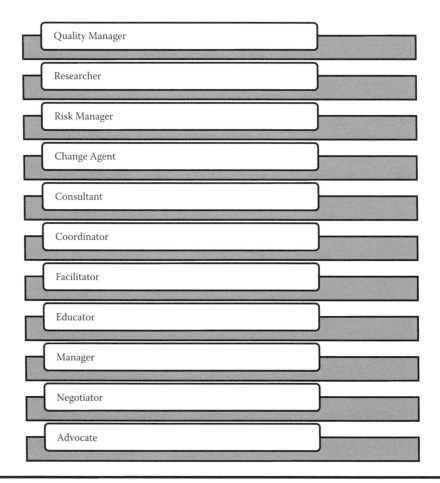

Figure 12.1 Components of being a medical tourism facilitator.

- Advocacy and the ability to act on behalf of clients to ensure that needed interventions are obtained and clients are progressing as anticipated
- Evaluation and continuous monitoring to ensure the usefulness and effectiveness of the facilitation plan and that client-desired outcomes and goals are reached
- Patient satisfaction measurement
- Feedback loop reporting to providers and the creation of measurable outcomes data

Regardless of the type of clients served or the practice setting for the health travel facilitator, the common characteristics of health travel facilitators should include the following:

- Education that includes medical terminology and anatomy, physiology, pharmacology, basic health history taking, and other general medical training
- Education that includes travel planning training, including geography, aircraft configuration, airport layout, a firm understanding of minimum connecting times, standard airport codes, standard carrier codes, tariff configurations, immigration and visa details, and refund and change restrictions related to airline and trouble ticketing, and hotel and ground transportation reservations

- Experience and expertise in the specialty to be facilitated
- Ability to have a holistic perspective and see the client as a whole person, rather than a disease or a case
- Knowledge of international protocols and health systems
- Knowledge of how to procure resources to accomplish your goals
- Medical communication skills and the ability to interact effectively with both the client and the healthcare team
- Ability to solve problems and overcome hurdles and obstacles and plan for the unexpected
- Ability to be creative and innovative
- Ability to be self-directed, because often there is no role model to follow

The health travel facilitator role has three dimensions. The first is the clinical role, which requires collaboration with the interdisciplinary team and involves the development of protocols for the key tasks or events that must be accomplished to assist clients through globally integrated healthcare access. Health travel facilitators then use these protocols to direct, monitor, and evaluate client treatment in the outcomes that are responses to the treatment. The second dimension is a managerial role, which refers to the scope of managerial responsibilities it takes to coordinate the care of clients. The third dimension involves the financial aspect of planning, and this involves access to information about the cost of each care service, and information on allocated length of stay or the number of treatments or procedures that will be necessary to accomplish goals. To be effective, health travel facilitators must have access to information on the cost of resources and consumption; and they must be familiar with payment systems including foreign currency, wire transfer, refund, cancellation, change fees, prepaid deposits, and overcharge policies and procedures.

One of the features that makes health travel management and facilitation appealing is that the structure must be extremely flexible. The design of each program can be modified to fit the needs and budgetary constraints in any healthcare setting. Therefore the facilitation theme can have many variations, and there is no right or wrong way to design a facilitation business. The key to the success of the business will be the roles and scope of functions that the facilitators are able to perform.

At the time of this writing there are no criteria as to who can perform health travel facilitation. The primary goal of providing superior customer service, and coordinating safe, quality patient care in the most cost-effective manner must flow. Golden designated timeframes must be established to achieve successful client outcomes. Because all care in today's healthcare arena is very time-sensitive, many facilitation firms will attempt a multidisciplinary collaborative approach so that many hands are helping to do the tasks of one. This can be efficient and cost-effective as long as there is transparency and accountability, and a clearly defined role for each member of the team.

A multidisciplinary team approach is often used in traditional case management because of the many organizations that utilize the case manager who may be a generalist, and not familiar with international patient service coordination. Although the generalist may have the expertise to handle most cases, the variety of cases that may present with special needs by their very nature in international cases, may present situations in which that case manager is not an expert in all areas or is unable to handle all the tasks required, especially with the rapid movement of clients between international healthcare systems.

To function appropriately, the generalist case manager will rely heavily on the sharing of information from the health travel facilitator and other professionals such as physicians, social workers, and other nurses, and mental health and other rehabilitation therapists as a case management plan is developed.

Health travel facilitators must be realistic and assume that many case management goals will remain unmet as a result of noncompliance by the patient or family or the lack of a source of payment for needed care and services. Unmet goals are often the result of factors such as the following:

■ Lack of understanding of the complexities of the disease process on the part of the facilitator
■ Lack of a formal training program for the health travel facilitator
■ Lack of the tools needed to do the job: policies and procedures, a computer system that can capture and report details and outcomes, and manage health data and medical records appropriately
■ Lack of strong leadership, or leadership that micromanages
■ Caseloads that are too high
■ Poor planning, resulting in crisis intervention or putting out fires as events occur
■ Lack of cooperation by physicians when specific requests are made
■ Lack of understanding by the health travel facilitator of the requirements, processes, and modalities of reimbursement and risk arrangements
■ Inadequate staffing by external organizations such as the social services support for the psychosocial aspects for care needed by clients during aftercare
■ Lack of providers who are trained to offer the level and type of care required, often resulting in fragmented care
■ Delays in services or lack of care altogether
■ Expensive or inappropriate levels of care
■ Fraud and abuse
■ Unnecessary readmissions or increased length of stay
■ Suboptimal use of healthcare resources, leading to either over- or underutilization
■ Patient and family dissatisfaction with care, and possible increased likelihood of lawsuits
■ Increased quality of care issues
■ Increased complications caused by ineffective or inappropriate care

Health travel facilitators should be expected to review efforts for continuous quality improvement (CQI) programs and ongoing management by healthcare providers and their own health travel facilitation organization. This is accomplished by identifying potential problems and then coordinating and channeling the delivery of care among providers and concierge providers by managing the clients' needs across the level, type, and scope of care needed. To identify issues and come up with solutions, the health travel facilitator should do the following:

■ Audit medical records to determine whether unnecessary tests, treatments, or procedures are planned or have been performed and whether other factors are contributing to increased costs, length of stay, or use of resources.
■ Review complaints and incident reports, as well as other documents that identify issues, to determine whether opportunities for improvement exist.
■ Interview key hospital staff, including the medical staff, to solicit their input and identify areas for improvement.
■ Review and analyze patient records to identify which costs could have been eliminated or which processes could be reviewed and improved.
■ Evaluate current data to ensure that the information obtained was indeed needed, and if not, what information should have been obtained to evaluate the areas that require change.

- Evaluate patient, physician, and staff satisfaction surveys to determine issues and identify areas that require change.
- Determine which additional costs associated with any wrong medications or treatments or placement of the client at the wrong level of care could have been avoided.
- Determine the source of increased costs related to the misuse of personnel, products, or resources.
- Evaluate delays in services and consequently added costs as a result of increased length of stay or additional treatments that may or may not have been medically necessary.
- Evaluate loss of sales or customers, and why clients might switch to other facilitators.
- Determine why high-quality providers may have dropped their contract with the facilitator, or refused to contract in the first place.

Regardless of what you try to study or the totals in the data that you study, the key to quality improvement is to have a process in place that measures the before and after events and to take the steps necessary to make changes, and then monitor the effect of the changes to ensure that they were effective. If the changes are not effective, the process should be re-examined and started again.

A powerful database and decision support system will enable interpretable and standardized reporting mechanisms that make continuous data monitoring and analysis occur, so the process becomes automatic, periodic, and standardized. This way, final outcomes may be compared and validated. Health travel goals and successful outcomes can only be reached if they're offered within a framework that includes total organizational commitment in which the business model is structured to meet the care needs of health travel clients. By ensuring that appropriate outcomes are achieved, health travel facilitators will be able to provide a framework for continuous and refined planning for client management to ensure multidisciplinary, multigeographic care and ensure appropriate and cost-effective use of healthcare resources, and precious healthcare dollars. Your model should contribute to the foundation of total quality improvement and attempt to ensure continued delivery of high-quality patient care.

Tools of the Trade

With health travel facilitation being a relatively nascent industry, it is important to understand the tools essential for the trade. These tools vary from human skills and expertise to actual training manuals and processes needed to accomplish the job. No health travel facilitation business should ever be paper driven.

As one evaluates the tools, it is important to examine the qualities necessary to perform health travel facilitation because the trade is not for the weak of heart or the uninitiated. Health travel facilitation realistically requires skills far above the clinical skills needed by general hospital floor duty nurses or even nurses in an intensive care unit (ICU). For this reason, this author has a tremendous disdain for those individuals who simply launch a website, purchase a smart phone, and attempt to coordinate international patient care without the requisite training, experience, or understanding of the risks involved.

Key to the field of health travel facilitation is good documentation. This requires expertise on the part of the facilitation business owner to develop the tools needed to ensure the documentation occurs and includes the periodicity or frequency expected for case events. An untrained inexperienced facilitator has no way to know this, and at the present time there are no software programs available to serve as an off-the-shelf guide to think through these necessities in the event that the facilitator lacks the requisite experience, training, or organizational skills. The importance of documenting the facts surrounding the case cannot be understated. Documentation is also what is used to protect oneself in the event of litigation. Keep in mind the two following quotes, "Keep it simple," and "If it's not documented, it didn't happen."

Job Description

Careful thought should be given to the description of the health travel facilitator's job. If your company grows, and you hire an assistant, you will need to convey the roles and responsibilities of the job and the culture of your health travel facilitation business to her.

A good job description should not only be used in the recruitment process, but also as an evaluation tool for periodic job performance evaluations. A well-developed job description may also help you as a defense in the event you are accused of wrongful hiring practices, discrimination, or failure to credential. The job description should be clear, and delineate the responsibilities and functions of the health travel facilitator, as well as reflect the expectations and level of educational background expected. If a budding entrepreneur opens a health travel facilitation business, without the requisite training, education, and experience, the job description may also serve as a tool to hire a proper medical case manager, and trouble manager, to work as employees of the firm.

Technology

Technology is often seen simply as an obstacle in the already multidimensional field of health travel facilitation. Although technology has proven in some situations to enhance process improvements and save valuable time, health travel facilitators must remember that technology is not always easy to use and may not meet all of their needs. Therefore, health travel facilitators should be familiar with the technology available so that they can make informed decisions when technological changes to current processes are necessary.

Business process improvement (BPI) is a process that is used to evaluate and redesign tasks with the goal of improving business processes, such as streamlining procedures and saving time and money. For every dollar saved and every hour saved, the result should be a lower cost, more competitive offering to potential clients, a direct advantage to the bottom line, and more cohesive, coordinated, client services.

In a perfect world, this evaluation should occur before the implementation of a new software program, to maximize the benefits of the software and to correct any problems such as duplication and unnecessary or outdated time-wasting processes. Business process reviews may include attention to both internal and external organizational activities and the creation of business process workflows.

Workflows

A workflow is a narrative; a graphic depiction of the flow of a process from beginning to end, either within one organization or across multiple organizations. Take a moment to give some thought to your planned workflow, and then have a few experienced nurses, physicians, or even your client hospitals, review and critique it to determine if you've left anything out, or could improve the workflow prior to implementation.

The purpose of the workflow is to segment each step in the process of health travel facilitation, from premarketing through case closure and postservice referrals. Give some thought to creating two workflows: The current "as-is" workflow and one that will be implemented at various stages of organizational and volume growth of your business. The inclusion of staff time, costs, and requirements can be helpful in planning technology expansions, staff expansions, and budget and cash requirements to grow your business.

Computer System Life Cycles

How well your business operates will be determined by how well you have successfully implemented software applications and databases designed to support you in day-to-day activities and follow-up. The interoperability of software utilized by health travel facilitators will be key to the efficiency, cost savings, and critical documentation necessary to run this complex business organization that likely functions across international time zones, cash currencies, languages, disparate health systems, and other cultural and organizational differences.

To plan what system you will need in order to run your business, Figure 12.2 depicts some of the stages you will need to take into consideration In the system analysis phase, you will take into consideration your health travel facilitation business' needs and define an approach and budget to guide system selection, software creation, or a decision to adapt existing software such as commercially available database managers, word processing, and spreadsheets.

In expensive and sophisticated case management software applications, disease management, referral, and prior authorization models are incorporated, which may be overkill for a small health travel facilitation business.

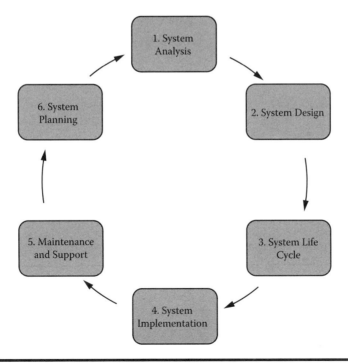

Figure 12.2   Health travel facilitator IT system development.

One company that offers these tools is CH Mack. CH Mack products are positioned to meet case management needs by offering solutions through their two products: the Q Continuum System, featuring a low price point, rapid implementation, and rich functionality, and MedCompass™/CaseCompass™, a sophisticated tool with advanced technology and robust functionality. Another company is TCS Healthcare Technologies with several products designed to accommodate a number of specialty focuses including outcomes-based care, case, disease, prevention, wellness, and utilization management, a tool for authorizations, assessments, and correspondence, and another tool for rules-based data management.

With health travel facilitation, for the time being, it may be necessary to create software that will meet this hybridized organization's needs. Creating a software system from scratch sounds appealing because it could be designed to meet your every specific requirement, but these types of projects are often abandoned due to lack of time, money, and subject matter expertise. Often this happens after a lot of time, money, and large quantities of staff resources have been used, leaving a host of internal issues unresolved. Keep in mind that in addition to case management tools, you will need a tool for credentialing and primary source verification (and periodic recredentialing) of physicians and allied health providers. To my knowledge, at the time of this writing, no physician credentialing engine exists today that can handle the myriad physician credentialing tasks for a globally integrated care delivery system.

To determine if you will make or buy, consider the following:

- Less than 80–90% of your needs may be met by existing off-the-shelf applications.
- You may only need a small component of a packaged solution.
- Your core business needs may not be met by packaged solutions.
- Your competitiveness may be enhanced by building a unique application.
- There may be only one vendor who has a product that almost meets your needs and they are not financially stable enough to remain viable through the end of the initial warranty period, or do not provide adequate customer support.

For the last part, consider the following criteria when evaluating vendors:

- Vendor corporate and financial information
- Business history
- Planning requirements documentation
- Vendor written proposals
- Vendor demos
- On-site visits to their established installations

Table 12.1 shows a technology evaluation grid that can be used for functional, technical, and business requirements.

If one is serious about purchasing software, one should develop a request for information (RFI) or a request for proposal (RFP) that would include the minimum information listed below:

- Description of the vendor company including the number of employees, location, time zone
- A description of the financial stability of the company including an annual report or financial statements, or a reference letter from their banker
- Specifications regarding hardware and software, including database or network requirements
- A sample contract
- Availability of training

Table 12.1   Technology Evaluation Grid

Item	Functional Requirements	Need or Want	Weight	Score	Comments
1	Generate activity list including patient name, priority, due date, and specific activities				
2	Generate standard reports listing and templates				
3	Enable health travel facilitator to create ad hoc reports without additional programming staff				
4	Generate customizable care plan templates				
5	Contain flags that notify the user of previous services and outcomes				
6	Track time and create invoices for client billing				
7	Enable nurse to view current and past medications, including ordering and treating physicians				
8	Track case complexity				
9	Track case savings by activity and total				
10	Track providers involved in care and categorize types of services delivered, by specialty				
11	Allow for desktop and laptop technology and simultaneous updating and versioning				
12	Enable health travel facilitator to access clinical criteria directly through the application				
13	Allow clients to electronically enter certain demographics with an electronic alert for missing required information				
Item	Technical Requirements	Need or Want	Weight	Score	Comments
1	Compatibility and interoperability with networks and existing databases				
2	Existing interfaces with other software				

Continued

Table 12.1 (continued)   Technology Evaluation Grid

Item	Technical Requirements	Need or Want	Weight	Score	Comments
3	Time to implement				
4	IT staff resource requirements				
5	Transaction response time				
6	Availability of vendor staff to support a project on a consultative basis				
7	Scalability: the ability to add additional users and increase transactions without compromising performance				
Item	Business Requirements	Need or Want	Weight	Score	Comments
1	Budget including costs for the following: • Software application • Internal resources needed to implement • Hardware • Database costs • Network costs				
2	Changes in future lines of business				
3	A consultant for software selection				

- A high-level list of other client demographics: types of organizations that have installed the software, number of clients, number of users
- Confidentiality or nondisclosure so that they won't tell other health travel facilitator companies what your business plans do, are doing, or have been in the past
- Customer references, including clients who have chosen the vendor software and who are similar in size and complexity to your business operation
- The frequency of upgrades and their associated costs
- Some sort of customer relations summary, including implementation support, hours of support after going live, response time, user groups, and customer input into future enhancements
- Product enhancements that are in the development process and any costs associated with those enhancements
- Annual software and maintenance estimates
- Their position regarding federal or state legislation or other industry-standard requirements such as HIPAA, HITECH, and other international healthcare privacy and security standards
- Coordination of an on-site visit to an existing customer of the vendor's office to evaluate how the software is being used and to elicit comments about experience with implementation of customer service and how well the software meets your organizational needs
- The availability of vendor consulting services for implementation or a specific task to support your organization or necessary resources may not be present

Your software review team should request that the vendors demonstrate their "out of the box" software packages, not some customized version, or beta. Although the vendor may provide the opportunity to customize the software, you should be mindful that customizing a software package is very costly and can create programming problems for the organization. It can also lead to enhancements that were proprietary when you designed them, and then are made available to all of your competitors, essentially eliminating any competitive edge. Obtaining multiple bids allows comparison of price, functionality, and customer support and adds to the ability to negotiate a more appropriate contract.

System Design

The system design phase is a point when business and technical needs are addressed to design the application to meet the health travel facilitator organization's needs. This assessment process begins after the software selection has been finalized. Depending on the vendor, an overview implementation meeting at the vendor, or client, site may be scheduled. Frequently, this is scheduled soon after the contract has been signed. It is also recommended that the training be scheduled early. Your organization should select and designate a superuser, one who will be very involved in the design and implementation of the system and will be considered a resource for training end-users or supporting the system after the go-live date. Keep in mind that vendor schedules are usually booked several months in advance, and scheduling a meeting as early as possible insures training dates that meet your project schedule. Once you have selected your software, you should request a sample project schedule, testing schedules, the software manual, any user training manuals, and an implementation manual.

Project Planning

The next phase is called project planning, which is one of the first steps in project management. Project management includes identifying the executive sponsor, the steering committee, the actual project manager, and project team members who will be essential to the initiation of the project. The executive sponsor supports the project from a high level and is updated on the project status and issues, and is responsible for executive decisions related to the purchase of the project. The executive sponsor is typically a member of the steering committee. The steering committee's function is to oversee the project and make high-level decisions about the project from an organizational team perspective. The project manager is the person responsible for the project and may be a member of an IT department or a medical department. If you're a small concern, you may be "all of the above."

Project managers typically use several tools including project management software that displays the projected schedule according to major tasks, staff resources, and timeframes. There may be many interdependencies within the schedule, meaning that a specific task cannot be initiated until another task is completed. The remaining members of the project team will also include technical and business analysts. Based on experience, the complexity of your project, and health travel facilitation management, both a competent nurse and a professional travel agent may be involved.

A technical analyst will be responsible for supporting the technical components of the implementation, for example, participating in the interface mapping of software fields from one application to another, followed by interface programming and testing. As you can see, properly establishing this kind of business is much more than setting up the website and enabling a cell phone to answer calls, and securing contracts with providers. It is also the reason why many start-up health travel facilitators fail.

Risk Management and Malpractice Protection

As a health travel facilitator you may find yourself in a dichotomous situation: you will be your client's advocate, and on the other hand, you must take steps to service your organization's advocate and ensure that health services are provided in the most cost-effective and appropriate manner.

Because there are no international or national standards, outcome criteria, or clear guidelines for such dual advocacy roles, the health travel facilitator is placed at risk of liability. To reduce your risk, you must first understand your role, and then practice in a manner that is consistent with your obligations.

As a health travel facilitator you have chosen a calling that directly affects your clients' lives and their pocketbooks. Clients who believe that they've been harmed at the hands of a health travel facilitator or a healthcare provider chosen or offered by the health travel facilitator, can bring suits against those they believed harmed them. In addition, your actions may damage the brand of a high-profile provider who may also feel that your actions caused them or their brand irreparable harm, for which they believe your organization or you are personally liable.

Malpractice occurs when a health travel facilitator fails to do what a reasonably prudent peer would do under the same or similar circumstances. In this case your actions may be compared not only to other health travel facilitators, but also with established case managers who have had years of nursing training and experience. The person making the claim of malpractice will be required to prove the following:

- The existence of the duty, in a client-to-professional relationship, to conform to a recognized standard of care
- The failure to conform to the required standard of care
- Actual injury or financial loss (damages)
- A reasonably close causal connection between the health travel facilitator's conduct and the client's injury or economic damages

Once the existence of a legal duty of establishing a malpractice claim occurs, the plaintiff must prove breach of duty. Breach of duty can be proven by showing that conduct fell below the applicable standard of care. The following list is a sampling of some of the health travel facilitation activities for which you may have liability for breaches of duty that can lead to professional liability on your part:

- Failure to develop a health travel care plan specific to the needs of the client
- Failure to adequately assess and implement that care plan
- Failure to evaluate the client's condition and modify the care plan to prevent deterioration and to maintain health
- Failure to ensure that all medications are listed along with any allergic reactions or sensitivities to pharmacotherapy agents previously prescribed and continued, by chemical or generic name, not brand names used in their home country

- Failure to document in a timely and proper manner the client's condition, care, and treatment rendered, and the client's response to that treatment
- Failure to follow the facility's or organization's policies and procedures, from whom the client will receive care
- Failure to document in a timely and proper manner in advance of the use of the service any driving histories or criminal background checks of any concierge vendors or destination managers and their drivers
- Failure to document appropriate teaching, including the client's responses and evidence of his or her understanding of your instructions
- Failure to provide a recognized the need for timely and appropriate aftercare and ensure adherence to the care plan
- Failure to properly assess and monitor clients
- Failure to implement safety measures to prevent substandard care, through primary source verification credentialing and recredentialing on a periodic basis
- Case abandonment

It's also important that as a health travel facilitator you mitigate the risk of medical liability by

- Working closely with the legal department of other organizations to prevent patient care problems from escalating into a medical liability
- Immediately investigating and resolving patient care problems
- Maintaining vigilance to review and ensure that only current versions of policies and procedures and standards of care and practice are utilized and that your providers are using appropriate and cost-effective resources, and not padding bills, or billing for fraudulent charges for services that were not rendered

Standards of Care

As a health travel facilitator, you should develop and review periodically an internal standard of care to protect and safeguard not only your clients but also the health professionals who are part of your vendor network. Standards of care have evolved to help clients avoid substandard care and to give guidance to professionals. They describe the minimal requirements that define an acceptable level of care, which is the provision of ordinary and reasonable care to ensure that no unnecessary harm comes to the client. However, standards are not absolute because they depend on subjective determinations and are bound by limitations of the surrounding technology, availability of treatments and interventions, provider training, and other local influences.

All providers, regardless of where they are in the world, have standards of care. The standards are the minimal level of expertise that must be delivered to the client. The standards of care are a starting point for greater expectations. These standards may be either externally or internally set. The healthcare professional is responsible for both categories of standards: those set on a national basis or on widely published evidence-based medicine guidelines and those set by the role of their profession. Each national medical association may publish a medical practice act, which may contain statutory minima for training, education, and experience for physicians and or nurses, to be permitted to care for your clients. Facilities may have their own policy and procedure manuals, which may or may not have been reviewed since the last accreditation survey that was conducted in that facility. Standards of care are determined by the judicial system, by expert witnesses. Such persons testify to the prevailing standards in the community, standards that the specialty, professionals are held accountable for matching or exceeding. Standards of care are broken down into four general categories: external, internal, national, and local. Internal standards are those set by the educational role of the healthcare professional or by individual institutions. Internal standards include job descriptions, education, and expertise, and policies and procedures. External standards are the rules and regulations and guidelines established by state boards and professional organizations, and are based on reasonable lists and are the average degree of skill, care, and diligence exercised by members of the same profession

Evidence-Based Medicine

Evidence-based medicine is now being used as the standard for making informed medical care decisions, developing practice guidelines, and evaluating the efficacy of alternative treatments. Outcomes researchers, practice guideline developers, and healthcare professionals are more frequently basing decisions on evidence found by taking the best from practice patterns of specific specialty providers who have the necessary clinical expertise and applying it to the delivery of healthcare.

The concept of evidence-based medicine gained momentum in the late 1980s and early 1990s as a response to both the new opportunity and a tough challenge. The opportunity was provided by better, less costly information systems that could gather research data and then disseminate the findings for decision making. The challenge was to apply the most effective modalities of treating patients, keeping up with them at the least cost and risk, while still maintaining quality of care in reaching treatment goals. There are many systems of published evidence-based medicine guidelines.

As a health travel facilitator, your concern with evidence-based medicine guidelines will be to contract with providers who are conscientious and judicious about the use of the best evidence by your hospitals, and surgery centers and physicians, in making decisions about the care of your individual clients; without current best evidence, practice may become rapidly outdated, often to the detriment of your clients. Evidence-based medicine is not cookbook medicine. It requires an integrative approach that combines the best external evidence with individual clinical expertise and patient choice. External clinical evidence can inform but never replace individual clinical expertise, and it is this expertise that is used to determine whether the external evidence applies to the patient at all and, if so, how it should be integrated into the clinical decision.

Documentation

Finally, as a health travel facilitator, the importance of documentation as you manage your client's case is clear because it is an essential component and tool of assessment, planning, communication and monitoring of your client outcomes. Documentation must be clear and concise. It is critical to effective case management practice.

During documentation, keep in mind these three things. Who is the audience? What is the objective? What information must be told? Keep in mind that in most states in the United States, case management agencies and providers are required to retain patient files for between 5 to 10 years. Thus records can be subpoenaed if a legal situation arises, underscoring that case

15 RULES TO LIVE BY

1. Always act first for client safety, taking into consideration the safety of the client in light of the client's conditions and needs.
2. Respond to the client's questions and don't extend answers beyond your own personal knowledge.
3. Educate the client to the best of your ability, and document that they understand.
4. Be mindful of standards of care in the locality in which you are coordinating care.
5. Supervise the episode of care from start to finish.
6. Adhere to your internal standards, policies, and procedures, as written unless there's a really good defense for why you didn't.
7. Document everything in a clear and concise manner without going overboard or adding superfluous comments.
8. Follow up beyond the discharge of the case and measurement of the outcomes.
9. Operate in an advisory role as plans are developed and implemented. Do not be dictatorial or issue ultimatums.
10. Be savvy when it comes to conflicts of interest—learn how to be open, honest, and willing to reveal contractual relationships with referral sources and your organization.
11. Be savvy when it comes to contractual arrangements with vendors and providers. Be open and honest with clients when options are limited to contracted providers. If a contracted provider is found to be at fault for poor quality care or services, be diligent about reporting such incidents.
12. Make use of a physician advisor in the appropriate specialty when questions arise, or communicate or negotiate with the attending physician when issues arise.
13. Consult with the treating physician as much as is needed to present options and promote discussions that ensure an informed consent.
14. Act promptly. Unnecessary delays cause conditions to worsen, compromise quality of care, and often cause increased financial expenditures.
15. Obtain signed medical releases of information and keep files in the client's chart to reinforce to the client that confidential and private information will be protected.

management documentation must be accurate and objective, without mention of suspicions, opinions, or allegations. From a legal standpoint, documentation is often the deciding factor in a case.

Keep in mind these rules:

- Be pertinent and concise and reflect client's current status.
- Identify your client's needs, problems, capabilities, and limitations.
- Indicate all interventions in the client's responses as you know them personally.
- Indicate the client status at the time of any transfer or discharge from care or supervision.
- Indicate when individual discharge counseling occurred and that the client requires ongoing care or supervision, the client's understanding, and include descriptive documentation that the client or the family has an understanding of what was taught, especially in cases of limited English proficiency on the part of the provider or the client.

The health travel facilitator should keep in mind that documentation in medical records and in e-mails is discoverable, which means that it must be disclosed before trial. Should the client's medical record require alteration or correction, this can be done if it is for valid purposes, such as transcription errors, changing erroneous dates, and notation or clarification of any new information that is relevant to that aspect of the client's care. If changes are made, they must be noted clearly by making a single line through the portion of the record to be altered, corrected, or appended, and the date of the change and the person's signature must be noted conspicuously as to who made the change. Also, if changes are to be made, there must be an explanation in the chart as to why the alteration occurred. State statutes, medical bylaws, or both, dictate which changes can be made to a medical record in each state or country. Changes to a medical record for purposes of fraud or intent to deceive are subject to criminal penalties that could result in a physician's loss of licensure and stiff penalties for the health travel facilitator.

Deep Pockets and Malpractice Coverage

Courts are increasingly holding nurses liable for malpractice and negligence, in part because of increased nursing responsibilities but also because of increased individual malpractice insurance coverage. There is no doubt in this author's mind that as insurance companies begin to offer professional liability coverage for health travel facilitators this too will be the case. Clients' attorneys are increasingly focusing attention on alternative deep pockets, in addition to hospitals and physicians. Remember to take proactive steps to prevent professional liability.

Chapter 13

Privacy and Data Security Concerns in Medical Tourism and Health Travel

Privacy is a bit of an Internet buzzword these days. Providers and facilitators are supposed to use reasonable commercial efforts to ensure that the data they transfer across the Internet is as secure as it should be. If you solicit business from countries all over the world, you may be subject to those companies' marketing and security regulations over the Internet.

Some of the E.U. regulations I have reviewed are much tougher than U.S. regulations. If you are not compliant, you could face criminal prosecution in those countries for failure to comply. Check with your professional trade association to see if they offer some insurance and guidance on global health data security practices, insurance, and defense sources in case you get into trouble. That's what trade associations are supposed to do. They are supposed to offer members industry updates and disseminate exemplary trade practices, objective resources, shepherd the updates, and locate and provide discounts for members on the sort of things gained through economies of scale, not just run conferences every year. If a trade association doesn't do that for its members, I don't join.

Among the measures you can take, the first would be to do what you can for yourself and then have what you've done checked by a Certified Internet Security Systems Professional (CISSP) consultant. We have such a consultant on our consulting team at Mercury Healthcare Advisory Group, and he's available to assist you, paid on an hourly or project basis. You don't want to know what a violation will cost you by comparison! He is very generous about answering quick questions. Although most hospitals will have this handled, most facilitators will not have even researched into the privacy and security laws, out of ignorance or bad advice.

For starters, HIPAA allows both civil and criminal penalties, including fines and possible time in jail. The Office of Civil Rights of the Department of Health and Human Services enforces civil violations, and the Department of Justice enforces criminal violations of the HIPAA standards.

Civil penalties are usually monetary fines. HIPAA allows fines of up to $100 for each violation of the law, to a limit of $25,000 per year for violations of the same requirement. Criminal sanctions for intentional misuse or disclosures, or flagrant disregard for your responsibility to use due care of PHI, carry fines of $50,000 to $250,000 and one to ten years' imprisonment. And, HIPAA is not the only U.S. regulation with which you may be required to comply. To learn more, and receive authoritative guidance on HIPAA, visit (http://aspe.hhs.gov/admnsimp/).

The Basics

First, an Anti-Virus Program Is Essential

There are many free and paid applications out there, and a good number of folks like Anti-Virus Guard (AVG). Others have tried Norton, Kaspersky, NOD32, and others. AVG offers free support through forums, and offers core protection for free. For what you'll need as a medical tourism provider or for your internal or external facilitators, review the options in their AVG Enhanced Firewall. (http://bit.ly/aWRgal). Watch for coupons that save money by purchasing a two-year subscription.

Next, Consider an Antimalware Application

What you are looking for is a contextual option to scan individual files. This option is handy for times when you have to download a file that you think is suspect, or need to open someone's flash drive with his medical records from an unknown source, or where the medical records file may have been through someone else's corrupted or vulnerable system, even the client's own laptop or computer.

Another thing to look for is some kind of shield that silently runs in the background and offers strong active protection against both known and unknown threats, and that schedules itself for automatic updates and fast spyware scans on a daily basis to ensure a clean environment.

While you are at it, document each step in a written policy form for your corporate record to demonstrate that you did use reasonable commercial efforts to keep a clean environment. As your business grows and you add staff, this will also serve as a great orientation document to show how you arrived at your current online data protection security procedures. It is also great backup in case you need to defend yourself in court or to demonstrate to your liability carrier exactly what precautions you take to remain compliant and secure.

Firewalls

Firewalls have an essential role in safeguarding your PC, your laptop, and smartphone. A firewall can block unauthorized remote attempts to access your computer as well as attempts to transfer data by locally installed programs. Unfortunately, not many people know about that.

Although many popular Windows programs have a default Windows Firewall, our team prefers a commercially available firewall protection application. Check out Comodo Firewall. Look for a program that consumes fewer precious system resources. Keep it under 5 MB if possible. Also, seek out a program that automatically monitors your connection and alerts you whenever some remote computer or locally installed program tries to initiate (hack) an unauthorized connection, and guides you as to what to do in the event of a hack attempt.

Script Blockers

To put it simply, script blockers make web browsing safer by blocking everything that can potentially be used to harm your computer. This includes JavaScript, Java, Flash, and other executable content. Despite its security, it can be a real hassle. You might find it annoying to constantly add sites to your "trusted sites" list. For instance, when you visit various video and hospital websites for the first time after installing it, the videos won't load unless you add the site to your trusted list. To add a site, you also may have to "allow" several sites before you are able to view them in full. In such cases you can simply select the "Allow all this page" option. One popular resource is a Firefox add-on called NoScript. (http://noscript.net/) One thing to keep in mind when you are designing your website, is that many individuals and businesses have this or a similar tool installed. Don't overdo the Flash and JavaScript!

One thing you should be aware of is "clickjacking." Think of any button on any website, internal or external, that you can get to appear between the browser walls: wire transfers on banks, Digg buttons, CPC advertising banners, YouTube, and so on. The list is virtually endless and these are relatively harmless examples. Next, consider that an attack can invisibly hover over these buttons below the users' mouse, so that when they click on something they visually see, they actually are clicking on something the attacker wants them to click on.

Say you have a home wireless router that you had authenticated prior to going to a problematic or malicious website. That website could place a tag under your mouse that frames in a single button an order to the router to, for example, delete all firewall rules. In other words, the attack is thrown by a malicious web page embedding objects, possibly from a different site, such as framed documents or plugin content (Flash, Silverlight, Java, etc.) which may lead to unwanted results if clicked by the current user (e.g., a "Delete all messages" button in your webmail or an advertisement banner in a click fraud scheme). Using DHTML, and especially CSS, the attacker can disguise or hide the click target in several ways that go completely undetected by the user, who's easily tricked into clicking it in a more-or-less blind way.

For even more security you can combine the two methods explained here: the database then requires the key file and the password in order to be unlocked. Even if you lose your key file, the database would remain secure. That's what we use at Mercury Healthcare.

We install the security piece directly onto the USB drive that we supply to our clients as a part of their package…and our branding. It's free and it adds a level of professionalism to our service.

Password Vaults

One of the most popular is KeePass, a free, open source easy-to-use password manager. You can put all your passwords in one database, which is locked with one master key or a key file. So you only have to remember one single master password or select the key file to unlock the whole database. The databases are encrypted using the best and most secure encryption algorithms currently known (AES and Twofish). KeePass has competitors, but this one works, works well, and is free.

When you provide a finished or predeparture medical records and imaging files package to your clients, you can use key files. Key files provide better security than master passwords in most cases. You only have to carry the key file with you, for example, on a floppy disk, USB stick, or burned onto a CD. Of course, you or your client shouldn't then lose this disk.

Website Trust Applications

Another extremely popular Firefox addon is WebofTrust (http://www.mywot.com/). The purpose of WebofTrust is to warn users about unsafe websites before they actually enter them. These unsafe sites can mean a site known to scam visitors, deliver malware, send spam, and so on. WebofTrust uses color-coded icons showing ratings for millions of websites: green for safe, yellow for caution, and red for stop. They have competitors out there and by the time you read this, there will be more.

Next, You Need to Consider VPN Options

A VPN, or virtual private network, is technology using hardware, software, or both to secure and privatize data across a network, usually the Internet, by building what techies call an "encrypted tunnel." A VPN allows you to connect your machine to a virtual network which in turn encrypts the data you send, hiding everything from the public domain. A good VPN will keep no records of your browsing history, meaning you're essentially an anonymous user.

Data pass through this "tunnel," protected from anyone who tries to intercept them. Even if the data are intercepted, they are hopelessly scrambled and useless to anyone without the key to decrypt them.

Health travel facilitators and healthcare providers should use VPNs between their site and hospitals, physicians, and others to secure company data, personally identifiable health information (PHI), and often to provide individual "remote access" VPN solutions to home-based or traveling clients to protect data between them and the company's network. A description of how it all comes together is in Figure 13.1.

With applications such as WiTopia's VPN service (www.witopia.net), you initiate the secure encrypted tunnel from your side, so it is not dependent on the websites you visit. Your security and privacy are now maintained whether you see an https:// or not.

It's also important to note that your protection and privacy are not limited to just browsing. WiTopia's VPN service encrypts all your Internet data to and from their VPN gateways. This includes Skype, IM, streaming, and e-mail, as well as browsing. You may want to consider using a VPN over a proxy server. VPNs encrypts all data (Surfing, IM, FTP, etc.) to and from your

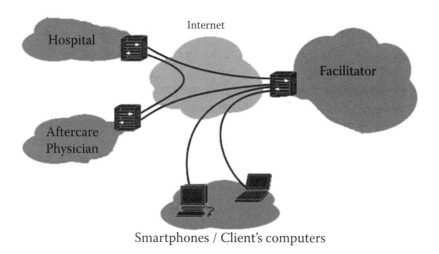

Figure 13.1 Internet VPN.

computer where a proxy typically only encrypts http (WWW) traffic. VPNs also tend to be much faster and more reliable.

Unfortunately, many try the free anonymous web proxy route. Using anonymous proxies means you may be pumping your passwords and personal data through a server set up by a couple of enterprising 13-year-old hackers in some foreign country over which you have no control. If you're really serious about security (and accessing your home PCs from anywhere) then you'll probably want to invest in a paid VPN service.

PCI Compliance

If you plan to accept credit card payments on the Internet, you need to know about Peripheral Component Interconnect (PCI) compliance. PCI compliance is important and serious. Repeated violations could cause a merchant to lose the ability to accept payment card purchases.

PCI compliance is not currently a federal law, but there are many state laws that are already in effect (and some that may go into effect) to force components of the PCI Data Security Standard (PCI DSS) into law. In addition, there is a big push by legislatures and industry trade association to enact a federal law around data security and breach notification.

Consumers, and their trading partners and the regulatory agencies of the government are all demanding that any organization (that would be your little basement-operation business or a downtown skyscraper corporation) that accepts credit card payments comply with the credit card industry's PCI DSS. Companies, including health travel facilitators and providers, have to protect consumer data. Failure to do so could result in severe penalties amounting to millions of dollars in fines. If you are not careful and do not maintain reasonable commercial efforts to remain in compliance, you may find that your professional liability insurance will not cover you, and many carriers may not underwrite you unless you pay very high premiums.

PCI DSS compliance is the full responsibility of the retail merchant, which in your case is the health travel facilitator, and the hospital, concierge vendor, physician, airline, hotel, and all your other trading partners. According to the law, the retail merchant is responsible for contacting the credit card processor for full PCI DSS requirements. Your contact information for your credit card processor should be found on your monthly account statement.

The PCI DSS, a worldwide set of comprehensive requirements for enhancing payment account data security, was developed by the founding payment brands of the PCI Security Standards Council, including American Express, Discover Financial Services, JCB International, MasterCard Worldwide, and Visa Inc. International, to help facilitate the broad adoption of consistent data security measures on a global, not just a U.S. domestic basis.

Certain versions of Windows are PCI compliant the time of this writing, including:

- Vista Business Edition (32-Bit)
- Vista Home Premium (32-Bit)
- Vista Home Basic Edition (32-Bit)
- Windows XP Professional Edition (32-Bit)
- Windows 2003 Server Edition (32-Bit)

As others are developed it is likely that they too will be released, to remain in compliance as customers upgrade or abandon certain popular operating systems.

A PCI audit can be conducted by a Qualified Security Assessor (QSA). This certification is offered by the PCI Security Standards Council or performed via a self-assessment questionnaire. The self-assessment questionnaire is for smaller establishments that have not had a serious non-compliance history. It will probably work for most, if not all, start-up health travel facilitators.

Qualys® (Qualys.com), a vendor in this space, has an entire suite of compliance status monitoring tools. They offer a great e-book *PCI Compliance for Dummies* (ISBN 978-0-470-74452-9) written at a beginner level. Our resident PCI expert, Lionel Bentkower, highly recommends it. You can download the material at http://bit.ly/c7CeW6. In addition, they offer several other helpful guides available for download. My favorite was *IT Policy Compliance for Dummies,* (ISBN 978-0-470-66535-0) available for download at: http://bit.ly/aO6jvf. These are the actual John Wiley & Sons, Ltd., books in e-form, compliments of Qualys. If you find them useful, thank Qualys for being so generous. As a start-up, every dollar saved is important!

Compliance with PCI DSS is daunting. The key is securing cardholder and other sensitive data and then maintaining a rigid policy and procedure to keep up with the standards. Otherwise, your access to cash will be restricted as it relates to accepting credit card payments for your health travel and facilitation services.

Chapter 14

Implications of U.S. Medical Tourism Facilitator Bankruptcy

Implications

What happens if a medical tourism facilitator goes bankrupt and the hospital or physician is owed for services rendered or was paid in the last 90 days? Creditors are often surprised to learn that they may be required to turn money over to a debtor's bankruptcy estate. Under the U.S. Bankruptcy Code, the debtor in bankruptcy or the trustee of a bankrupt debtor can seek the return of payments made to creditors that were made during the 90 days preceding the filing of the debtor's bankruptcy case (known as the Preference Period) if the transfers are "preferential" [11 U.S.C. § 547(b) (4)]. A payment made during the Preference Period may be "preferential" if it "enables a creditor to receive payment of a greater percentage of his claim against the debtor than he would have received if the transfer had not been made and he had participated in the distribution of the assets of the bankrupt estate."[*] In medical tourism, providers and other vendors who are owed money for services rendered are creditors of the facilitator or insurer that owes them payment for services and supplies.

The U.S. Bankruptcy Code provides various defenses that a creditor may assert to the recovery of preferential transfers.[†] One such exception is the ordinary course of business exception of 11 U.S.C. 547(c)(2). For this exception to apply, the transfer must be in payment of a debt that was incurred by the debtor in the ordinary course of business or financial affairs of the debtor and the creditor and the payments be: (1) made in the ordinary course of business or financial affairs of the debtor and the creditor (subjectively ordinary), or (2) made according to ordinary business terms in the applicable industry (objectively ordinary).[‡] The "subjective prong" of this defense requires proof that the debt and its payment are *ordinary* as compared to other business dealings between the creditor and the debtor.[§]

---

[*] Barrett Dodge Chrysler Plymouth, Inc. v. Cranshaw (In re Issac Leaseco, Inc.), 389 F.3d 1205, 1209 (11th Cir. 2004) (quoting Union Bank v. Wolas, 502 U.S. 151, 160–61, 112 S.Ct. 527, 533 (1991)).

[†] 11 U.S.C. § 547(c)

[‡] 11 U.S.C. § 547(c)(2)

[§] Logan v. Basic Distribution Corp. (In re Fred Hawes Organization, Inc.), 957 F.2d 239, 244 (6th Cir. 1992).

In order to avoid preference exposure or preserve the subjective prong of the ordinary course defense, here are a few points hospitals, physicians, and other providers and suppliers should keep in mind in contracting with and selling services to medical tourism facilitators who might be on shaky financial ground. These same admonitions apply to some insurance companies that may not be in a strong financial positions as well as some self-insured employer-sponsored health benefit plans that may be underfunded for claims payment for medical tourism client services.

A key factor that the U.S. bankruptcy courts consider when determining whether a payment was made in the "ordinary course" as compared with previous payments made by the debtor to the creditor is the timing of the payment. If a preferential payment was made much more quickly or much more slowly, as compared to the timing of payments made historically by the debtor to the creditor, the ordinary course defense may not be accepted by the court.

To help protect the ordinary course defense, a creditor should be aware of the amount of time it typically takes a debtor to pay. It should also be stated in the contract as a timely payment requirement. If payments come to the provider that deviate from the typical practice, either because they are paid more quickly or more slowly, the hospital or physician (hotel, concierge, and other vendors also) should determine the reason why the payment frequency and timing have changed and are not the same as in the past. If the change in payment timing relates to financial difficulties being experienced by the facilitator or payer, a court might ultimately reject an attempt by the creditor to rely on the ordinary course defense.

A payer report card is a good tool to use as a dashboard to monitor payment trends from all payment sources, not just insurance companies. It can highlight slow payers, payment variances that don't follow the contract, lost claims, an increase in audits that give rise and defense to payment delays, and so on.

The Method of Payment: Has It Changed?

Did the facilitator pay the provider by the same method as in the past? U.S. bankruptcy courts consider any deviation of this type to be an indicator as to whether a preferential payment was made in the ordinary course as compared to previous payments made by the facilitator. For instance, if the facilitator typically made payments to the creditor by wire transfer but the preference payments were made by check, the ordinary course defense may be rejected by the court.

Many facilitators make payment by check or wire transfer according to the terms and conditions of payment I have seen in medical tourism facilitator contracts. Hospitals and other providers should specify the payment method in their contract with facilitators and then use the payer report card to follow and track any change in the debtor's method of payment and determine the reason or reasons why the change was made. If the change in method of payment did not relate to a deteriorating financial condition of the facilitator, the ordinary course defense may still apply.

If within the 90 days before the facilitator's bankruptcy, the facilitator requested a change in payment terms and conditions, the U.S. bankruptcy court might also consider whether there has been a change in the written payment terms between the debtor and the creditor. Was the contract amended or was it an oral change? Was there any written or oral or implied understanding?

If the facilitator asks for such a change, the hospital or other provider may wish to ask some very detailed due diligence questions. Any request for a change in terms should be a red flag to the provider that the debtor may be experiencing financial difficulties. If a debtor makes such a request, the creditor should be sure to be clear about why the debtor is making the request. This is not only applicable to requests to pay later, but also if payment is accelerated, remember the first point above: slower or faster changes are seen by the courts as a change in habit that may indicate the payment is no longer ordinary.

A change in the terms by a facilitator may not be problematic, if the facilitator is financially healthy. For instance, if a debtor requests a change from payment in net 15 days to payment in net 30 days, and the reason for the request for the change does not relate to any deteriorating financial condition of the facilitator, if both parties abide by the new terms, there might be enough time between the change in terms and any future bankruptcy filing by the facilitator to allow the new terms to become the ordinary course between the parties.

Payment Variances, Partial Payments, or Payment in Full

If the facilitator with whom you are contracted typically pays invoices for medical tourism services in full, but then changes this practice during the 90 days before the bankruptcy filing, the subjective ordinary course defense might be rejected.

Whoever has the responsibility at the hospital or physician group/dental group for monitoring the relationship with the facilitator, including the financial punctuality and accuracy of payments should track and be informed about how the facilitator typically handles outstanding invoices. They should also know whether the facilitator typically makes payments that cover individual invoices or whether they pay the fees owed to providers of service in batches. Here again, if the change in payment practice relates to financial difficulties, a court might ultimately reject an attempt by the creditor to rely on the ordinary course defense.

Has the account standing deteriorated to the point that collection activities have been initiated? If the payments were made in response to a change in debt collection activities by the provider, the bankruptcy courts may compare the pattern of historical collection activities of the parties against the collection activities that happened prior to the preference payments. They will do this to determine if the activities preceding the preference payments fit the historical pattern. Providers need to monitor carefully any collection efforts necessary with their facilitators. Collection activities that precede preference payments are often stepped up and more intense compared to historical necessity for any collection efforts. These changes can cause the payments to be considered by the courts as outside the ordinary course between the parties. If a medical tourism provider has to start chasing a facilitator for payment, they need to determine whether the need for increased collection activity relates to a deteriorating financial condition. If so, they may be classified as a preferential creditor by the courts and have to pay back the money they were paid, to be redistributed to other secured creditors.

If a medical tourism provider learns that any of the above changes in the typical practices established between themselves and the facilitator relate to the debtor's deteriorating financial condition, they need to carefully consider if they wish to continue doing business together. When the provider is unable to persuade the facilitator to conform to its prior pattern of payment, the provider may need to reconsider the relationship. The medical tourism provider may ultimately determine that the benefit of continuing to do business with the facilitator is worth the risk of potential preference exposure in the event the facilitator files for bankruptcy. On the other hand, the provider may decide that the benefits do not outweigh the risk and decide to end their dealings with the facilitator.

Chapter 15

Considerations in Working with Hotels

Medical tourism programs that don't have their own serviced apartment facilities will find that they must collaborate with hotels, and deal with hotel room rates, resort fee waivers, booking incentives and overall negotiation.

Higher costs and lower availability at hotels are not good things for medical tourism program operators, however, there is a positive force behind the trend: corporate travel is also expected to rebound as companies increase their budgets and send more people out on the road to meet and conduct business.

PWC actually has a Hospitality and Leisure Practice, which monitors not only hotel and travel but now also monitors and consults in the area of medical tourism business development and strategy. I only became aware of this when they began to call me for specific market insight and consulting assistance on various projects.

Consulting houses such as PricewaterhouseCooper (PwC) and Smith Travel Research publish information about Average Daily Room Rates (ADR). It is important that you follow these reports because as the travel market continues to fluctuate, prices and availability will no doubt affect health travelers. As a medical tourism program director, you will need to exercise some creative strategies at the bargaining table. Don't depend on others to look out for your best business interests here.

When a seller's market exists, it is because there is generally less availability, with a lot fewer hotel rooms coming online, especially in the upscale hotel segment. Given this scenario, medical tourism program directors and their international department staff are wise to book hotel rooms as far in advance as possible. If the hotel will let you, you can plan further out. Most hotel managers negotiate with the current state of the market in mind. If you drive volume to a particular market, book for as far in the future as you can. However, booking a hotel stay far in advance doesn't always guarantee good rates, inasmuch as some hotels will cancel a reservation outright if they can easily fill rooms with higher-paying business in a group.

Your medical tourism clientele may also not be the most attractive client to them. Think about it. They may have soiled sheets from wound seepage, more service intensity, special requests, and other reasons for not necessarily wanting your business, even if it is a longer stay than most business travelers. If your bookings are no longer good for the hotels, they will want to get a higher rate of return.

Second-Tier City Considerations

The best chance of finding favorable rates and availability are in second-tier cities (STCs). Second-tier cities are hard to define because they can moves as they are redefined by market and economic structure rather than by size. They are generally distinct from large urban metropolises, and are spatially distinct, rather than suburbs of larger metropolitan areas. This is something to think about when considering hospitals and medical spas for your health travel network.

Second-tier cities possess a specialized set of activities (paralleling the cluster concept in economic development), and trade-oriented industries (wealth generation), both of which take root (through attraction and growth) in those communities. STCs have comparatively strong growth characteristics in terms of both population and employment. As you seek opportunities to add hospitals and other suppliers to your provider network, keep in mind that government officials will view your expansion into their market quite favorably on a number of fronts if they are ready for that expansion and can accommodate your clients and take good care of them, bringing honor and economic development to the community.

To narrow the concept down for you, Meeting Planners International (MPI; which I follow because we facilitate a fair amount of executive health travel and executive checkups, paired with strategic planning retreats for corporate executives and their significant others), offers a more practical definition, in which a second-tier city is a city with a population of more than 300,000 and less than one million. This statement highlights that STCs are not just defined as "smaller" but also as "larger." STCs have a significant presence of their own that distinguishes them from small cities, micropolitan areas, and rural towns. So, STCs have a ceiling ("no bigger than") and a floor ("no less than").

A precise definition of an STC can be hard to come by, and will always be subject to debate. In the practice of network providers and site selection, the discussion of second-tier city usually occurs with large corporate-oriented projects, including headquarters and research and development facilities that are nearby. Construction may be newer in the area, and roads may be wider, and medians and landscaping at the side of the road may be more familiar to an American health traveler.

STCs will have many of the characteristics that meet the needs of health travelers who are not going for the electricity of the downtown touristic inclusions, while offering a mix of advantages that make them highly competitive with the largest locations. The STC will have what the large cities have, and have more of it (responsive government, labor growth), enough of it (transportation infrastructure, financial services), and less of it (congestion, hotel accommodation costs) in a mix that makes them especially attractive. The fundamental value proposition of STCs in placing your health travel clients is the right size at the right cost.

RevPAR—Watch Out for "Ancillary" Fees

Room rates are far from the only factor to consider when cutting deals with hotels. Hotels focus on RevPAR, an acronym that stands for revenue per available room. Increasingly, add-on fees, sometimes called "resort fees," for everything from parking to use of the fitness center and even maid service, are being added to hotel bills. RevPar is the strongest indicator of hotel profitability.

Industrywide, hotels are following what the airlines are doing in terms of fees. Depending on the nature of your booking and business volume, and how much it's worth to the hotel, you can negotiate these fees out.

In addition to asking for fees to be waived, as a medical tourism program director, you will need to guard against any new fees that could crop up after your booking is arranged. Contract provisions should protect you from fees being added on later, upon guest arrival. Once the contract is signed, you'll need to stay on top of how the hotel implements that contract. They sometimes hand the contracts over to reservations people who don't necessarily read them to see what concessions are in there. You have to follow up or your client satisfaction ratings will drop to damaging levels. Keeping an eye on fees has become a necessary part of the negotiating process. For example, your clients who drive to a particular medical tourism destination could be assessed an unexpected $25 daily parking fee. Once they have arrived, your leverage has essentially disappeared. Nobody is going to start looking for a new hotel room under the stress of impending medical care.

You never know what the next money-grabbing gimmick will be, so you really have to stay ahead of the game. I tell the hotel that I want no hidden fees tacked on to the room rate. When I give people a price for the room, I want that to be the price.

Keeping the Terms of the Negotiated Rates Are Key

Creative long-term negotiating tactics for favorable rates will be important, along with traveler compliance to keep costs under control. When ADR goes haywire, negotiated rates are used by hoteliers to lock in volume business commitments. You also need to inquire if the companies that your clients work for have already negotiated savings with certain brands, which can save you and your client money and help their employer meet volume commitments. Companies forfeit a lot of savings when employees book outside preferred agreements and channels and end up paying consumer rates.

Pointers on How to Negotiate

Egencia, a division of Expedia that publishes a Travel Forecast and Annual Hotel Negotiability Index, suggests the following recommendations for how travel managers and facilitators can get the best value from hotels depending on market conditions:

- Negotiating with three- to four-star hotels is likely to be easier than with hotels in the luxury category, when luxury category hotels are "in the money."
- Encourage travelers to book hotels that offer free amenities such as Internet, shuttle service, breakfast, and evening events.
- Negotiations with specific hotels will yield better results than chainwide negotiations, particularly for business concerns without a high volume or average daily spend.
- Consider independent hotels. Without costly loyalty programs to subsidize, these properties may offer better rates and amenities.
- Negotiate last-room availability clauses. This means that properties must offer negotiated rates even if only one room type is available, resulting in lower ADR throughout the year.

Last words of advice, always walk your hotels with the same attention to detail as you walk through your hospitals and clinics. Your clients expect you to be the expert and match up their preferences with the best choice for them, their pocketbook, their comfort, their safety, and their culture. The pretty pictures might not show everything as it is without staging and retouching.

Consider their safety as physically challenged travelers. One rule I instituted for our programs is that we will not offer a hotel property where the handicap access room was above the third floor.

The reason for this is that most fire trucks equipped with a ladder apparatus can usually only reach the third floor. If the guest requires assistance and alternative egress, or escape, elevators are typically automatically programmed to descend to the ground level and stop upon activation of the fire alarm enunciator panel. That means that any disabled client trapped above may truly be trapped. Let that not happen on your watch.

Also consider the comfort of your morbidly obese clients who may come for gastric bypass and other weight loss surgeries. They will need larger furniture pre- and postoperatively. Once they have had surgery, and their abdominal muscles have been cut, even if only laparascopically, they may need to steady themselves as they arise from chairs, beds, or in and out of bathtubs. Make sure you know what furniture arrangements will be in the rooms they are assigned, and spare them embarrassment and possible injury if they lean on something that may give way underneath them. Also check with the kitchen staff to ensure that they are able to provide details on all ingredients, as hidden sugars of any kind will be devastating to gastric bypass patients (even in yogurts, juices, teas, and soups such as carrot purees, etc.),

Last but not least, check the shuttle vehicle that may be used to collect them from the airport or to transfer them to your hospital or clinic. Stepping into many vans without a stepstool or ladder, or stairs into a minibus can be a challenge to persons who cannot ascend or descend stairs of any kind, like knee patients, hip patients, back patients, and those with fresh postoperative wound sites.

Chapter 16

Ultimate Customer Service: A Collaborative Effort

Healthcare organizations are in the early stages of customer experience maturity. There's very little customer delight in medical tourism, and the index is likely very low in healthcare service delivery overall. Across different interaction types and different channels, very few hospitals in medical tourism regularly delight customers. If they did, there would be numerous published studies, the legitimate media (not press releases and social media blog posts) would be echoing the findings, and customers and employers would be clamoring for appointments instead of fearful and apprehensive about the health travel and destination medicine complex.

The results are most problematic for online interactions;[*] only 16% of respondents regularly delight customers using online customer service. Because most medical tourism engagement originates as an online transaction, one can safely assume that if Temkin's report analyzed survey results from more than 140 large North American firms that have annual revenues of $500 million or more, there wasn't even a high sampling of healthcare organizations included in the mix. Where am I going with this?

In traditional healthcare, service is not sourced online, but instead by personal referral from a physician to a lab, a hospital, or a consulting provider. All those physician referral portals online rarely have any real ROI for the people who pay to be listed on them, except perhaps the utility of finding one's address or telephone number, and even then many fail miserably. Other than by physician or other professional referral, encounters happen by what I call the "Venus fly trap" method: you capture what flies by and lands at your door on the stretcher of an ambulance through the emergency ("casualty" for my non-U.S. readers) department.

Health travel and medical tourism are different. Although the media fail to acknowledge that the real referrals come from physicians in markets where specialized tertiary healthcare is essentially scarce and unavailable (e.g., the Middle East, North Africa, and the Caribbean), the media prefer to echo one or two now-proven-flawed "research" (*promotional*) reports from large

---

[*] Bruce Temkin, Temkin Group. *The Current State of Customer Experience.* June 2010 doi May 13, 2011, http://www.rightnow.com/pdf/Current-State-Of-Customer-Experience.pdf

consulting firms published in 2007 and 2008 that projected super growth potential >35% compound annual growth rate (CAGR) for the industry, that was never based on factual or reliable indicators, but has exploded the market for Internet-marketing start-up facilitators on the medical tourism "bandwagon to riches."

According to an article published on medicaltourism.com,* "Either way it is advisable to contact the hospital or clinic directly if only to gauge the quality of their responses and response time, which will probably give you a good indication as to the level of service and attention you will receive once you've arrived at the hospital or clinic."

The article also states that when a patient attempts to contact an international destination hospital, "48 hours or less is a pretty normal response time for facilities that receive a large influx of international patients. If you have not received an answer within 48–72 hours, then try again, or think of calling the hospital." That's absurd to suggest as an acceptable waiting time, but then, there is no author listed for the article, so one cannot judge the actual expertise or experience with medical tourism, healthcare marketing, customer service, or international patient relations operational realities of the author.

The problem, as I see it, is that it sets the expectation bar so low to the ground that to regard this suggested benchmark as acceptable will never result in the industry as a whole creating customer delight with an online medical tourism transaction or interaction.

Because many of us in the industry know the back-story of what happened to the bid on this domain back in 2008, we discount the unoriginal claptrap published on this website, but the unsuspecting consumer market and uninitiated media sees this domain as "authoritative" and therefore would grant credibility to its ghost author(s). And yes, I wear my harsh disdain on my sleeve, but it is not personal; instead, it is my disdain for the "red ocean strategy" demonstrated on the site, when that site could be so much more valuable to the consumer, the industry, and the media, but instead competes in the existing market, with beginner articles, copycat drivel, and an attempt to exploit existing demand. The industry should demand more at this stage. Medical tourism is no longer nascent, it is growing slowly and steadily in some markets and just starting out in others, but is by no stretch of the imagination "just coming into existence and beginning to display signs of future potential" which is how nascent is generally described. We are beyond *Medical tourism 101*, worldwide. If we don't challenge ourselves as an industry to reach up and raise the bar, who should do it for us?

Okay—diatribe over. But, my deeper contempt for this farcical benchmark of 48–72 hours delayed response also reveals my concerns about serious operational problems in most medical tourism programs.

Organizational readiness is a key issue. I have visited a number of hospitals with new medical tourism programs that believe (and have told me to my face after I've spent thousands of dollars from Mercury Healthcare corporate funds (not sponsored familiarization tours) and many days' time to travel to inspect their facility) that "we have doctors, a hospital, a website, hotels and an airport nearby, if someone really calls about this program we advertised on the Internet, we'll figure out (a) whose job it will be to answer them authoritatively, (b) which doctors we will involve, (c) the price we'll quote for (d) the 'package' we have not really fully developed yet." Sorry, that's not a "program," you are not ready for prime time, and you shouldn't even activate your website if you don't have these basic elements fleshed out. You don't even have a product to sell yet. What you have is a medical staff, a facility, a website, some nearby hotels and an airport, and a dream.

---

* "Should I Contact the Hospital Directly or Use a Medical Tourism Facilitator?" *Medical Tourism*. Web. 12 May 2011. <http://medicaltourism.com/related-topic.php?topic=18>.

Period. You'll be lucky if you can respond meaningfully with a package price within two weeks. That does not produce customer delight.

Another important element is having a fully trained medical tourism department staff. A medical tourism department is not the same as an international patient relations department. The entire phenomenon of health travel to intentionally access care in a place other than where one resides is meaningfully different from the traditional pattern of international medical travel. Medical tourism is driven and shaped by complex interactions of a multitude of medical, economic, social, and political forces. Here are only three reasons why the department either needs to be split operationally or distinctly different in staffing and service orientation.

For one thing, the typical hospital that routinely receives international patients manages the episode of care for locals who either become ill or injured while on vacation or business travel, and medevac patients who are transported there by various modes of transportation from someplace elsewhere they fell ill or were injured, that didn't have adequate care available. This usually involves travelers with some form of insurance coverage based on a travel insurance policy that covers certain (not all) medical conditions, has tremendous pre-existing limitations, is supported by case managers and translators hired by the insurer, and subject to prenegotiated reimbursement rates for services rendered and billed as line item services, not a predetermined package price.

Local patients who are expatriates are often tended to by this international relations department. Some of the differences are shown in Table 16.1. These expatriates can be very forgiving about failure to delight them. Medical travel patients on the other hand, will not tend to be as forgiving. If you want referrals to their employers, their friends, and their families, you will have to delight them with customer service. Differentiating your organization and your product with customer service, I will argue is an uncontested space in medical tourism. When coupled with a good surgical outcome, it is what will produce new opportunity for profitability and rapid growth to an entirely new market, that is completely distinct from the international business of expatriates and travel illness, and accident patients routinely attended by your designated "international department." The skills sets will be different, the expectations of the customer have to be managed differently, and the product development

Table 16.1 Difference between Expatriates and Medical Travel Patients

Expatriates	Medical Travel Patients
Often speak at least a smattering of the local language	Probably don't speak the local language at all
Have a home to return to where their luggage remains	Bring their luggage to a hospital that has no real place to put it in a regular hospital room
Different expectations that are based on familiarity with the local culture and infrastructure conditions,	Often unprepared and surprised by local culture and norms in third-world and developing nations
Know their way around the town and its local market resources	Lost, scared, and preoccupied by fear and anxiety of the entire medical tourism experience
May have local health insurance	Probably paying cash out of pocket
Selected the hospital of their own volition or by local reputation among other expats	Chose the hospital by Internet referral or friends or physician referral

is different (usually involving packaging services in a bundled pricing schema with a default price established for "extras" outside the bundle).

The level of coordinated stakeholder involvement is drastically different. Medical travel patients will usually be accompanied by a companion traveler who requires accommodation in a hotel, a sofa bed, a serviced apartment, or elsewhere. They could become a patient too. They could become ill or injured while on the trip (unexpected) or they could be incorporated into the event (wellness checkups, screening exams, health promotion activities, featured in media interviews) or otherwise occupied by sightseeing activities planned by the hospital staff, or a facilitator or destination manager. These days, many people travel with pets as a companion. How will your organization accommodate that detail? The international department may be much busier with established expatriate and case management traffic from the aforementioned sources. It should be more closely tied to admissions coordinators, bed control, case management, discharge planners, social workers, billing, collections, third-party payer relations, government payers, and philanthropic foundations that pay for this care, and the revenue management department.

By contrast, the medical tourism program office will instead be more closely affiliated with many external stakeholders who will tend to details and arrangements with hotels, ground transportation, attractions, kennels and pet boarding accommodation, language interpretation, hosting, and other necessities of the elective, out-of-pocket, self-paid health traveler or medical wellness tourist.

So let us return now to the challenge that brought us down this path—that of customer service delight. As medical tourism and wellness travel continue to evolve and progress through the age of customer capitalism. The era of shareholder capitalism, that is, pushing products and services at customers, tweaking the supply chain, parsing and manufacturing demand, with the goal of making money for shareholders, is over. Those of you who deny this will compete in a bloody red ocean of crowded competitors vying for the same market share in an undifferentiated product and price-driven strategy.

Savvy organizations will quickly accept that the medical travel customer is in charge, as a result of an epochal shift of power in the marketplace from seller to buyer. Making money and corporate survival now depend not merely on satisfying customers but delighting them. To prosper, your hospital or clinic must offer a continuing supply of new value, and deliver it sooner. This will be largely dependent on the response of that international department, measured in minutes, not days, and with a meaningful message, not an e-mail auto responder. It is why at Mercury Healthcare, we invest in the expense to provide live-answer telephone coverage 24 hours per day, 365 days per year from two continents. We don't want the prospect to have time to query other suppliers. We don't want them to have to fill out forms online, and we don't want them to have to leave voice-mail messages on a mechanical or digital system. We want to delight them with responsiveness, immediately, and with the answers they require. The new bottom line of business is: is the customer delighted? They cannot be if we have to then call a hospital and wait days to weeks to receive a quote for service.

There are five ways to measure something as insubstantial and mercurial as client delight.

Measure Customer Delight at the Organizational Level

Measure loyalty and delight by giving priority to the most enthusiastic customers. Identify your heroic and triumphant outcomes, customer service "home runs," and keep a tight focus on your evangelists, those customers who would sing your praises to friends and colleagues so you don't have to toot your own horn.

This is where your real engine of growth lies. These evangelists are employed by someone who may provide employee benefits, they may be a business owner, a member of a social club or professional association, they may be bloggers, Tweeters, or friends on Facebook. These outliers—the enthusiasts who loved your product and are inclined to talk it up to their friends and colleagues—are in effect the unpaid marketing department of your medical tourism program.

You may notice that asking people directly whether they are delighted doesn't always correspond with program growth, repeat purchases, or even referrals. Instead, a more reliable question is an indirect question, that is, a question about customers' willingness to recommend a product or service to someone else. This is the litmus test. It correlates to a term I use in a few paragraphs called the Net Promoter Score or NPS®, coined by Fred Reichheld and his colleagues at Bain & Company.

You must also take care not to just count the cheerleaders. Reichheld et al. discovered it wasn't enough to count the enthusiasts. He also had to take into account those customers who had been turned into detractors by poor or even unscrupulous business practices that might have been very profitable but which undermined customer loyalty. When customers are unhappy about their experiences, they share that too. The old adage used to be if they were happy they told one, and if they were unhappy they told ten. Now, with social media, bad experiences can quickly become viral and even reach millions of people. To get a sense of whether a firm is making any headway in the marketplace, it has to take into account not only the total amount of delight it has created, but also the level of frustration and disappointment among those who were likely to become active detractors.

Once Reichheld brought detractors into the mix, along with promoters, he saw a strong correlation between survey responses and relative growth rate across competitors. Client delight is thus measured with this equation:

$$\% \text{ Promoters} - \% \text{ Detractors} = \% \text{ Net promoters}$$

Measure Customer Delight at the Working Level

I am a firm believer in employee engagement. One way to engage the international or medical tourism patient relations department is to create a pay-for-performance incentive program that rewards an increased NPS outcome month after month, tied to identification of the individual or team that is responsible for the success.

The organization can only consistently delight its customers if each individual work team is focused on that goal. This is not just the work of the CEO or the marketing department; it's the job of everyone in the organization. That means that each team's work goals must be spelled out in terms of client outcomes, not merely output from within the firm. This granular, organizational philosophical approach is probably closely related to my admiration and respect for Planetree-designated hospitals (www.planetree.org). Planetree is a non-profit organization in Derby, CT that provides education and information in a collaborative community of healthcare organizations, facilitating efforts to create patient-centered care in healing environments. Patient-centered care creates and sustains customer delight in the healthcare setting.

A Humble Beginning and a Not So Delightful Experience

As Angelica Thieriot battled a rare viral infection, she sat staring at the cold, blank walls of her hospital room. Nurses hurried in and out without regard to Angelica as an individual, leaving her to spend hours feeling lonely and afraid. She was disheartened to find that this lack of personalized care threatened to overshadow the benefits of the hospital's high-tech environment.

Angelica's experiences led her to envision a different type of hospital where patients could receive care in a truly healing environment that would also provide them with access to the information needed to become active participants in their own care and wellbeing. In 1978, Angelica founded Planetree, taking the name from the roots of modern Western medicine, the tree that Hippocrates sat under as he taught some of the earliest medical students in ancient Greece. Today, Planetree is an internationally recognized leader in patient-centered care. In healthcare settings throughout the United States, Canada, and Europe, Planetree is demonstrating that patient-centered care is not only an empowering philosophy, but a viable, vital, and cost-effective model.

Our affiliate sites operate in diverse healthcare settings, with each site adapting the Planetree model as required by its unique needs. These facilities range from small rural hospitals with 25 beds to large urban medical centers with over 2,000 beds. The Planetree model is implemented in acute and critical care departments, emergency departments, long-term care facilities, outpatient services, as well as ambulatory care and community health centers.

Planetree has received recognition in numerous publications including *The New York Times*, *JAMA*, *Prevention Magazine*, *Healthcare Forum Journal*, *Hospital & Health Networks*, *Nursing Times*, *The Quality Letter for Healthcare Leaders*, *Health Facilities Management*, and *Newsweek Japan*. Mercury Healthcare recognizes and applauds hospitals with Planetree designation and will fast-track any hospital with that designation through our lengthy and detailed credentialing and privileging process, because we recognize what a difference this commitment means to customer delight and high-quality patient-centered care. In fact, because we are deeply familiar with both the accreditation standards and the Patient-Centered Hospital Designation Program, we assign more points in our baseline internal assessments for Planetree designation than we do for Joint Commission International (JCI) hospital accreditation, because Planetree actually measures different elements of direct patient care and organizational readiness to provide care for human beings caring for other human beings in a medical setting.

Equally important, an intelligent NPS measurement system must be able to register that outputs which irritate or disgust the customer are failures. They are negative events for the firm because they undermine its capacity to survive. These are the very things that Planetree designees strive to avoid. In practical terms, the real revolution in management practice comes when the hospital or clinic starts defining the goals of its medical tourism program in the form of patient stories and case studies from the voice of the client (VOC). This is the Rubicon where a medical tourism provider hospital or clinic or physician crosses from traditional to radical management.

Stories catalyze other prospects' understanding by providing direct access to past clients' actions, thoughts, and feelings. They enable prospects to climb out of their own self-centered world and see things from someone else's perspective. With that understanding, they can begin to imagine what kind of product or service they will be likely to experience if they choose your organization for their episode of care.

Sizing and Prioritizing Client Delight Measurement

In a world of rapid change in the marketplace, of an increasing proportion of knowledge work, of increasing technical complexity of the work, and where customers who do not even know themselves what will delight them, Reichheld states that stable predictable work environments are largely a thing of the past. I tend to agree.

Many medical tourism program developers simply copy what others have done, offering the same specialties, competing prices, and the same bundle of advertised packaged services. Proceeding with this traditional competitive strategy approach in today's environment will result in a specification of output that will include a variety of things: some things that the customer really wants, others that the customer would consider nice to have but are not essential, and still other things that the customer doesn't really care about it at all, that have been included in the specifications, "just in case."

When work is organized in such "big chunk" specifications, there are usually serious productivity problems, which become bigger gaps with a small or nonexclusive workforce to handle the workload and business development:

■ Because of a lack of primary customer research, and a reliance on what associations organized and owned by neither health administrators nor tourism experts churn in unidentified blogs and frequent media-play interviews, coupled with no real access to the customers because they don't "send" patients for medical tourism referrals by their association actions, a great deal of time and effort is often spent on things that are of low priority to the ultimate customer, thereby delaying delivery of the things that the customer most dearly wants. This was pointed out to me by our medical director on a long flight to South Africa from the United States, as we were headed out to speak at a conference there. He found this to be a problem for most medical tourism associations, not just one of them. They don't produce referrals, so they cannot directly measure patient satisfaction outcomes through primary research because they are not stakeholders in the episode of care. Fair enough.

■ Because the program manager has often not examined the relationship between the amount of effort that each individual component of the specifications will take, or how much delight it will generate, no sensible decision can be made on tradeoffs and no assignments can be made with a specific measureable objective to warrant the assignment. Cultural differences in a workforce also play a big part here, because in certain cultures, the worker does not take the initiative to design the measureable objective or define the research to be undertaken. One waits to be told what to do, when to do it, and to what exact specifications the work should be done. Without that direction, "It ain't gonna happen."

■ Again, both because of cultural differences in a global health arena, and because many tasks are grouped together into a large single specification, the overall project typically takes a long time to complete, with the likelihood that the customer's situation will have changed by the time of delivery. As a result, the eventual product of service, even if it corresponds to the project specifications, will not be what the customer wants at the time of delivery. This is the crippling component of most healthcare business strategic initiatives, be they developing a written contracted reimbursement strategy, a defined set of business rules, or the entire schema of a medical tourism program and product development initiative.

■ Despite media and provider hyperbole, the reality is that there are not as many medical tourism cases happening as have been reported. Therefore, when it is ultimately discovered that the output does not delight the customer, a significant amount of rework is probable. For those who lack sufficient capitalization for staying power, there may be no one to perform the rework and devise the corrective action plan, especially not someone from the international relations department who is otherwise engaged with ongoing traffic from the other "traditional" international patient relations activity.

In the traditional approach of "big chunk" specifications, these problems will remain largely invisible, because measurement and management attention are focused on output, not outcomes. In the healthcare revenue cycle, we see a similar problem with managers who focus on reducing the number of days in accounts receivable (A/R days) instead of the dollars collected in cash per episode of care and average daily net revenue performance by payers. Thus the goal assigned is to get contracts with good payers and bad payers, and maintain the "busy-ness" of departmental output and the number of contracts and bodies in the door, instead of revenue performance outcomes by payer. But, alas, that's another book.

Once management undertakes the more strenuous goal of achieving stated as opposed to hypothetical desirable customer outcomes, then a more targeted and agile approach to planning and measurement is required, so as to optimize the prospects of delighting the customer. Without revealing the entire story, I recommend Fred Reichheld's book, *The Ultimate Question: Driving Good Profits and True Growth* (ISBN: 9781591397830).

Similar to tradeoffs in managed care contracting, where negotiators have to size up what the customer wants to purchase and contract to sell it to them, in medical tourism, the program developers have to similarly determine what the customer wants to buy, and let me assure you, it is not "just" a new hip or a heart surgery. It is a total episode of care experience, one that encompasses service, quality, access, and price.

Horn & Hardart was a food service company in the United States noted for operating the first food service automats in Philadelphia and New York City. An automat (sometimes referred to colloquially as a *wall*) is a fast-food restaurant where simple food and drink are served by coin- and bill-operated vending machines.

Originally, the machines took only nickels. In the original format, a cashier would sit in a change booth in the center of the restaurant, behind a wide marble counter with five to eight rounded depressions in it. The diner would insert the required number of coins in a machine and then lift a window, which was hinged at the top, to remove the meal, which was generally wrapped in waxed paper. The machines were filled from the kitchen behind. All or most New York automats also had a cafeteria-style steam table, where patrons could slide a tray along rails and choose foods, which were ladled out of steaming tureens.

The format was threatened by the growth of suburbs and the rise of fast-food restaurants catering to motorists (with their drive-through windows) in the 1950s. I didn't use the word "catering" by accident. To "cater" is to provide service.

Consider this: If I want a sandwich from a place other than my home kitchen, do you think for a minute that as the CEO of an international organization, I am going to eat food prepared who-knows-how-long-ago, and purchased self-service from a wall or a drive-through window? Served in a paper bag? No! I am going choose a vendor restaurant, probably from a social networking referral source such as OpenTable.com, Yelp.com, or FourSquare.com, and read the reviews if I don't have a favorite that is well-known to me in the vicinity. I will read the reviews on my Smartphone, and then review the directions to travel there using that device or my global positioning system (GPS or SatNav to my non-U.S. readers) in my car. On arrival, I will either select or be shown to a seat at a table, visit the washroom and wash my hands, then return to the table, place a napkin on my lap, place my beverage order to be served in a clean, spot-free glass or cup that is not made of paper or cardboard, take my meal on a clean porcelain or ceramic plate instead of a plastic basket lined with waxed paper, and then eat my sandwich. Then I will request a bill and pay for my meal by cash or credit card, obtain a receipt for the meal and leave the server a gratuity for their "s-e-r-v-i-c-e." Yes, it will cost me more than the automat or drive-through, but my preference is for a higher level of civility and customer service. My expectation is that the food will be prepared to my order at the time my order is placed, it will be served at the appropriate temperature, on clean china, by a professionally experienced wait staff in appropriate professional wait staff attire, in accordance with established service techniques, and that they will then vanish and leave me to enjoy my sandwich, only interrupting me to check my level of satisfaction or my desire for anything else, or to refill my beverage or replace a utensil I might accidentally drop on the floor.

What is my delight score for that customer experience? "ZERO" "NEUTRAL". Nothing there was worth reporting to friends, posting on a social media channel, telling my employees, my family, or clients what a memorable experience I had; it was baseline acceptable. Will I come back? Perhaps, if I am hungry again and willing to take a chance on them again to gauge consistency, but I was not "delighted" with any aspect of normal, routine, expected service.

Call me difficult to please? Hardly! Call me unappreciative? Why? I paid at the price asked for what I received; it was not a gift. If that baseline level of service was not meant to be available, my customer delight score would have immediately plummeted to negative integers. Also notice that my entire example did not focus even one tiny "bite" on the food preparation, taste, freshness of the ingredients, the aesthetic quality of the presentation of the sandwich, the condiments and relishes (don't ever forget my pickle!), or the quality of my beverage. What could have contributed to ultimate customer delight? Ambiance, an unhurried, calm dining atmosphere, entertainment, and so on, For me to rate the restaurant high in the customer delight scale, all four elements of service, quality, access, and price need to be "delightful," not just at baseline acceptable or satisficing.

My point is that the automat is like a do-it-yourself (DIY) medical tourism experience. The drive-through is like most medical tourism facilitator experiences from novice facilitators who believe they are entitled to be paid (I didn't use the word "earn" intentionally) a commission for making a phone call or referral instead of providing superb customer service. And, the restaurant example is tantamount to our experience in dealing with most multipurposed international patient relations desks, instead of working with a dedicated medical travel department representative at a medical tourism program hospital, with a well-trained team and a well-organized and -developed medical travel or wellness tourism product.

Measuring a Key Aspect of Customer Delight: Response Time

When was the last time you were delighted with the delivery time or turnaround time on a project, an Internet order, or a cup of coffee at a busy restaurant during breakfast rush hour? With their hierarchical bureaucracy, with multiple vertical layers of authority and many different departments and divisions, work jams are occurring all over medical tourism hospitals on a daily basis. Typically no one recognizes them or does anything about them. Price quotes, contracts with facilitators and payers or referral organizations such as ours sit waiting in queues. Approvals hold things up. Lack of preplanned program development holds things up. Product design not taken seriously holds things up.

Your potential customers are trying to get answers and waiting for responses, or price quotes or appointments to chat online with the physician for ten minutes. Well-intended cost savings or long, slow approval processes implemented in one part of the organization are slowing things down in another part of the organization, retarding the overall delivery of value to both internal and external customers. We are all guilty of it, because we are all used to that mode of business as usual, and because we are all trying to manage multiple priorities. That's not delighting our customers, and let's face it: they don't care one bit about our excuses. They care about outcomes.

In 1958, Jay W. Forrester of MIT published a pioneering article in the *Harvard Business Review* which established a model of time's impact on an organization's performance.[*] The article showed how time flows through a system, and how focusing on time-based competitive performance results in improvements across the board. When work is done quickly, costs come down naturally. No wonder the American health delivery system is so costly to manage: the contracting process alone, from cold call to negotiation, has taken an average of eight months for the contracting cycle. The article noted that companies generally become time-based competitors first by correcting their manufacturing techniques, then by fixing sales and distribution, and finally by adjusting their approach to innovation. Ultimately, it becomes the basis for a company's overall strategy. We don't manufacture goods in medical tourism, but we do have a product development cycle that takes collaboration of numerous internal and external stakeholders, each with their own intricate piece of the puzzle and their own availability and timeframe to produce the deliverable. This is why Mercury Healthcare provider relations team inspectors are no longer permitted to independently plan visits to hospitals without first assessing and demonstrating the provider's readiness level to the executive team.

For example, if a hospital does not have a roster of credentialing details that it can produce by reflex e-mail for the physicians who will participate in the medical tourism program, it is an indicator that it has not pulled its program together to the extent that we want to invest thousands of dollars in staff time, travel, and travel costs to visit them. If prices will be quoted on the fly, the hospital is not ready. If the hospital cannot indicate that it has inspected hotels, committed to its guests with negotiated prices in several comfort and price categories, vetted local drivers and destination managers prepared to meet flights and escort departures, and has limited English proficiency by the nursing staff, they are not ready. The international department designee is merely the tip of the iceberg. That simply takes a role designation, printed business cards, and an e-mail address. I discussed the development and preparation for familiarization tours in Chapter 5. This too creates internal customer delight, as we have a relatively narrow window of time to visit a hospital, assess the program for consistency with our standards, and execute a contract. If they send us all the little pieces, and then waste our time showing us yet another cath lab, or labor and delivery department, or present scientific research papers on the intricacies of salt molecules as they relate to gastric cancer, that time costs us money. Not just for my company, but for all concerned.

Better stated, as Professor Ranjay Gulati has pointed out in his book, *Reorganize for Resilience* (2010), program managers throughout the hospital, not just in medical tourism, need to replace the inside-out perspective (what the hospital wants to sell), with an outside-in perspective (from the customer's point of view). Instead of trying to "parse and manufacture demand for medical tourism hips, knees, hearts and bariatric cases," they need to be considering what the noncustomer needs and wants, and compete in a different space and time to convert that noncustomer to a customer. Then it is back to the role of that international desk. They have to be the ones to deliver the service to accompany the technical product that the doctors and nurses will deliver.

For a medical tourism strategy to be deployed by the international or business development department, they need the freedom to delight their customers with actions that come from a philosophy that market boundaries and industry structure are not a "given" and can be designed to those delight specifications established by the clients and the cheerleaders, and carried out through the actions of the medical tourism provider complex, not just the hospital or the doctor involved. Assuming that program design structure and market boundaries exist only in managers' minds,

---

[*] Jay W. Forrester: Industrial dynamics: A major breakthrough for decision makers. *Harvard Business Review* (July–August 1958).

hospital and medical business executives who hold this view do not let existing market structures limit their thinking. To them, extra demand is out there, largely untapped, and yearning to be delighted so they can post something salient on their Twitter and Facebook blogs. The crux of the problem is how to create it. This, in turn, requires a shift of attention from supply to demand, from a focus on competing to a focus on value innovation, that is, the creation of innovative value that is measured in degrees of customer delight to unlock new demand. This is achieved via the simultaneous pursuit of differentiation and affordable cost for value received, not cheap medical care.

As market structure is changed by breaking the value/cost tradeoff, so are the rules of the game. Competition in the old game is therefore rendered irrelevant. Every medical tourism provider sells hips, knees, hearts, and gastric bypasses. By expanding the demand side of the economy new wealth is created. Such a strategy therefore allows a medical tourism provider to largely play a nonzero-sum game, with high payoff possibilities.

Short medical tourism product development cycle times can give a medical tourism or wellness provider an enormous competitive edge by increasing its ability to offer a wider array of products and services sooner than its competitors: the advantage of getting there first. But that's only the beginning. The key step in managing time comes in identifying where delays in delivering products and services to the ultimate customer are occurring and systematically eliminating them. This brings us back to the international department once again. If they are busy with existing business and a different set of priorities for existing patients, who will look after new inquiries from medical tourists that require more handholding, a different product, different pricing, and more logistical coordination? One key tool that can be used for this purpose is value-stream mapping (VSM).

With VSM, business development strategists for medical tourism can measure time by identifying workflow and eliminating delays in getting value to customers. Anyone who has ever studied Lean in healthcare is no stranger to this idea. Through VSM, one analyzes the flow of materials and information currently required to bring a product or service to a customer. In effect, the workplace is viewed from the ultimate customer's point of view, with the object of accelerating or eliminating any step or activity that does not add value, to them.

Although VSM emerged in the manufacturing sector, it is also used in logistics, supply chain, service industries, healthcare, software development, and new product development. Funny, as I listed those, unlike traditional healthcare, medical tourism is much more closely connected to logistics, supply chain, service and tourism industries, health delivery, information and communication technologies (ICT), and software development in one neat and tidy package. That is probably why in my head, this seems so natural and a part of healthcare business and medical tourism program administration.

To learn more about VSM, I strongly recommend Stephen Denning's book, *The Leader's Guide to Radical Management* (Jossey-Bass, 2010; ISBN-13: 978-0470548684), which provides a comprehensive overview of the concepts. I found his suggestion practicable and indispensable as he lays out a no-nonsense roadmap for shifting your hospital and management team into this new competitive way of thinking and acting.

Tracking Client Delight in Real-Time: Social Media— Where the Magic Begins!

Social media has changed everything for modern business management. Unfortunately, too many of my peers and colleagues in my age bracket choose to deny this to the extent that they need to spend time to learn more, do more, and experiment more. Instead, they continue to head to the local printer to print brochures and market the way they marketed their businesses 10 or 15 years ago. This is also true of hospitals; they may have a website, but it is dreadfully nonfunctional, full of misspelled words, stock photography, broken links, and "stuff." They have a Twitter account, but for the most part the American hospital Twitter account is underutilized, the Facebook Fan page is inactive and also underutilized, and nobody is responsible for its development.

The explosion of social media from practically nothing five years ago to over a half-billion participants has created major threats to traditional management that is focused on output and making money, as well as major opportunities for organizations that are committed to delighting their customers by generating positive outcomes. Fear about HIPAA might make the hospital nervous about "tweeting" and "liking," but if customers are the cheerleaders, there's no HIPAA violation. That's what social media is all about! It is the voice of the customer, good or bad, laudatory or shameful; it is what it is.

In April 2010, Christopher Meyer and Julia Kirby in the *Harvard Business Review* wrote "[Social Media have] changed the rules of business forever." When customers know everything, it becomes important that management be equally informed, particularly when customers have the ability to videotape the experience and transmit it, potentially to millions of other customers. Most traditionally-managed firms are just one YouTube video away from a major brand disaster." Amen!

Consider the following two case examples.

When United Airlines broke Dave Carroll's guitar, he made a singing YouTube video that told the story of the incident; the video has now been viewed by more than 8 million people. Read the story and view the video at (http://bit.ly/iLupWR).

In 2010, my husband and I made a reservation at a Holiday Inn in Madrid near Barejas International Airport to arrive late and grab a few hours sleep before an early morning departure back to the States. We found the hotel dirty, the bed uncomfortable, the free Wi-Fi was not free, and the location of the hotel was not in a place that appeared safe. We asked to cancel the reservation and be allowed to find a different hotel. The desk clerk refused. I used my smart phone, posted a tweet on Twitter about my displeasure to see if anyone was listening at Holiday Inn corporate back in the United States and sat in the lobby to wait for 10 minutes. Within 7 minutes customer service was on the phone with the desk clerk. The desk clerk handed me the telephone receiver, and said, "Somebody wants to speak with you from our corporate office in the U.S.A."

We had already returned the rental car. Holiday Inn arranged a room at another property, a ride there, and a glass of wine for both of us to calm down and make nice. They charged us the same rate as we would have paid in the other hotel, but gave us the Wi-Fi in the room at no charge, which was important to me, and was part of my originally negotiated rate quote at the other hotel.

Customer Experience Organization and Obstacles

Although many hospitals and medical tourism providers do have some kind of customer experience effort going on across their company, few hospitals centralize this process. In most of the hospitals I have visited throughout the world, it is as if medical tourism exists in a vacuum. Much of the hospital is essentially unaware that a medical tourism program is operational in their hospital. Staff members have no clue what that term means, or why they should know it. This is a warning sign to our inspection team that tells us immediately that the hospital and its nursing staff are not committed to developing the program to the point that every person on the staff, from the CEO to the person who mops the morgue floor, is a brand ambassador. And that can be a problem.

In very few hospitals, is there an executive in charge of customer experience efforts across their organization. More often, that remains at a manager or department supervisor level. If this is the situation at your hospital, fix it! Fix it now, before someone embarrasses your organization with an unaddressed complaint handled by someone who is not empowered to facilitate customer delight, and the next tweet about your company is the voice of an angry consumer who is less than delighted.

Voice of the Customer and Net Promoter: Actionable Business Intelligence

Do you have a formalized VOC program? More than three-quarters of those Fortune 500 firms have a process for contacting customers based on their feedback and get feedback from customers about their overall relationship with the company. What do you do to obtain feedback from customers?

Temkin recently posted a nice blog article about VoC best practices. Here is what I learned from his post. Basically, he refers to 6 Ds:

- Detection
- Dissemination
- Diagnosing
- Discussing
- Designing
- Deployment

These 6Ds are what he calls the elements of a good closed-loop voice of the customer program. I look at them as the fundamental elements of any good business intelligence program.

- First, you need to listen to your consumers. How you do it may be passive or active and solicited in the form of surveys and calls and solicited information. He cautions that program managers should be strategic about to what sourcing information they listen.
- In the next step of dissemination, he explains that the success of VoC programs does not come from collecting customer feedback, but instead about getting the information gleaned from the data into the hands of the right people at the right level and at the right time.
- Temkin then calls the next part "diagnosis," but really it is about the age-old maxim that data are useless unless they are converted into useful actionable information. This is tantamount to listening to the last employee I fired, who always started a sentence with "You know what the problem is?" One day I told him that the problem was him not having the solution and that he should go clear out his desk. Just having raw data only highlights potential problems or opportunities. That's the easy part. It doesn't give you any answers. Your VoC program should help you develop processes for uncovering the insights and testing hypotheses. Otherwise, send it to "John." He likes that kind of thing and now he has lots of time to gather more.
- Discussions are very important. Temkin explains that although some issues can be handled within a single department, VoC insights often highlight issues and opportunities that span multiple organizations. This is true in medical tourism, as you may need to confer with airlines, hotels, drivers, insurers, case managers, facilitators, technicians, nurses, doctors,

healthcare information systems, external medical directors, aftercare providers, and external case managers. Medical tourism program organizers need to put in place cross-functional forums, to make sure that VoC insights don't get lost across organizational silos which are particularly problematic in healthcare.

■ Once your team finds a problem or opportunity for improvement, you have to be ready to take action. That doesn't mean you simply act. There has to be an established and stream-lined policy and protocol to follow that is effective, measureable, and accepted by all the stakeholders, so that turf wars are not created, and so that someone owns the action. Do this by design so that your actions are not always one-offs taken by mavericks who have no buy-in from the people who have to work within the system day in and day out.

■ Like parachutes, VoC programs only succeed when action is taken to deploy them, so have a plan for when and how they will be evaluated, timeframes for action plans, and planned effectiveness measurement.

Here are some ways you can develop a VoC program for your hospital.

1. Obtain feedback on how customers view their overall relationship with your organization by direct communication in the form of telephone calls, surveys, or online questionnaires.
2. Establish a process to contact certain customers based on their feedback, both good and bad.
3. Obtain feedback from customers immediately after interactions with your inquiry desk (just as when you are asked at the checkout counter in most groceries and home improvement companies "Did you find what you were looking for today?" and then again immediately upon discharge from your hospital or clinic (checking that they got home OK, how are they feeling, any comments, difficulties, or suggestions to make it easier for others?).
4. Analyze customer feedback across different customer segments; it is up to you to define the segments based on the type of data you are seeking.
5. Provide access to customer feedback widely across the company; if it's great news, make a fuss. If it shows an opportunity for improvement, get those brand ambassadors busy on making things better. Heads should only roll if nobody cares.
6. Create executive dashboards that highlight customer feedback results and trends. There should be a daily report and flash notices if something really crucial happens. I hate those kinds of surprises; I'd rather deal with them while there's still a chance to recover.
7. Provide customized views of results for different stakeholders across the program. Make the data informative and actionable by those who need to take action, rather than mired in too much information.
8. Have a formalized process for reviewing feedback with cross-functional teams (physicians, nursing, dietary, information systems, marketing, international relations, contracting, revenue cycle, and others).
9. Analyze customer feedback across different stages of a customer's episode of care.
10. Text mine to analyze comments and other unstructured data. This is often done in the form of sentiment extraction and is applied to
    ■ Reputation management
    ■ Competitive intelligence
    ■ Quality improvement
    ■ Trend spotting

11. Respond to feedback in social media channels immediately, or at least the same day.
12. Tie compensation to customer feedback scores (pay for performance).
13. Track the impact of corrective actions.
14. Analyze feedback in social media channels.
15. Notify people with alerts when a piece of feedback meets specified criteria.

Next, you will want to determine your organization's Net Promoter® Score. Net Promoter is both a loyalty metric and a discipline for using customer feedback to fuel profitable growth in your business. Developed by Satmetrix, Bain & Company, and Fred Reichheld, the concept was first popularized through Reichheld's book *The Ultimate Question*, and has since been embraced by leading companies worldwide as the standard for measuring and improving customer loyalty.

Fred Reichheld's 2006 book, *The Ultimate Question*, challenged the conventional wisdom of customer satisfaction programs. It coined the terms *bad profits* and *good profits* and pointed to a faster, much more effective way of gauging customers' real loyalty to a company, introducing a quantitative measure (the Net Promoter Score) for establishing a baseline and effectively tracking changes in customer loyalty. To explain:

> The right goal for a company is to deliver customer experiences of such high quality that customers recognize the value in the relationship and become Promoters. These Promoters generate good profits and fuel true growth. They become, in effect, part of a company's marketing department, not only increasing their own purchases but also providing enthusiastic referrals.
>
> By contrast, companies can boost short-term profits by exploiting customer relationships, raising prices when they can get away with it, or cutting back on services to save costs and boost margins. Those practices boost bad profits by extracting value from customers at the expense of loyalty, creating Detractors. Companies cannot achieve long-term sustained growth on the basis of bad profits.
>
> Conventional accounting can't distinguish a dollar of good profits—the kind that lead to growth—from a dollar of bad profits, which undermine it. The Net Promoter Score fills this gap. Just as managers use financial reporting to make sure they are meeting profit goals, they can use NPS to make sure they are meeting customer-relationship goals. Therein lies the path to true growth. (Reichheld, *The Ultimate Question*, p. 28)

Reichheld's *The Ultimate Question* builds on the link between Net Promoter Scores and business growth and profitability. It was an easy read that helped me to find a way to combine our operational discipline to increase Promoters and reduce Detractors. The Net Promoter concept can foster a potential win–win for medical tourism program operators and their customers because it offers rapid access to data near-real-time metrics closely coupled and correlated with precipitating actions. Instead of waiting months for long, drawn-out surveying, analysis, and interpretations, the system can help you initiate positive changes if you apply it correctly.

In a medical tourism setting, the Net Promoter Score, or NPS®, is a straightforward metric that holds medical tourism program organizers and facilitator companies and employees accountable for how they treat customers. Across other industries, it has gained popularity thanks to its simplicity and its linkage to profitable growth. Employees at all levels of the organization understand it, opening the door to customer-centric change and improved performance.

Calculating Your NPS Score

NPS is based on the fundamental perspective that every company's customers can be divided into three categories: Promoters, Passives, and Detractors. By asking one simple question, "How likely is it that you would recommend [Company X] to a friend or colleague?" you can track these groups and get a clear measure of your company's performance through its customers' eyes. Customers respond on a 0–10 point rating scale and are categorized as follows:

■ *Promoters* (score 9–10) are loyal enthusiasts who will keep buying and refer others, fueling growth.
■ *Passives* (score 7–8) are satisfied but unenthusiastic customers who are vulnerable to competitive offerings. (Remember my sandwich experience?)
■ *Detractors* (score 0–6) are unhappy customers who can damage your brand and impede growth through negative word-of-mouth. (Remember my Madrid example and my use of Twitter to complain from the Holiday Inn lobby?)

To calculate your organization's Net Promoter Score, take the percentage of customers who are Promoters and subtract the percentage who are Detractors.

Net Promoter programs are not traditional customer satisfaction programs, and simply measuring your NPS does not lead to success. Companies need to follow an associated discipline to drive improvements in customer loyalty and enable profitable growth. They must have leadership commitment, and the right business processes and systems in place to deliver real-time information to employees, so they can act on customer feedback and achieve results.

That accountability to an associated discipline is what Owen and Brooks describe, in *Answering the Ultimate Question*, as Customer-Centric DNA*. Real breakthroughs in program performance are achieved only when medical tourism organizations move from a research model to an operational model embedded in their hospital or clinic culture. That culture is what I enjoy so much when I experience Planetree-designated hospitals' cultures. It is that patient centricity created from the operating culture transformed into action. You can feel it, patients can feel it, and it creates delight with your product, your service, and instills confidence in your ability to care for patients who selected you and traveled from far away to place their lives in your hands.

Asking the ultimate question allows your hospital or clinic to track promoters and detractors, producing a clear measure of your organization's performance through its customers' eyes, its Net Promoter Score. Bain analysis shows that sustained value creators—companies that achieve long-term profitable growth—have Net Promoter Scores two times higher than the average company. And NPS leaders outgrow their competitors in most industries, by an average of 2.5 times.

Customers can be categorized based on their answer to the ultimate question. The best way to gauge the efficiency of a company's growth engine is to take the percentage of customers who are promoters (P) and subtract the percentage who are detractors (D). This equation is how we calculate a Net Promoter Score for a company.

$$P - D = NPS$$

---

* Net Promoter Operating Model, *NetPromoter*®, accessed May 12, 2011, http://www.netpromoter.com/np/model/index.jsp.

Although easy to grasp, the NPS metric represents a radical change in the way companies manage customer relationships and organize for growth. Rather than relying on notoriously ineffective customer satisfaction surveys, companies can use NPS to measure customer relationships as rigorously as they now measure profits. What's more, NPS finally enables CEOs to hold employees accountable for treating customers properly. It clarifies the link between the quality of a company's customer relationships and its growth prospects.

How does your hospital or clinic stack up on this measurement? How do your doctors and nurses stack up? The average firm sputters along at an NPS efficiency of only 5–10%, but the average firm is not rendering healthcare. In other words, promoters barely outnumber detractors. Many firms, and some entire industries, have negative Net Promoter Scores, which means that they are creating more detractors than promoters, day in and day out. These abysmal Net Promoter Scores explain why so many companies can't deliver profitable sustainable growth, no matter how aggressively they spend to acquire new business. Companies with the most efficient growth engines—companies such as Amazon, HomeBanc, eBay, Harley-Davidson, Costco, Vanguard, and Dell—operate at NPS efficiency ratings of 50–80%. So even they have room for improvement.

In concept, it's just that simple. But obviously, a lot of hard work is needed to both ask the question in a manner that provides reliable, timely, and actionable data, and, of course, to learn how to improve your Net Promoter Score.

Customer Experience Competencies

I keep returning to the international department staff because for medical tourism that staff may be too wrapped up in other duties. The jobs that need to be done are extremely vital to the growth, development, sustainability, and profitability of your program. Don't skimp here.

Your team will need to master four core customer experience competencies in order to build and sustain your customer experience leadership, namely:

1. Purposeful leadership to guide them
2. Compelling brand values and taking pride in being brand ambassadors
3. Employee engagement through pride, and pay-for-performance
4. Remaining connected to the customer; not taking 48–72 hours to answer an e-mail

In order to develop these competencies, senior hospital and clinic executives have to lead by example and regularly communicate that customer experience is one of the hospital's key strategies. If you don't feel it, live it, and breathe it, your employees and subordinates will see right through you.

In today's millennial workforce, you will have to celebrate, recognize, and reward employees who exemplify your core values. Unless your young workforce has been living in a cave, the millennial workforce culture is present worldwide, not just in the developed nations.

Your executive team must have a clearly defined set of values to guide how it makes decisions, and not just make decisions on the fly. Otherwise you will be grooming impetuous workers instead of leaders. The succession plan and professional development, including leadership training, are what creates leaders, not "winging it" every time a decision has to be made and action taken.

Your nurses, case managers, admissions coordinators, technicians, and others across the entire organization need to understand that you are developing a medical tourism product, and understand the core values of the hospital and the program, and understand how those values relate to their role. To fail to plan and explain this, is to plan to fail.

Your human resources department has to understand what is needed in professional development and staff development so that they can arrange training. This can start with cultural competency training and continue to functional medical English, for starters, outside of the United States and United Kingdom and English-speaking nations, and for functional medical languages other than English when the native language is Hungarian, Croatian, Romanian, Polish, German, Russian, Turkish, Arabic, Portuguese, French, or another language. The organization has to provide industry-leading training for employees in all competencies of the healthcare organization, not just clinical areas.

Senior executives need to have enough of a budget cushion for a start-up medical tourism program so that they can support decisions to trade off short-term financial results for longer-term customer loyalty.

I strongly believe that if your medical tourism/international patient relations team is not involved in all of these efforts, they have too much time on their hands or you don't have a real commitment to developing and improving your program, and are back to the category of a hospital, a website, some doctors, and an e-mail address.

NICHE MARKET OPPORTUNITIES

Chapter 17

Medical Tourism Growth Potential for the United States

Most medical practices and many rural medical centers and critical access hospitals (CAHs) qualify to be designated as a small- and medium-sized enterprise (SME). Small- and medium-sized enterprises, which the Small Business Administration's (SBA) Office of Advocacy defines as SMEs for research purposes, as independent businesses having fewer than 500 employees account for about half of all employment and economic activity in the United States.[*] SMEs represent about 97% of all identified exporting firms and roughly 31% of total U.S. export value.[†] To a large extent, healthcare exports have not been well tracked, and I believe the market is actually much larger than most people estimate. Take, for example, neighbor markets such as Canada, Mexico, and the Caribbean. Hospitals in Miami report significant revenues from the Caribbean market from healthcare exportation, and it continues to grow.

Conversely, large firms represent 3% of all exporting firms and are responsible for 69% of total U.S. export value.[‡] Market forces explain much of the difference. Large firms have a bigger presence in the manufacturing sector (which represents most U.S. exports). Large firms can also take advantage of economies of scale and other efficiencies. Nonetheless, there is a clear opportunity for SME hospitals, medical groups, and other types of providers to increase their exports in healthcare services.

For medical tourism and health travel market expansion, healthcare SMEs are less likely to look beyond the large domestic market for revenue growth. Failure to realize the revenue and excess capacity-filling potential of neighbor markets for SMEs in the U.S. northern boundary communities that serve the Canadian market and Iceland, and those in the southern border areas that serve Mexican and Caribbean nearshore markets, is a flaw in strategy. Most small hospital executives assume that all that market potential makes a bee-line straight for tertiary hospitals and teaching

---

[*] SBA Office of Advocacy, Frequently Asked Questions, September 2009.

[†] U.S. Department of Commerce, U.S. Census Bureau, "A Profile of U.S. Exporting Companies, 2007–2008," April 2010, p. 3.

[‡] *Ibid*. The data cover wholesalers as well as manufacturing companies. Small businesses that supply components that go into a large company's product are not counted as exporters, so more SMEs may be involved in exporting, but not as the exporter of record.

institutions. Both those alternatives offer large, busy, and often impersonal environments, often have a low patient "delight" hospitality index, usually charge much higher prices than their local hospital counterparts, and frequently deliver care by residents and fellows rather than attending the specialists and experts upon which the brand is based. The unique selling proposition (USP) of the SME hospital (not just in the United States but in every medical tourism market) is different, and until now has failed in its promotion and marketing.

Unlike in the manufacturing sector, the costs of exporting may not have as significant an effect on SME healthcare providers. With manufacturing, exporting can involve a substantial initial cost, limiting a small firm's ability to participate in global trade.[*] On the other hand, with healthcare, the cost of establishing the hospital, staffing, and so on, is already committed, and the opportunity to export can actually provide new cash revenues paid in advance or at the time of service.

A fuller appreciation of SME exporting and the role of SMEs in job creation, innovation, and entrepreneurship is essential for defining the government's role both in unlocking SME export potential and broadening the benefits of trade to a wider segment of American society.[†] For hospitals and healthcare providers in the United States, however, I have not been privy to any written plans that demonstrate how the U.S. Department of Commerce plans to support this initiative for those hospitals, healthcare providers, ambulatory surgery centers, and others who might have an ability to make a commitment to join in this NEI and increase healthcare exportation at the SME level. Rather than delay the manuscript to the publisher any longer, I guess we will have to assume that time will reveal the plans and resources available. The office at the U.S. Department of Commerce does seem responsive to e-mails and calls, however, so if you have interest, do call them.

SMEs are the biggest drivers of jobs and new job creation in the United States. They accounted for almost 55% of private sector employment in the first quarter of 2009.[‡] They were also responsible for creating 64% of net new jobs during the 16 years from 1992 to 2009.[§] In addition to providing employment opportunities, they are important sources of innovative processes, products, and services.

Canada and Mexico are the largest export markets for both SMEs and large firms. However, SMEs have demonstrated their capability to export to emerging and developing countries. For example, China is the third-largest destination for SME exports after Canada and Mexico. From 2007 to 2008, the markets with the largest percentage increase in the number of SME exporters were markets such as the United Arab Emirates (21%), Saudi Arabia (14%), and Brazil (11%).[¶]

[*] International Trade Commission, Small and Medium-Sized Enterprises: Overview of Participation in U.S. Exports, January 2010, p. 1–1.

[†] Understanding of the role of U.S. SMEs in trade is being considerably advanced by a series of International Trade Commission reports requested by U.S. Trade Representative Kirk in October 2009. The first report, released in January 2010, focused on the role of SMEs in U.S. trade. The second report, released in July, provides a comparison of U.S. SME performance with SMEs in the European Union. The final report, due this fall, will examine SME services trade, key tariff and nontariff barriers that may disproportionately affect SMEs, and the role of indirect exports (i.e., SMEs that provide inputs to larger firms that export the final product).

[‡] U.S. Department of Labor, Bureau of Labor Statistics, Business Employment Dynamics, Table F: Distribution of private sector employment by firm size class, not seasonally adjusted. www.bls.gov/bdm/bdmfirmsize.htm.

[§] International Trade Commission, Small and Medium-Sized Enterprises: Overview of Participation in U.S. Exports, January 2010, p. 2–7.

[¶] U.S. Department of Commerce, U.S. Census Bureau, "A Profile of U.S. Exporting Companies, 2007–2008," April 13, 2010, p. 3.

What mystifies me is how other than one large health system, Kaleida, in upstate New York associated with State University of New York (SUNY) Buffalo, few hospital providers in U.S. border regions along the Great Lakes, and across Minnesota, North Dakota, Idaho, and so on really have shown any articulated interest in serving cross border-patients from Canada.

SMEs face a wider range of resource constraints and scarcities than large firms do. For example, SMEs are more likely to need external financing to undertake an export transaction of hard goods that require trucking and transportation, a particularly daunting task currently with the tightening of credit markets and increased fuel costs. As noted by FedEx in comments submitted in response to the NEI Federal Register notice, "We continue to hear from many of our customers that inadequate trade financing remains the top issue for SMEs."*

In addition, SMEs, especially in healthcare, are often quite insular and therefore have insufficient knowledge of foreign markets, in contrast with a larger firm's access to market intelligence and its direct presence in targeted foreign markets. Finally, unlike their manufacturer counterparts, healthcare SMEs face lower real and perceived risks of exporting services, as the export markets are not as litigious or prone to seeking damage awards beyond restitution for actual economic damages. Other than a good international business consultant for market information and introductions, there are actually fewer trade barriers than other service and hard good industries might face abroad. It is questionable how likely they are to have a diversified foreign customer base.† Significant revenues might be generated with a few solid direct G2B (government to business) contracts from abroad, or employer health services contracts from employers with expatriates deployed in the United States and its territories.

For manufacturers, the effect of one deal falling through has a greater impact on an SME's bottom line. This is not the same, however, in healthcare services. Although a deal that has fallen through might be felt temporarily, most of these cases will tend to be one-off cases, requiring prepayment in cash, and if the case or admission is cancelled, it would be rare that nurse staffing ratios for coverage on the floor affected would change significantly.

The International Monetary Fund (IMF) forecasts indicate that nearly 87% of world economic growth over the next five years will take place outside the United States.‡ Just as trade typically falls faster than GDP in a recession, trade typically grows faster during a rebound. Accordingly, exports can be expected to rise rapidly as the world recovers from the economic crisis. In support of this, the IMF forecasts imports of advanced countries§ to grow by 7.2% in 2010, and emerging and developing country imports are forecast to grow by 12.5%.¶ At the time of this writing I was unable to locate more recently released updated statistics.

As global markets become increasingly interconnected, it is critical that the U.S. maintain and promote a highly competitive export economy. I know that our company, for which we have obtained the trademark on the phrase "globally integrated health delivery system®," as well as the future competitiveness of the United States, depends on its ability to remain fully engaged in the growing

---

* U.S. Department of Commerce, "Request for Public Comment To Inform Development of National Export Initiative Plan," Docket Number 100624279-0279-01, June 30, 2010.

† International Trade Commission, "Small and Medium-Sized Enterprises: Overview of Participation in U.S. Exports," January 2010, pp. 2–15 and 2–16.

‡ United States Trade Representative, President's 2010 Trade Policy Agenda, March 2010, p. 2.

§ Terms similar to advanced country include developed country, industrialized country, more developed country (MDC), more economically developed country (MEDC), Global North country, first world country, and post-industrial country.

¶ IMF, "World Economic Outlook Update: Restoring Confidence without Harming Recovery," July 7, 2010, Table 1.

global marketplace. We see the opportunity, but we need buy-in from U.S. healthcare providers interested in health export to support our efforts, join the network, and care for inbound and intra-bound medical tourism patients.[*] The NEI provides an opportunity to amplify the Administration's export promotion activities in support of the highly competitive U.S. services sector.

As the largest component of the U.S. economy, services account for nearly 70%[†] of U.S. GDP. This dynamic sector encompasses such services as financial (banking, securities, and insurance), telecommunications, computer, energy, environmental, express delivery, distribution services, audiovisual, construction, professional (architecture, engineering, accounting, and legal), health-care, education, and travel and tourism services. The United States is the world's largest services market and the leading services-exporting country, with exports of $502 billion in 2009, or 14% of all global services exports.[‡]

The United States has enjoyed a consistent surplus in the services trade, and the current sur-plus of $132 billion is larger than that of any other country, reflecting the highly competitive and innovative nature of U.S. services firms. Indeed, U.S. services firms act as force multipliers for American manufacturing firms and agricultural producers, providing the express delivery, bank-ing, insurance, accounting, legal, retail, and other services necessary for these firms to expand domestically and globally. In every U.S. state, services employ more workers, pay more wages, and account for more business sales than any other sector.

Global trade in services is important to the continued expansion of the U.S. economy, and international markets offer significant growth opportunities for U.S. services. To seize these opportunities, the federal government will pursue a variety of services export trade promotion activities designed to achieve the broadest possible expansion of exports by U.S. services firms. These activities will complement U.S efforts to reduce barriers to trade, as outlined further in Part II, Priority 7: Reducing Barriers to Trade.

The complexities of a changing global economy require an export strategy that is both bal-anced and targeted. Current and projected economic growth rates point to many of the emerging and developing countries as the fastest-growing economies, representing great opportunities for experienced U.S. exporters. Meanwhile, traditional trading partners such as Canada, Mexico, and many European Union countries still offer highly accessible markets for most U.S. exporters, many of them SMEs.

Targeting other key "next tier" emerging markets,[§] and the Asia–Pacific region as a whole, is critical to continued and sustained U.S. export growth in the long term. More countries are enter-ing the ranks of relatively stable, fast-growing markets, offering significant commercial opportuni-ties. Key next-tier economies such as Colombia, Indonesia, Saudi Arabia, South Africa, Turkey, and Vietnam are anticipated to experience high GDP growth rates in the next few years.[¶] As with

---

[*] Those patients who travel within the country to access health services.

[†] 68.8% of U.S. GDP in 2009. Source: U.S. Department of Commerce, Bureau of Economic Analysis, 6/10/2010.

[‡] U.S. Department of Commerce, U.S. Census Bureau/Bureau of Economic Analysis, U.S. International Trade in Goods and Services: Annual Revision for 2009, June 10, 2010, p. 1.

[§] Given the intersection of trade promotion, trade policy, and economic development issues in such markets, closer interagency coordination is essential. Therefore, the TPCC has worked through a Next Tier Working Group to identify priority markets. The initial six markets identified by this group are: Colombia, Indonesia, Saudi Arabia, South Africa, Turkey, and Vietnam. Each market meets a set of criteria including population, GDP and projected GDP, inflation, ease of doing business, diversity of market sectors, and U.S. market pen-etration and room for expansion. At the same time, the Next Tier Working Group will continue to periodically review strategies and the priority markets themselves as the global marketplace evolves.

[¶] IMF, World Economic Outlook Database, April 2010, pp. 49, 54, 61, 65, 67.

many of these markets, foreign competition is intensifying, and these countries also present many and varied hurdles and market access barriers for U.S. companies.

In addition, although several individual countries in the region are among the next-tier economies, the Asia–Pacific region as a whole also continues to grow in importance to U.S. export and job expansion prospects. The Asia–Pacific region is growing rapidly and already constituted 23% of the world economy in 2009.* As discussed in the president's 2010 Trade Policy Agenda, countries in the region must see the United States as a committed and engaged trading partner if the United States is to remain at the center of their network of intensifying trade relationships.†

Canada and Mexico, the United States' neighbors and North American Free Trade Agreement partners, are the largest export markets for U.S. goods and services and are therefore an ideal starting point for new exporters. I can envisage a few hurdles though, particularly on the immigration side of the chain. Crossing either border lately has been more and more of a hassle, and I am a returning American citizen! Because the trading relationship (in other areas where we are shipping hard goods out) is well established and market access barriers are relatively low, these markets are a high priority in terms of broadening the base of exporting U.S. companies. That might not be as easy in healthcare, inasmuch as the export is services and the only way to perform the exportation is to bring someone into our country. In addition to benefiting from the competitive advantages of doing business with an FTA partner country, U.S. companies will find these markets more accessible from a shipping, logistics, and payment standpoint. Something tells me that they forgot the nuance of medical tourism: that we need the body on this side of the border to operate on it.

Europe remains an important market, given the huge baseline trade and deep commercial ties. Average annual U.S. goods exports to the European Union (EU) are about $250 billion, about 25% of total U.S. merchandise exports to the world. Therefore, any market access gain with the EU can translate into major commercial benefits. In 2008, U.S. services exports to the EU totaled more than $224 billion, representing 43% of all U.S. services exports to the world. The European Union is a natural target for U.S. export promotion efforts that encourage companies to begin exporting or to expand to new markets.

The United States has FTAs in place with 17 countries.‡ Free Trade Agreement partner countries offer attractive and increasingly transparent business environments. These FTAs provide dramatic improvements in market access, from tariff elimination or reduction and stronger trade rules, to general improvements in business practices and dispute resolution. In addition to seeking congressional approval of pending FTAs or negotiating new FTAs, the administration must continue to promote greater participation of U.S. companies in the current FTA partner countries. United States' exports to FTA partners have seen strong, above average increases, particularly for SME healthcare organizations.§

---

* As used in this paragraph, the Asia–Pacific region includes TPP members Australia, Brunei, Chile, New Zealand, Peru, Singapore, and Vietnam, as well as China, Indonesia, Japan, Korea, Malaysia, and Thailand.

† USTR, The President's 2010 Trade Policy Agenda, March 2010, pp. 7–9.

‡ These countries are Canada, Mexico, Costa Rica, Dominican Republic, Guatemala, Honduras, Nicaragua, El Salvador, Australia, Bahrain, Chile, Israel, Jordan, Morocco, Oman, Peru, and Singapore. See www.export.gov/fta/ for more information on each FTA.

§ For example, since implementation of the U.S.–Singapore FTA in 2004, two-way trade with that country has increased 20%, and U.S. exports to Singapore have increased 35%. In 2009, total trade with Singapore reached $38 billion.

Chapter 18

Medical Tourism Benefit Introduction for U.S. Health Insurance Plans

Almost weekly, I receive questions from our international network providers about why it takes so long for U.S. health insurers to approve medical tourism coverage for medically necessary and routine care for patients.

I have listened to a handful of speakers from the United States, some who have neither the expertise or education to present this subject. Others, who are novice facilitators lacking any work experience or professional education in the insurance sector have announced to hospitals and providers abroad that they intend to "market" their provider network to insurance plans and employers in the United States. I heard one that was neither qualified to present this subject, nor was he a facilitator, but was instead a public relations consultant who stated that he intended to bring his client list of represented providers to more than ten million insurers and employers in the United States ready to seek services abroad. To add insult to injury, the Associated Press syndicated the story without vetting the facts, so that this impossible and confusing assertion was echoed around the world.

Strategic Implications for International Providers

Although I am sure that some of these speakers and so-called experts were simply misinformed and uneducated, with no nefarious intent, such claims and predictions can create problems for hospital administrators, doctors, and dentists charged with the responsibility for strategic development of a medical tourism program. This is especially true if those responsible may not be as familiar with the myriad U.S. healthcare reimbursement systems and benefit models offered through insurers, and other plan designs and options available to self-funded health benefit trusts under the Employee Retirement Income Security Act of 1974 (ERISA). Without this knowledge, it would be unfair for me to judge these providers too harshly for their failure to apply critical thinking skills before making costly errors in strategy and investment. To begin, one must first understand critical thinking, and what it entails. Critical thinking calls for a persistent effort to examine any belief or supposed form of knowledge in the light of the evidence that supports it and the further conclusions to which it tends. It also generally requires the thinker to gather and marshal pertinent (relevant) information, to recognize unstated assumptions and values, to comprehend and use language with accuracy, clarity, and discrimination, to interpret data, to appraise evidence and evaluate arguments, to recognize the existence (or nonexistence) of logical relationships between propositions, to draw warranted conclusions and generalizations, to put to the test the conclusions and generalizations at which one arrives, to reconstruct one's patterns of beliefs on the basis of wider experience, and to render accurate judgments about specific things and qualities in everyday life.

Understand the Benefit Addition Process

Next, one must understand benefit design in a number of settings: first, the insurance benefit setting, and second, the ERISA benefit setting. In the insured setting, in order for a benefit to be added to a health coverage plan, many things must happen.

Long before (possibly two to three years) the benefit is available for use by an insured plan member who has a policy that includes this benefit, the health plan must prepare to manage and administrate the new benefit through a step-by-step process. If the process is not followed, or doesn't meet the requirements to advance to the next step, the process stops until the requirement is met or the attempt to add the benefit is abandoned.

The first step in adding a medical tourism or global medical care benefit to a plan benefit design is to determine if there is a real need to add this benefit. In a country where insurance benefits are provided under a system of managed care, insurance companies and health plans work with designated providers who are contracted to be "in-network." These providers of care negotiate discounts and maximum allowable fees for the services rendered. Although the billed charges may be high, the payer exerts market force and often drives down the actual amount paid to 45–55% of billed charges. Therefore, a hip replacement may be billed at $60,000 dollars, however, the actual revenue is somewhere between $27,000 to $33,000. When the provider adds in the cost to collect deductibles and copayments, which are often contractually stipulated to be billed only after the claim is adjudicated, the provider must invest in an entire revenue management department to manage billings and collections to the patient or responsible party long after the service is rendered, and perhaps also deal with payment variances and appeals for additional payment if the claim was paid at an amount that was less than the negotiated rate.

Health Insurance Company Benefit Design Due Diligence

Once a determination is made to begin the investigation of adding this benefit, an investigative task force is assembled to have a high-level discussion about the addition. The task force may include brokers, marketing department representatives, claims managers, information systems representation, the medical director and utilization management and quality management managers, actuaries, underwriters, and provider relations managers. The task force is then charged with the responsibility to research and report back: the validation of the financial risk associated with adding the benefit, the benefits to the plan, the ability to manage and administrate the process, the plan licensure and accreditation requirements, which standards and metrics will be used to measure quality and provider competency, and finally to draft the benefit for presentation to decision makers at the executive level of the plan. This process could take four to six months, minimum.

There are many difficult hurdles to overcome at this first step, because in addition to validating the argument that the benefit should or should not be added, certain assumptions and predictive models must be developed. For years, managed care companies and insurers have long used some form of experience rating (claim dollars paid out/premium dollars paid in) to help price their products for large companies.

Every few years, the health care insurance community comes up with the latest and greatest "silver bullet" to address the rising cost of healthcare. Most of them have familiar acronyms: PPO (preferred provider organization), FSA (flexible spending account), HMO (health maintenance organization), POS (point of service), MSA (medical savings account), HRA (health reimbursement account), and most recently, HDHP (high-deductible health plan) and HSA (health savings account), and now, medical tourism and globally integrated healthcare. The industry has also tried self-funding, wellness programs, disease- and case-management programs, health-risk assessments, provider profiling, and more. All of these ideas and strategies helped, for a while, then typically were abandoned or placed in the background as costs once again started to escalate.

Cost–Benefit Analysis

Statistics show that approximately 80% of healthcare costs are being generated by less than 20% of the population. In addition, a high percentage of those costs tend to come from individuals with comorbidities (people with two or more disease states; i.e., a person with heart disease and diabetes). One of the primary hurdles for the task force is to estimate accurately how many people might actually be inclined to use such a benefit if it were offered and what the actual cost benefit would be to the plan to put in place all the necessary elements to offer and manage the benefit.

To understand this more completely, one must first understand what is at stake for the insurer and the cost of network development. Insurers seek accreditation under an accrediting body known as the National Committee for Quality Assurance, (NCQA). The NCQA seal is a widely recognized symbol of quality. Organizations incorporating the seal into advertising and marketing materials must first pass a rigorous comprehensive review and must annually report on their performance. For consumers and employers, the seal is a reliable indicator that an organization is well managed and delivers high-quality care and service. The cost for a health plan to undergo an NCQA accreditation survey is many times the cost of a typical hospital accreditation survey and preparation and must be repeated every two years.

NCQA has helped to build consensus around important healthcare quality issues by working with large employers, policymakers, doctors, patients, and health plans to decide what's important, how to measure it, and how to promote improvement. Their programs and services reflect a straightforward formula for improvement: measure, analyze, improve, repeat. NCQA makes this process possible in healthcare by developing quality standards and performance measures for a broad range of healthcare entities. These measures and standards are the tools that organizations and individuals can use to identify opportunities for improvement. The annual reporting of performance against such measures has become a focal point for the media, consumers, and health plans, which use these results to set their improvement agendas for the following year. In short, employers who purchase healthcare for their employees demand accreditation for the plans they offer to their employees. That accreditation comes with some very specific standards of network development, credentials verification, and privileging of the medical and dental panel. To fail to meet those rigorous standards means facing the threat of loss of accreditation. Loss of accreditation by NCQA can result in employers dropping a plan mid-year and purchasing coverage from another insurer that meets that standard.

To prepare to manage a new benefit such as medical tourism, a provider panel of international hospitals, laboratories, physicians, allied health practitioners, dentists, and others must be developed in accordance with the standards set forth to maintain health insurance plan accreditation. This includes professional credentials verification. Before a network can be empanelled, professional providers must submit lengthy applications, answers to very personal questions about their lifestyle, professional liability history, drug use, psychosocial profile, and more, and agree that the information may be verified by primary source verification from educational institutions, clinical training programs, medical education institutions, and peer recommendations. This must be done initially prior to granting privileges and must be repeated every two years.

As for the hospital, the plan's provider network development team must review certain documentation of the hospital, and perform an annual site inspection. There is no NCQA requirement that the hospital be Joint Commission International (JCI) accredited.

These two requirements present a serious challenge to the task force. In my role as a CEO of an international PPO (Mercury Healthcare) that has implemented and maintains these NCQA network development standards, I am very familiar with the costs associated with the professional provider recruitment and credentials verification process. For physicians and dentists, the cost to recruit and process the credentials verification for one physician is in excess of USD $100. The cost to engage a hospital into our network inclusive of the contracting process, the site inspection and the due diligence review, can escalate to an investment of more than USD $15,000 in time, staff involvement, and travel costs. For any other health plan, the cost is the same if they do it but not as efficient. Worse yet, the provider has to fill out the same redundant paperwork multiple times; once for each insurance plan. If the insurance plan outsources both network development and credentialing to an entity like Mercury, the provider wins, because the provider only has to complete one set of this tedious paperwork that takes hours to complete for each physician and each hospital. The insurance plan also wins because the cost to perform the credentialing is included in the network leasing fee paid to the PPO.

One very distinct difference for health plan quality metrics that is not present in international hospital accreditation programs is the measurement of provider and patient satisfaction. This is measured externally by a contracted outside vendor-performed survey of the plan's participants and participating providers. These two surveys also come with a hefty price tag on the domestic side, but can escalate dramatically if the survey takes on international translation, cultural sensitivities, and international communications costs to perform the survey.

Finally, from a network adequacy and competitive standpoint, it would be insufficient and not compelling enough for the plan to offer providers in only one nation, or have only one option of a sole provider in a city or country so the network development that must be undertaken must be done according to a contracting strategy of global proportion.

All this would be very costly if the employers and the covered employees are primarily the 20% of that population that is responsible for the high cost utilization, and even more costly if those 20% were not of the ilk to utilize services from a hospital or healthcare professional in another country, or might be willing, but the medical appropriateness of their condition finds them to be an unfit candidate for such travel.

Concerns about Regulatory Compliance

Health insurance companies must be licensed in the state in which policies are sold. This means that although the major insurance companies, Blue Cross, CIGNA, AETNA, United HealthCare, and others may be recognizable brands, each must operate their company in accordance with certain insurance laws that differ from state to state. Each of the 50 states and the various territories in the United States requires that the plan be licensed and that certain standards be met in order to protect the interests of the consumer who has purchased the policy.

Each year, each licensed insurance company files an annual audited financial report, market conduct statistics, and files an application to increase or decrease rate structures. They also file the results of audits and projections prepared by actuaries. Actuaries are experts in: evaluating the likelihood of future events, designing creative ways to reduce the likelihood of undesirable events, and decreasing the impact of undesirable events that do occur. In order to prepare for a rate increase or a benefit design change, often these filings must be prepared two years in advance. This allows the state regulators and actuaries to verify the risk projections, determine the provider network adequacy to manage the benefit, determine that the premium increase or decrease supports the risk projection, and if not, adjust the cash reserves or excess loss insurance to cover the projected cost of claims. If all is reconciled, the state will then authorize the inclusion of the benefit.

Other regulatory concerns, with which the plan must deal operationally, include compliance with patient privacy and personally identifiable health information (PHI) under HIPAA. These data and privacy security regulations must be addressed and the providers required to uphold the privacy standards, fraud prevention requirements, billing standards, pricing transparency standards, and other regulatory concerns, regardless of whether they are located in or out of the United States. There is a reasonable expectation that most U.S. providers are prepared for such compliance, however, the plan or its agent (such as Mercury Healthcare) must be prepared to train the provider to satisfy any deficiencies in education, training, process, and procedure. The cost of the training is the financial burden of the provider (similar to how it is in the United States) but there is still a matter of the delay and time involved to ensure compliance by both the contract and in practice. In addition, the provider must also be willing and able to submit bills in the required format using proper standardized U.S. claim forms, procedure and diagnosis coding nomenclature, and other revenue cycle requirements, in order for claims to flow smoothly through the system at the insurance plan in order to get claims paid.

Education of the Brokers and Employers about the Benefit

Once the provider network is empanelled, and the benefit authorized, the brokers who will sell the plan must be educated about medical tourism and the specifics about the benefit and its advantages to the purchaser, whether it is an employer or an individual purchaser. Brokers sometimes work as consultants who educate their clients, and sometimes work as policy sellers, either individually as an agent or as an employee of the insurance plan.

The brokers work on a sales cycle that is determined by the period of "open enrollment" for most employers. This open enrollment period often occurs from October 1 to December 31 each year. In some cases, that open enrollment period can also happen from April 1 to June 30, depending on how the company closes its financial books.

If an employer group is likely to evaluate a new benefit such as medical tourism and international healthcare access, the broker must receive the training about the new benefit and be able to answer questions about the providers, quality standards, and other plan participant and employer concerns prior to these dates. In addition, the insurance plan marketing collateral must be developed and printed and prepared for distribution by the brokers so that employees can review the options with their families, make the necessary elections, submit the paperwork to the human resources department and be issued a benefit booklet or "Evidence of Coverage" and a membership card.

The success or failure of medical tourism plan design implementation is dependent on many factors. If the benefit design preparation, regulatory compliance and other arbitrary deadlines are missed, the process could take an additional year to bring to market. If this happens, the actuarial projections must be restated or adjusted in accordance with current economic realities, market trends, underwriting conditions, and any new laws or requirements that affect rate setting and premium increases or supplemental costs for excess loss coverage or reinsurance for the plan.

Without a thorough understanding of the entire process described above, it is unlikely that a novice well-intentioned facilitator without the requisite education and experience could make good on a promise to steer insurance and employer business to a foreign hospital, or medical or dental professional, in the near term.

Strategic implications for foreign hospital administrators, doctors, dentists, and investors include making your best effort to seek to comprehend the language used in seminars, news articles, and press releases with accuracy, clarity, and discrimination. I challenge you to interpret and validate data, to appraise evidence and evaluate arguments, to recognize the existence (or non-existence) of logical relationships between business proposals, and to draw warranted conclusions, and to test the conclusions at which you and your executive team arrive.

Chapter 19

Medical Tourism for U.S. Employer-Sponsored Health Benefit ERISA Plans

The Employee Retirement Income Security Act of 1974 (ERISA)[*] protects the interests of participants and beneficiaries in private-sector employee benefit plans. Governmental plans and church plans generally are not subject to the law. ERISA supersedes state laws relating to employee benefit plans except for certain matters such as state insurance, banking and securities laws, and divorce property settlement orders by state courts.

An employee benefit plan may be either a pension plan (which provides retirement benefits) or a welfare benefit plan[†] (which provides other kinds of employee benefits such as health and disability benefits). ERISA was signed into law by President Gerald Ford on Labor Day, September 2, 1974. ERISA consists of four titles. Title I sets out specific protections of employee rights in pensions and welfare benefit plans. Title II specifies the requirements for plan qualification under the Internal Revenue Code. Title III assigns responsibilities for administration and enforcement to the Departments of Labor and Treasury. Title IV of ERISA establishes the Pension Benefit Guaranty Corporation. This chapter focuses only on Title I as it relates to health and welfare benefit plan concerns.

The number of employer-sponsored, ERISA self-funded health benefit plans in the United States that have the option to design benefits to include a health travel option currently number 201,567[‡] (Table 19.1). The table does not include the tens of thousands of state, county, and municipal government-sponsored, self-insured plans that also offer coverage to the teachers, firefighters, police officers, judges, state and local government office workers, and pensioners and retirees who also have the option to design benefits to include a health travel option without the

---

[*] P.L. 93-406, 88 Stat. 829 (Sept. 2, 1974). ERISA is codified at §§1001 to 1453 of title 29, United States Code and in §§ 401–415 and 4972–4975 of the Internal Revenue Code.

[†] See ERISA § 3(1), (29 U.S.C. § 1002), for the different types of welfare benefit plans.

[‡] Mercury Healthcare International Inc. Market Research (May 2011).

Table 19.1 Number of ERISA Employer-Sponsored, Self-Funded Health Benefit Plans by U.S. State

State	No. of ERISA Plans	State	No. of ERISA Plans
Alabama	2,331	Missouri	4,838
Alaska	291	Montana & Wyoming	738
Arizona	2,243	Nebraska	2,952
Arkansas	1,150	Nevada	865
California	14,965	New Hampshire	1,152
Colorado	3,553	New Jersey	6,964
Connecticut	3,652	New Mexico	649
Delaware	606	New York	16,341
District of Columbia	1,289	North Carolina	6,112
Florida	7,184	N. & S. Dakota	1,573
Georgia	5,454	Ohio	9,613
Hawaii	1,639	Oklahoma	1,956
Idaho	673	Oregon	2,436
Illinois	10,692	Pennsylvania	10,853
Indiana	5,588	Rhode Island	957
Iowa	3,021	South Carolina	2,401
Kansas	2,666	Tennessee	3,906
Kentucky	2,702	Texas	12,974
Louisiana	2,015	Utah	1,813
Maine	1,218	Vermont	959
Maryland	3,918	Virginia	6,250
Massachusetts	7,498	Washington	4,048
Michigan	6,916	West Virginia	949
Minnesota	7,030	Wisconsin	6,856
Mississippi	1,133		
		Total Plans	**201,567**

Source: Mercury Healthcare International, Inc. (May 2011) internal research. © 2011. All rights reserved. No reproduction or storage without written permission. To obtain permission, contact info@mercury-healthcare.com.

interference of traditional insurance companies that may be reluctant to add a health travel coverage option to plan participants.

Although most of the companies represented include Fortune 1000 companies, there is a growing trend by small to medium businesses (SMBs) of 2–100 employees to move away from high-cost renewals charged by traditional insurance plans, and convert their plan to an ERISA self-funded health benefit plan coupled with a leased network of providers with negotiated rates and hired services of third-party administrators to reprice and process their claims, cost containment firms to negotiate out-of-network prices with providers, case managers to monitor and manage high-cost and complex cases, and health travel logistics teams to coordinate care in alternative locations away from the plan participant's hometown. When coupled with an affordable reinsurance policy, self-funded plans hold the risk of a limited exposure on the cost of claims, and only pay out plan benefit dollars when a claim is incurred. This saves millions of dollars per company over traditional risk-transfer insurance policies where premiums are paid monthly regardless of whether claims are incurred or not.

It should come as no surprise that healthy employees boost a company's bottom line. They experience less sick time, take fewer disability days, and suffer lesser risk of premature death. According to the Centers for Disease Control, more than 75% of employers' healthcare costs and productivity losses are related to employee lifestyle choices. Self-funded health plans that couple a voluntary wellness program with their self-funded health benefit plan are currently experiencing a return on investment (ROI) of up to seven times every dollar invested in the traditional local health delivery setting. Coupled with a health travel program that includes a comprehensive physical, age–gender appropriate screening exams, and case management campaigns for high-cost chronic disease management and surgical interventions, that program option can easily bring in excess of quadruple those savings.

Once an employer has decided to add a domestic or international health travel benefit option to their ERISA self-funded, group health benefit plan, they'll need to design their benefit option and add the details of their unique program to their Summary Plan Description (SPD). ERISA sets fiduciary standards that require employee benefit plan funds to be handled prudently, and in the best interests of the participants. It requires plans to inform participants of their rights under the plan and of the plan's financial status, and it gives plan participants the right to sue in federal court to recover benefits that they have earned under the plan. To be qualified for tax preferences under the Internal Revenue Code (IRC), plans must meet requirements with respect to pension plan contributions, benefits, and distributions, and there are special rules for plans that primarily benefit highly compensated employees or business owners.

ERISA specifies what the SPD must contain.[*] The Summary Plan Description is the main vehicle for communicating plan rights and obligations to participants and beneficiaries. As the name suggests, it is generally a summary of the material provisions of the plan document, which is understandable to the average participant of the employer. However, in the context of health and welfare benefit plans, it is not uncommon for the SPD to be a combination of a complete description of the plan's terms and conditions, such as a certificate of coverage, and the required ERISA disclosure language.

Under Section 104(b)(1), a plan administrator must provide a summary of any material modification (SMM) in the terms of the plan as well as any change in information required to be included in the SPD.[†] This summary must be provided, in most cases, within 210 days after the

---

[*] Hicks v. Fleming Cos., 961 F.2d 537 (5th Cir. 1992).

[†] 29 U.S.C. § 1024(b)(1), ERISA § 102(a); 29 U.S.C. § 1022(a); 29 C.F.R. § 2520.104b-3.

close of the plan year in which the modification was adopted, and also must be furnished to the Labor Department upon request.* Similar to the SPD, the materials must be written in a manner that can be understood by the average plan participant. ERISA does not define "material modification" and does not specifically cover what changes warrant an SMM;[†] however, the courts have addressed this issue.[‡] Courts have held plan amendments such as the establishment and elimination of benefits are material modifications.[§] However, as courts have also pointed out, not all plan amendments are material modifications.[¶]

Note: An insurance company's master contract, certificate of coverage, or summary of benefits is not a plan document or SPD.

An SPD must contain all of the information shown in Table 19.2.

Wrap SPD Document Requirements

Group insurance Certificates of Insurance are typically not SPDs because they do not contain all of the language required by ERISA. An employer must prepare an ERISA "wrapper" to supplement the Certificate of Insurance. Together, the wrapper and Certificate of Insurance comprise a proper SPD.

The plan's annual report must include a detailed financial statement containing information on the plan's assets and liabilities, an actuarial statement, as well as various other information, depending on the type of the plan and the number of participants. (Manual review of these reports is the only way we know of to obtain the plan participant size for ERISA plans. To date, we have found no single source that offers such statistics for public review.) Plan administrators must make copies of the annual report available at the principal office of the plan administrator and at other places as may be necessary to make pertinent information readily available to plan participants.[**]

The annual report must be filed within seven months after the close of a plan year, and extensions may be available under certain circumstances.[††] The annual report is to be filed with the Department of Labor (DOL) on Form 5500.[‡‡] In 2006, the DOL published a rule requiring electronic filing of Form 5500 annual reports for plan years beginning on or after January 1, 2008.[§§]

---

* ERISA § 104(b)(1), 29 U.S.C. § 1024(b)(1); 29 C.F.R. § 2520.104a-8.
† However, regulations provide a special rule for health plans. Subject to an exception, an SMM shall be furnished if there is a "material reduction in covered services or benefits." 29 C.F.R. § 2520.104b-3.
‡ Employee Benefits Law (Matthew Bender 2d ed.)(2000).
§ See, for example, Baker v. Lukens Steel Co., 793 F.2d 509 (3rd Cir. 1986)(elimination of an early retirement benefit option was a material modification); American Fed'n of Grain Millers v. International Multifoods Corp., 1996 U.S. Dist. LEXIS 9399 (W.D.N.Y. 1996) aff'd, 116 F.3d 976 (2d Cir. 1997) (amendment to a medical plan requiring retirees to pay a portion of premiums considered a material modification).
¶ See, for example, Hasty v. Central States, Southeast and Southwest Areas Health and Welfare Fund, 851 F. Supp. 1250, 1256 (N.D. Ind. 1994) (amendments more specifically providing for a trustee's discretionary authority under an employee benefit plan were not a material modification because the amendments "simply clarify a power").
** ERISA § 104(b)(2), 29 U.S.C.§ 1024(b)(2). Under this section, other materials, such as a bargaining agreement or trust agreement affecting the plan may also be made available.
†† See 29 C.F.R. § 2520.104a-5.
‡‡ Although ERISA and the Internal Revenue Code provide that other annual reports must be filed with the PBGC and the Internal Revenue Service, these reporting requirements can be satisfied by filing Form 5500 with the Labor Department.
§§ 29 C.F.R. § 2520.104a-2.

Table 19.2   An SPD Must Contain All of the Following Information

- The plan name
- The plan sponsor/employer's name and address
- The plan sponsor's EIN[a]
- The plan administrator's name, address, and phone number
- Designation of any named fiduciaries, if other than the plan administrator, e.g., claim fiduciary
- The plan number for ERISA Form 5500 purposes, e.g., 501, 502, 503, etc. (Note—each ERISA plan should be assigned a unique number that is not used more than once.)
- Type of plan or brief description of benefits, e.g., life, medical, dental, disability
- The date of the end of the plan year for maintaining plan's fiscal records (which may be different than the insurance policy year)
- Each trustee's name, title, and address of principal place of business, if the plan has a trust
- The name and address of the plan's agent for service of legal process, along with a statement that service may be made on a plan trustee or administrator
- The type of plan administration, e.g., administered by contract, insurer, or sponsor
- Eligibility terms, e.g., classes of eligible employees, employment waiting period, and hours per week, and the effective date of participation, e.g., next day or first of month following satisfaction of eligibility waiting period
- How insurer refunds (e.g., dividends, demutualization) are allocated to participants. Note: This is important to obtain the small plan (<100 participants) exception for filing Form 5500.
- Plan sponsor's amendment and termination rights and procedures, and what happens to plan assets, if any, in the event of plan termination
- Summary of any plan provisions governing the benefits, rights, and obligations of participants under the plan on termination or amendment of plan or elimination of benefits
- Summary of any plan provisions governing the allocation and disposition of assets upon plan termination
- Claims procedures—may be furnished separately in a *certificate of coverage*, provided that the SPD explains that claims procedures are furnished automatically, without charge, in the separate document (e.g., a certificate of coverage), and time limits for lawsuits, if the plan imposes them.
- A statement clearly identifying circumstances that may result in loss or denial of benefits (e.g., subrogation, coordination of benefits, and offset provisions)
- The standard of review for benefit decisions (we recommend consideration of granting full discretion for plan administrator or authorized fiduciary to interpret plan and make factual determinations)
- ERISA model statement of participants' rights
- The sources of plan contributions, whether from employer and/or employee contributions, and the method by which they are calculated
- Interim Summary of Material Modifications (SMMs) since SPD was adopted or last restated

Continued

Table 19.2 (continued)

- The fact that the employer is a participating employer or a member of a controlled group

- Whether the plan is maintained pursuant to one or more collective bargaining agreements, and that a copy of the agreement may be obtained upon request

- A prominent offer of assistance in a non-English language (depending on the number of participants who are literate in the same non-English language)

- Identity of insurer(s), if any

Additional requirements for Group Health Plan SPDs:

- Detailed description of plan provisions and exclusions (e.g., copays, deductibles, coinsurance, eligible expenses, network provider provisions, prior authorization and utilization review requirements, dollar limits, day limits, visit limits, and the extent to which new drugs, preventive care, and medical tests and devices are covered). A link to network providers should also be provided. Plan limits, exceptions, and restrictions must be conspicuous.

- Information regarding COBRA,[b] HIPAA,[c] and other federal mandates such as Women's Health Cancer Rights Act, preexisting condition exclusion, special enrollment rules, mental health parity, coverage for adopted children, Qualified Medical Support Orders, and minimum hospital stays following childbirth.

- Name and address of health insurer(s), if any

- Description of the role of health insurers (i.e., whether the plan is insured by an insurance company or the insurance company is merely providing administrative services)

- Recommended, but not required provisions in an SPD:

- For insured arrangements, attach the Summary of Benefits provided by the insurance companies to help assure you have provided an understandable summary of the certificate of coverage

- Language that in the event of a conflict between the plan document and the SPD, the plan document controls

[a] Employer Identification Number.
[b] Consolidated Omnibus Reconciliation Act of 1985.
[c] Health Insurance Portability & Accountability Act of 1996, Kennedy–Kassenbaum Bill Privacy A bill enacted by Congress in 1996 which established a comprehensive and uniform federal standard for ensuring privacy of genetic information.

One reason that plan administrators cite in their reluctance to jump on the health travel bandwagon is a fear of breach of fiduciary responsibility potential for lawsuits by employees. ERISA imposes certain obligations on plan fiduciaries, persons who are generally responsible for the management and operation of employee benefit plans. ERISA Section 3(21)(A) provides that a person is a "fiduciary" to the extent that the person: (1) exercises any discretionary authority or control with respect to the management of the plan or exercises any authority with respect to the management or disposition of plan assets; (2) renders investment advice for a fee or other compensation with respect to any plan asset or has any authority or responsibility to do so;[*] or (3) has any discretionary

---

[*] See 29 C.F.R. § 2510.3-21, which provides guidance as to when a person shall be deemed to be rendering investment advice to an employee benefit plan.

responsibility in the administration of the plan.* Every plan governed by ERISA must have one or more named fiduciaries, and these fiduciaries must be named in the plan document.

Section 404(a)(1) of ERISA establishes the duties owed by a fiduciary to participants and beneficiaries of a plan. This section identifies four standards of conduct: (1) a duty of loyalty, (2) a duty of prudence, (3) a duty to diversify investments, and (4) a duty to follow plan documents to the extent that they comply with ERISA.†

1. *Duty of Loyalty.* Section 404(a)(1)(A) of ERISA requires plan fiduciaries to discharge their duties "solely in the interest of the participants and beneficiaries" and for the "exclusive purpose" of providing benefits to participants and beneficiaries and defraying reasonable expenses of administering the plan.‡ The duty of loyalty applies in situations where the fiduciary is confronted with a potential conflict of interest, for instance, when a pension plan trustee has responsibilities to both the plan and the entity (such as the employer or union) sponsoring the plan.§

   However, just because an ERISA fiduciary engages in a transaction that incidentally benefits the fiduciary or a third party does not necessarily mean that a fiduciary breach has occurred.¶

   In one noted case, the court in *Donovan* noted that it is not a breach of fiduciary duty if a trustee who, after careful and impartial investigation, makes a decision that while benefitting the plan, also incidentally benefits the corporation, or the fiduciaries themselves. However, fiduciary decisions must be made with an "eye single to the interests of the participants and beneficiaries."** The court articulated that the trustees have a duty to "avoid placing themselves in a position where their acts as officers and directors of the corporation will prevent their functioning with the complete loyalty to participants demanded of them as trustees of a pension plan."††

   A plan fiduciary must also act with the "exclusive purpose" of "defraying reasonable expenses of administering the plan."‡‡ The Department of Labor has stated that "in choosing among potential service providers, as well as in monitoring and deciding whether to retain a service provider, the trustees must objectively assess the qualifications of the service provider, the quality of the work product, and the reasonableness of the fees charged in light of the services provided."§§

2. *Duty of Prudence.* Section 404(a)(1)(B) of ERISA requires fiduciaries to act "with the care, skill, prudence, and diligence under the circumstances then prevailing that a prudent

---

* Plan fiduciaries may include plan trustees, plan administrators, and a plan's investment managers or advisors. See Department of Labor, Fiduciary Responsibilities, available at [https://www.dol.gov/dol/topic/retirement/fiduciaryresp.htm#doltopics].

† ERISA § 404(a)(1), 29 U.S.C. § 1104(a)(1).

‡ This section is supplemented by Section 403(c)(1) of ERISA, which provides that the "assets of a plan shall never inure to the benefit of any employer and shall be held for the exclusive purposes of providing benefits…and defraying reasonable expenses of administering the plan." 29 U.S.C. § 1103(c)(1).

§ Craig C. Martin & Elizabeth L. Fine, ERISA Stock Drop Cases: An Evolving Standard, 38 *J. Marshall L. Rev.* 889 (2005).

¶ *Ibid.*

** 680 F.2d at 271.

†† *Ibid.*

‡‡ ERISA § 404(a)(1)(A)(ii), 29 U.S.C. § 1104(a)(1)(A)(ii).

§§ U.S. Department of Labor, Employee Benefits Security Administration, Information Letter, July 28, 1998. [http://www.dol.gov/ebsa/regs/ILs/il072898.html].

man would use in the conduct of an enterprise of a like character with like aims."[*] When examining whether a fiduciary has violated the duty of prudence, courts typically examine the process that a fiduciary undertook in reaching a decision involving plan assets.[†] If a fiduciary has taken the appropriate procedural steps, the success or failure of an investment can be irrelevant to a duty of prudence inquiry.[‡] Regulations promulgated by the Department of Labor provide clarification as to the duty of prudence in regard to investment decisions. These regulations indicate that a fiduciary can satisfy his duty of prudence under ERISA by giving "appropriate consideration" to the facts and circumstances that the fiduciary knows or should know are relevant to an investment or investment course of action.[§] "Appropriate consideration" includes (1) "a determination by the fiduciary that the particular investment or investment course of action is reasonably designed, as part of the portfolio...to further the purposes of the plan, taking into consideration the risk of loss and the opportunity for gain (or other return) associated with the investment," and (2) consideration of the portfolio's composition with regard to diversification, the liquidity and current return of the portfolio relative to the anticipated cash flow requirements of the plan, and the projected return of the portfolio relative to the plan's funding objectives.[¶]

Simply checking a list of high-level criteria such as "hospital accreditation status" by one organization or another is insufficient to meet this test. Most plan fiduciaries will tell you that they know nothing about any particular brand of hospital accreditation in their own country, let alone international hospital accreditation. They do, however, recognize the procedures and merits of the primary source verification vetting process suggested by the National Committee for Quality Assurance, (www.ncqa.org) which is the organization that accredits health plans and member provider satisfaction, member satisfaction, health delivery outcomes, and plan documentation of its credentialing and privileging activities by primary source verification.

Because most medical tourism facilitators have no healthcare industry background or insurance industry background, in most cases, they are unfamiliar with any of these standards and tend to parrot what is published on the Internet and in the popular media about accreditation and provider empanelment. Most form their business strategy on the assumption that the market is lucrative for seekers of inexpensive care, rapid access to providers and technology, and last or fairly new last chance therapies and clinical trials.

Furthermore, most have never invested the several hundreds of dollars required to purchase, or taken the time to read, a copy of the Joint Commission's credentialing and privileging standards, or those of the Joint Commission International, the National Committee for Quality Assurance,

---

[*] 29 U.S.C. § 1104(a)(1)(B).

[†] See, for example, GIW Industries v. Trevor, Stewart, Burton & Jacobsen, 895 F.2d 729 (11th Cir. 1990) (investment management firm breached its duty of prudence after investing primarily in long-term, low risk government bonds and failing to take into account the liquidity needs of the plan); Donovan v. Mazzola, 716 F.2d 1226, 1232 (9th Cir. 1983) (court stated that test of prudence is whether "at the time they engaged in the challenged transactions, [fiduciaries] employed the appropriate methods to investigate the merits of the investment and to structure the investment").

[‡] See, for example, Unisys, 74 F.3d at 434 ("[I]f at the time an investment is made, it is an investment a prudent person would make, there is no liability if the investment later depreciates in value"). A plan fiduciary must also act with the "exclusive purpose" of "defraying reasonable expenses of administering the plan."

[§] See 29 C.F.R. § 2550.404a-1.

[¶] *Ibid.*

or any other accrediting bodies. (Without a medical background, it would be frustrating at best, as the standards are technically written and laden with medical terminology, for which relatively few have an adequate command or familiarity with hospital operational procedures.) As a result, many medical tourism facilitators make incorrect assumptions about the available international hospital accreditation standards and the significance of international accreditation of hospitals, and which brand of accreditation the hospital or clinic has chosen for its survey.

Therefore, when facilitators make claims that they will coordinate referrals of employer group health plan participants to a healthcare provider, providers may wish to question the facilitator's familiarity with these standards and vet their familiarity through a critical assessment of their network infrastructure, contracting standards and application forms, and other network development standards and criteria. The likelihood is extremely low that an employer will feel comfortable with the vetting process that will meet the duties of prudence and loyalties explained above and be eager to revise their SPD to include a health travel benefit on the basis of plan savings alone.

To participate with those organizations with the required industry knowledge, established procedures and standards, many healthcare providers within the United States readily submit to network credentialing and verification procedures. Providers outside the United States who are unfamiliar with this level of intense vetting are often unprepared, and reluctant to become involved in the amount of probing, paperwork, vetting, and inspecting that must be carried out before the network organizer can represent to the employer that the duty of prudence has been taken seriously and addressed thoroughly. Many have given me the argument that they don't want to invest the time or effort in this level of vetting, because medical tourism has not yielded the volume of business about which everyone has prattled on.

To them, I offer three rhetorical questions:

First, do you believe that the uninsured and underinsured markets have the strongest real growth potential for health travel referrals?

Second, if the employers face this vetting duty before they will alter plan design and do business with a health travel provider, without doing the paperwork and undergoing the vetting process and being represented by a network, do you truly have a chance to ever see increasing volumes of patient referrals?

Third, do you really believe that a sole medical tourism facilitator with a smart phone, a laptop computer, and a basement office has the staff and wherewithal to sustain the preliminary cost of constructing a network with the appropriate documentation, vetting procedures, and sales staff to market such a network to enough providers to produce the volumes you anticipated?

An employer may wish to consolidate the various component benefit plans into a single plan for reporting and disclosure. A few group health employer benefits consultants can help benefits managers and plan administrators and fiduciaries save the time and expense of preparing an SPD, a Form 5500, and a Summary Annual Report (SAR) for each separate component benefit plan, by replacing them with one comprehensive wrap plan. If they understand the health travel benefit options, they can incorporate this valuable savings option and can design a solution that is right for each plan.

The problem is, most benefits consultants are not experts in ERISA or health travel benefit options. Most medical tourism facilitators have no clue how to spell ERISA, let alone to understand its regulatory intricacies or how it can be connected to employers. Also, if an employer or benefits management consultant listens to propaganda disseminated by the Jonathan Edelheit,

CEO of the Medical Tourism Association on FOXNews,[*] they may be misled to believe that "medical tourism" or health travel only involves people traveling to other countries to receive care. That's clearly not a standard definition or limitation of medical tourism or health travel.

My opinion is that it will take several more years for employers to feel comfortable with international health travel as a normal option for their domestic workforce's health delivery, and a shorter time for those expatriate employees. Internal and unpublished industry statistics from the health plans that currently offer traditional coverage for expatriate employees already demonstrate a decrease in the number of expatriates returning back to the domestic healthcare providers for high-complexity care. My educated guess as to how acceptance will increase is that as these expatriates sample the care of the international marketplace and are queried for patient delight and clinical outcomes, the word will spread and the plan fiduciaries will test the waters, first with a limited number of service lines, and eventually for any services covered by the plan for which the plan participant chooses to travel for care, providing the travel can be done safely and with pricing transparency, regardless of whether the care provider is located across town, across the county, across the state, across the nation, or outside the national borders of the country in which they reside.

---

[*] http://video..foxnews.com/v/4667707/medical-tourism/

Chapter 20

Health Travel Conceptual Challenges for ERISA Health Benefit Plan Managers

Employers throughout the United States have been experimenting with directing employees to designated providers for medical care for some time. The designated provider program has been in use in many workers' compensation programs for at least 20 years. In the 1990s, Delta Airlines sent employees with heart conditions to Atlanta to a designated hospital for all cardiac care. The Atchison, Topeka, and Santa Fe Railway Company sent employee psychiatric cases to Menninger Clinic in Topeka, Kansas. More recently we heard about Lowes, Alpha Coal West, Serigraph, Blue Ridge Paper, Hannaford, and a Union Health Services Coalition in Las Vegas all getting onboard with the trend.

What is the difference now, and why all the media hyperbole? Because healthcare reform and high costs and low value make news. Innovation makes news. A significant change in direction makes news. Abandoning a long-time practice of obtaining employee healthcare in the local neighborhood simply because it is convenient and the way we've always done it before, makes news.

Did This Just Happen Overnight?

Not at all! For years, we have had designated providers in the form of health maintenance organizations (HMOs) and preferred provider organizations (PPOs) and exclusive provider organizations (EPOs). Each of these health delivery systems depended on local market suppliers at first, but corralled the subscribers into provider networks or "panels."

How Did We Get Here?

The Advent of the HMO (1973)

Promoted by the Nixon Administration, in 1973, the U.S. government passed the HMO Act of 1973. The Health Maintenance Organization Act of 1973 (Public Law 93-222), also known as the HMO Act of 1973, 42 U.S.C. § 300e, is a law passed by the Congress of the United States that resulted from discussions Paul Ellwood had with what is today the Department of Health and Human Services. It provided grants and loans to provide, start, or expand a Health Maintenance Organization (HMO); removed certain state restrictions for federally qualified HMOs; and required employers with 25 or more employees to offer federally certified HMO options IF they offered traditional health insurance to employees. It did not require employers to offer health insurance. HMOs were defined simply as plans that: specified list of benefits to all members, charged all members the same monthly premium, and were structured as a nonprofit organization. Eventually, for-profit HMOs were also permitted. The Act solidified the term HMO and gave HMOs greater access to the employer-based market.

Federal legislation required employers to give their employees the option to enroll in a local health maintenance organization rather than in the conventional employer-sponsored health program. The dual choice provision expired in 1995.

Unlike traditional indemnity insurance, an HMO covers only care rendered by those doctors and other professionals who have agreed to treat patients in accordance with the HMO's guidelines and restrictions, in exchange for a steady stream of customers. In the HMO, if all the plan participants stayed within the confines of the ropes, the providers could be paid a capitation (a per-member-per-month flat fee to cover the cost of all included care afforded by the plan contract of coverage) which essentially transferred the risk of the provision of care to the provider and left the health plan organizer to manage margins, develop the networks, collect premiums and oversee data. Unwitting providers who were never trained to negotiate or understand the contracts, and didn't know what they didn't know, negotiated less than equitable contracts with the plans.

The result to providers: untenable financial risk, no reinsurance to cover excess losses beyond what was projected (perhaps because the providers didn't know how to model the risk and didn't know whom to ask for help) such that the provider backlash caused capitation to disappear for all but a few savvy professionally managed provider groups. At the same time, consumers balked at the narrow networks where coverage (plan payment) for healthcare services was available if the care was first "deemed" medically necessary, not by their personal physician, but by the administrators of the health plan, and then accessed from the designated providers in the narrow network rather than the entire local market of doctors and hospitals, and dentists, and other allied health and ancillary services.

To add to the complexity and expense of HMO operation, HMOs are regulated at both the state and federal levels. They are licensed by the states, under a license that is known as a certificate of authority (COA) rather than under an insurance license. State and federal regulators also issue mandates, requirements for a health maintenance organizations to provide particular products. In 1972 the National Association of Insurance Commissioners adopted the HMO Model Act, which was intended to provide a model regulatory structure for states to use in authorizing the establishment of HMOs and in monitoring their operation. What that meant was that there was no national CIGNA, AETNA, Blue Cross, UNITED, or other health plan. Each state had its own redundant plan, redundant COA, redundant license costs and operating expense.

Many people call that "managed care." That's wrong! Care wasn't managed; access and cost was managed. Those narrow networks did nothing to vet quality; they monitored cost of delivery and under capitation, cost was predictable. Other than the initial and re-credentialing of the providers, which was a rote procedure of completing an application and vetting the information from the primary source, the only time quality was vetted was if someone raised a complaint, or some anomaly occurred. Otherwise, essentially, all was copacetic.

Preferred Provider Organizations (PPOs) (1982)

In 1982, California legislation was enacted allowing selective contracting for Medicaid and private insurance, paving the way for other states to enact similar laws facilitating preferred provider organizations (PPOs). In the PPO, payers who had no other means to negotiate a discount with a provider of care paid an access fee to lease a network of providers organized by someone else. The PPO organizer does not bear risk for the cost of claims. It never did. PPOs are not organized to assume claims cost risk. They are simply a network that organizes discounts from providers and makes the discount available to PPO members authorized to access the discount.

HMOs could also lease out their network of contracted providers paid on a discounted fee-for-service basis. Instead of receiving premiums for the transfer of the risk of the cost to provide care, they provided administrative services only (ASO) and created a product named just that, the ASO. The risk associated with the claims cost was borne by an entity authorized to access the network providers at a discount. These were most often smaller insurance companies that did not have a provider relations contracting department, purchasing coalitions, unions, and employers with self-funded health benefit plans organized under the rules of the U.S. Labor Code (Section 29 of the Code of Federal Regulations) and that comports with the Employee Retirement Income Security Act of 1974 (ERISA) (Pub.L. 93-406, 88 Stat. 829, enacted September 2, 1974). ERISA is sometimes used to refer to the full body of laws regulating employee benefit plans, which are found mainly in the Internal Revenue Code and ERISA itself. Responsibility for the interpretation and enforcement of ERISA is divided among the Department of Labor, the Department of the Treasury (particularly the Internal Revenue Service), and the Pension Benefit Guaranty Corporation.

Self-Funded Employer-Sponsored Health Benefit Plans and ERISA (1974)

In most cases, ERISA employers establish a 501(c)9 trust fund to pay the claims for health benefits incurred by plan participants. The Internal Revenue Code lists eligible healthcare expenses paid for care as described in Section 213 (d) of the Code.

ERISA does not require that an employer provide health insurance to its employees or retirees, but it regulates the operation of a health benefit plan if an employer chooses to establish one. Employers are free to develop their health benefit plan and author (often with the help of a benefits consultant) a Summary Plan Description (SPD) to describe the health plan, and can include any of the eligible items listed in Section 213 (d) of the Code. One point I want to bring out is that travel expenses for the purpose of accessing care is an eligible expense under Section 213 (d) of the Code.

Limited Expense Reimbursement and Healthcare Reimbursement Arrangements (HRAs) (2003)

In 2003, as part of the Medicare Modernization Act, an ERISA employer could opt to organize a Limited Expense Reimbursement Healthcare Reimbursement Arrangement (HRA). The contribution cannot be paid through a voluntary salary reduction agreement on the part of an employee. It is 100% employer funded. Because of this, an ERISA employer may designate which qualified (under IRC 213(d)) expenses may be payable using the HRA money. Employees are reimbursed tax free for qualified medical expenses up to a maximum dollar amount for a coverage period. An HRA may be offered with other health plans.

Generally, distributions from an HRA must be paid to reimburse the plan participant for qualified and eligible medical expenses they have already incurred. The eligible expense must have been incurred on or after the date they are enrolled in the HRA. Sometimes the employer issues debit cards, credit cards, and stored value cards provided by the employer to be used to reimburse participants in an HRA. If the use of these cards meets certain substantiation methods, the plan participant may not have to provide additional information to the HRA.

Qualified medical expenses are those specified in the plan that would generally qualify for the medical and dental expenses deduction under IRC213(d). These are explained in Publication 502, Medical and Dental Expenses, published by the Internal Revenue Service. However, even though non-prescription medicines (other than insulin) do not qualify for the medical and dental expenses deduction, they do qualify as expenses for HRA purposes.

Qualified medical expenses from your HRA include the following.

- Amounts paid for health insurance premiums
- Amounts paid for long-term care coverage
- Amounts that are not covered under another health plan

One additional thing that few providers and many plan participants don't realize is that since the 1980s, under the ERISA Act with its pre-emptive effect on state common law tort lawsuits that "relate to" employee benefit plans, HMOs administering benefits through private employer health plans have been protected by federal law from malpractice litigation, on the grounds that the decisions regarding patient care are administrative rather than medical in nature. (See "Cigna v. Calad," 2004.) This means that either the employer or the provider is ostensibly and vicariously liable for acts by network providers in the event of negligence or in some cases poor outcomes of care. This alone creates serious implications for employer-sponsored health plans that might offer coverage for care delivery outside the United States because of the difference in malpractice and professional liability coverage, responsibility and dispute resolution methods.

Innovative Coverage Options

Point-of-Service Plans (POS)

A point-of-service (POS) feature was added to many benefit plan designs. This feature enabled plan members to choose where to access the care at the time they needed care. Access care from network providers and receive a higher discount and a lower copayment and deductible. Wander outside the network, some coverage would be afforded for your medical costs, but at a lower discount and higher out of pocket copayment and deductible. After a few years of plan membership, folks would look back and think, "I have only used network providers and I've been paying for this POS option; I might as well not pay the POS option surcharge anymore and just make it a point choose in network providers." A few years later, the employer offered fewer or eliminated the POS and instead offered an HMO option with a "lock-in" feature.

Exclusive Provider Organizations (EPO)

An exclusive provider organization (EPO) is a type of managed care plan that combines features of HMOs and PPOs. As a managed care organization, it is similar to a PPO in purpose and organization, which allows a plan participant to go outside the network for care, but the participant must pay the full cost of the services received; it is similar to an HMO in that primary care physicians or case managers act as gatekeepers to access the network of providers on the panel and includes an authorization system, precertification and other cost containment measures.

Designated Medical Provider Programs

A designated medical provider program is a narrow network model that has been used in the workers' compensation system where physical medicine and rehabilitation providers combined with occupational health specialists and case managers cover the needs of an employee suffering from a work-related illness or injury sustained while on the job. Reinsurers have also utilized this narrow network model for years. Both utilize the designated provider programs for certain high-cost or high-complexity episodes of care for at least 15 years that I am aware. An episode of care is defined as care for a specific medical problem or condition. It may be continuous or it may consist of a series of intervals marked by one or more brief separations from care, and can also identify the sequence of care (e.g., emergency, inpatient, outpatient), thus serving as one measure of health care provided. There are many evaluation procedures that focus on both the outcome or status of the patient at the end of an episode of care: presence of symptoms, level of activity, and mortality; and the process is what is done for the patient diagnostically and therapeutically. The statistical quality and value outcomes combined with the price negotiated to cover the episode help the workers' compensation carrier or reinsurer to determine if that provider will continue to be designated in the future.

Indemnity Insurance

Indemnity insurance plans allow purchasers of the insurance to choose their own doctor and the plan pays a contractually established percentage of the total bill after a deductible has been incurred without managed care limitations, protocols, or precertification and preauthorization procedures. For many U.S. -based multinational corporations, those employers currently purchase coverage beyond the public health option for expatriate workers, which in some cases is a local indemnity insurance plan and in rare instances may have a few managed care features. Of course, this is in accordance with whatever employment contract was negotiated by and between the employee and the employer. American companies are bound to option COBRA benefits to American employees and provide workers' compensation for work-related illness or injuries.

Multinational ERISA Employers with Self-Funded Health Benefit Plans

The traditional model for delivery of employee benefits is to provide competitive benefit packages in each location. Usually overlaying this is an expat benefit program for those sent on assignment from their country of hire ("home" country) to another country ("host" country) for a specific project or length of time.

Regulatory Compliance and Expatriate Benefit Management

The typical package is handled as follows. If a social security agreement exists between the home and host countries, the company will sometimes take advantage of this, so that the employee is maintained in the home-country social security system, where possible. Medical benefits will be provided in the host country. However, the company may consider use of the home-country arrangements or an international plan, where appropriate. This package applies for a limited period, typically five years, often to align with the maximum period the employee can be retained in the home-country social security system. At the end of this period, the employee is either repatriated or localized. Two dozen countries have entered into treaties of Friendship, Commerce, and Navigation with the United States. Those treaties generally permit companies of those countries to favor citizens of the particular country in certain circumstances. However, courts allow this defense in only narrow circumstances.

Multinational corporations also have to deal with an increasing number of "global nomad" employees, that is, employees who move from country to country on varying assignments. Given the number and frequency of assignments, and the nature of the roles, these employees often quickly lose any link with the country of hire and so maintaining a benefits package linked with a home country makes no sense. A common alternative approach for these employees is to provide competitive benefits in each country. However, this may not be satisfactory, as it can result in fragmented retirement coverage under multiple plans around the world and is often problematic for risk benefits coverage. In addition, where these employees are assigned to more challenging locations, such as some emerging economies, there may be no local employee benefit programs provided.

The sheer complexity and increasing number of locations where an organization has operations means it will inevitably encounter restrictions affecting ongoing home-country benefits provision. This might simply create potential for double provision, for example, where participation in a local retirement arrangement is mandatory, or in more serious circumstances, it might create a legal exposure for the company or employee. It can also expose the corporation to liability for richer or less than equal benefits than their home-country counterparts. Multinational employers need a globally consistent approach to benefit provision; ensuring that expatriates are not disadvantaged by accepting international assignments; and with regards to healthcare, maintaining high standards of quality, access, and cost containment.

Employers are bound by the law of the place where the contract is to be performed, by the law of incorporation or any other law that may be nominated as the governing or proper law of the agreement. In general, employers cannot reduce entitlements below the minima imposed by the relevant laws. It is usual to find that health benefits are most carefully defined in agreements to achieve compliance with all laws (indeed some laws will have a mandatory status). But, to make employment in some countries more attractive, employers are always able to offer better terms than any relevant law requires. In such cases, the exact wording of the contract of employment will determine the scope of the benefits and their duration. However, if an employer provides self-insured or self-funded health benefits, then there are discrimination rules that apply.

Most jurisdictions impose general employment discrimination laws that protect specified traits or groups, such as gender/race/religion, in hiring, firing, and terms of employment. Examples include: Brazil constitution art. 7 items XXX-XXXI; EU Equal Treatment Directives 76/207/EC and 200/78/EC; South Africa Employment Equity Act 55/1998; Spain labor code arts. 4.2 (c), 17.1; and US Title VII/ADEA/ADA. Because rewards such as pay, benefits, and equity grants are vital terms of employment, discrimination in rewarding employees can violate these protected-group employment discrimination laws. Many countries include as illegal discrimination a concept of "adverse impact" (called in Europe "indirect discrimination") by which an "on-its-face" neutral compensation system may be held illegal if it disadvantages employees in some protected group.

Beyond gender, another specific group subject to special protection under some countries' pay-specific discrimination laws is local citizenship. Some developing countries prohibit compensating aliens more generously (the policy here is to keep multinationals from rewarding their expatriates more than comparable locals). For example, Bahrain labor law art. 44 mandates that "wages and remuneration" of "foreign workers" not exceed pay for local "citizens" with "equal skills" and "qualifications" unless necessary for "recruitment," and Brazil labor code art. 358 requires that "salary" of a local citizen not be "smaller" than pay of a "foreign employee perform[ing] an analogous function." Employers need to watch for these laws in structuring expatriate packages.

Looking into the future, with the increasing demands and complexity of globalization, Mercury Healthcare expects to see the demand for international plans increase as globe-trotting employees expect to be offered an arrangement that keeps healthcare benefits consistent throughout the corporation and that eliminates the fragmentation that occurs when employees move from plan to plan and country to country.

Health and Group Benefits for Expatriates

A 2008 Mercer Benefits survey found that 66% of companies now provide an international medical program specifically aimed at expatriates. Insurance vendors offer increasingly sophisticated products that give companies opportunities to tailor their plans to regional requirements, such as reimbursement levels or integration with local social security coverage. However, they offer this in the form of insurance. And that presents problems and creates silos that contribute to inefficiency, increase healthcare administrative management costs, add costs for premiums for risk transfer and loss of control of cost avoidance. It also impedes wellness and health status monitoring of the population for which the corporation bears financial risk for the cost of claims.

The employers surveyed in the Mercer study also noted that some employers require employee contributions to share the cost of coverage and coinsurance or deductibles to share the cost of claims.

Medical benefits, in particular, can be an emotive issue for expatriates as an area that affects not just them personally, but also any family members accompanying them on assignment. The majority of companies Mercury Healthcare has casually surveyed say they provide high- or medium-level medical benefits to their expatriates. This could create problems under the new healthcare reform rules because those benefits could be deemed "Cadillac plans" and cause the corporation to sustain hefty tax consequences (40%) and lose their Grandfathered status.

In 2008, the Mercer comparative study identified a difference in approach between North American and European multinationals, especially where medical benefits are concerned. European employees did not expect to make a contribution toward the cost of coverage for themselves or their families, and they expect full reimbursement for the cost of any treatment. By contrast, although North Americans normally expected a lower overall level of benefits, they preferred a wider choice—including such items as optical and dental benefits. The typical expatriate benefits package is shown in Table 20.1.

With U.S. healthcare reform, the only thing that changes is that now the North Americans will expect a higher level of benefits, both expatriates and domestic workforces alike. That will undoubtedly add to the cost of the premiums on the expatriate population. Premiums that must be paid whether or not claims are paid in the month. It makes sense that both the expat employee

Table 20.1   North American Multinational Corporation Benefits

Business travel accidental death and dismemberment	Normally provided
Medical benefits	A standard policy with an international provider, offering no restrictions on choice of provider and family coverage provided at employer cost. Employees are not expected to contribute to the cost of treatment
Other benefits	Provide dental, vision, emergency assistance/evacuation, dependent medical, critical illness and short-term disability benefits

and the corporation would benefit if the SPD were able to be applied globally, integrated by data, benefits parity, and with the same standards applied to determine which providers should be included in an approved panel of network and which should be bypassed except in the case of a bona fide emergency. It would make even more sense if this could be done on a leased access, self-funded basis, augmented by reinsurance for excess claims costs, such that plans incurred expenses only when a claim arose, not on a monthly premium, risk-transferred basis.

With healthcare reform combined with global multinational expansion, employers are likely to receive pushback from existing expatriates as well as future global nomads on benefit limitations of any kind. Numerous self-help websites caution expats to negotiate cost of living and hardship adjustments based on expatriate life style rather than the life style of local people. The articles and blogs all echo that expatriates living in some developing countries may find that local food, basic accommodation, and basic healthcare is relatively inexpensive, while maintaining their old lifestyle with imported food, "expatriate" accommodation, private healthcare, and entertainment/recreation is very expensive. The cost of living for local people is not always the same as it is for an expatriate, nor is the access to care or the local public health coverage for preventive health services required under PPACA.

Health and Group Benefits for Domestic Employees

Self-funded employers reportedly cover of 77% of the U.S. workforce. They have to be concerned that if they reach certain expenditures on healthcare per employee, they will be deemed a "Cadillac" plan and lose the "grandfathered" status they may currently enjoy, as well as take a 40% tax hit in accordance with PPACA. All this leaves employers scrambling for options. This translates to benefit cuts, higher copays and deductibles, higher premium contributions from employees, and some of these may not be able to be passed on to employees who are members of unions (15.3 million in 2009, according to the Bureau of Labor Statistics). Some benefit cuts may also place them into noncompliance or cause them to lose their grandfather status as well. What's an employer to do?

An increasing number of employers are offering financial incentives to encourage workers to consider in-network "domestic health travel" options. Using a globally integrated health care provider network such as Mercury's, employers can choose from providers throughout the United States and abroad. By steering workers to facilities with high-quality care and competitive prices, employers are able to reduce their costs 20% to 40%, or more, more than enough to cover the travel expenses.

The Devil Is in the Details

Most of the employers mentioned in recent feature articles are not buying "insurance." Therefore, it is inappropriate to refer to this new domestic health tourism curiosity and popularity within the framework of "insurers" getting on board. Instead, these employers have had long-established ERISA trust funds or use the assets of the corporation to pay for employee and dependant health care and operate their plans under the regulations in ERISA. Only in rare cases do they buy insurance and transfer risk to an insurer by using some of that money to pay premiums. In most cases, they hire a third-party administrator, and a reinsurance carrier covers excess losses to the fund beyond a certain multiple of predictable financial risk. This confuses a lot of people, including hospitals and employees, because they see a logo, or two or three logos, from recognized health plans.

When employers take on this self-funded risk, they use the ASO or a third-party administrator. The two function in similar ways as previously described above. An employer provides the human resources specialist to operate the plan, in effect acting as custodian. A trustee provides direction for investment of the plan's funds, usually in a self-directed investment account. Trustee plans are gaining in popularity as both the employer and employees seek more control over pension fund investments. In a self-insured health benefit plan, the group may have an ASO contract with an insurance company or several companies (hence the multiple logos) or a third-party administrator to handle claims processing and administration, and to access their network of providers.

Unlike insurance, where risk for the cost of claims is transferred to the insurance company in exchange for payment of premiums, the risk of the cost of claims stays with the employer trust fund. Therefore, employers, employees, and providers have an opportunity to initiate a change to the way business is done that meets all three stakeholders' needs.

Chapter 21

U.S. Retiree Health and the Challenges of GASB 45 Regulations

Millions of former state and government retired employers are responding to the challenges of Governmental Accounting Standards Board (GASB) 45 regulations (United States) by exploring alternative benefit strategies including globally-integrated healthcare options

A September 2008 issue brief by the Center for State & Local Government Excellence, "After GASB 45: Solving the Unfunded Liability Problem in Retiree Health Care," reveals that many state and local governments are responding to the challenges of GASB 45 by exploring alternative benefit strategies that employ cost-containment, efficiency improvements and prefunding mechanisms.

The Government Accounting Standards Board 45, an accounting rule that went into effect in 2007, states that public employers can no longer report postretirement health benefits on a pay-as-you-go basis, but rather must account for and report the annual cost of other **postretirement benefits for retirees.** A key challenge for these public U.S. employers is how to fund health care benefits for their retiree workforce.

As a result, billions of dollars in unfunded OPEB liabilities have been uncovered nationwide, causing local city and state government and union employers to **scale-back significantly on** healthcare benefits for early retirees or **reduce other benefits or expenses.** Therefore, for millions of early retirees ages 55–64 within the public sector, the implications of GASB 45 pose the threat of them being left without medical coverage until they qualify for Medicare benefits.

Global Health Benefit Options as a Viable Alternative

One cost-containment strategy, case managed, employer-funded medical travel, offers a promising solution to providing cost-effective health benefits to early retirees in the public sector. Everyone in the industry has read the 2009 Deloitte Center for Health Solutions study on outbound medical tourism projected to reach upwards of 1.6 million patients by 2012, with sustainable annual growth of 35%. The concept of medical travel or global health care in the third-party-payer market is that individuals receive a medical benefit offered through their employer, which gives them the option of traveling to international hospitals for major surgical procedures. After all, in California, four major insurers currently pay for binational care, two of which have done so for more than 10 years, with excellent quality outcomes and high levels of patient satisfaction.

Employers who incorporate a medical travel program typically allow individuals to waive their copays, deductibles, and coinsurances. Employees who receive medical care internationally are then able to retain dollars they would have otherwise spent if they had chosen to have their procedure done domestically. Besides, most retirees have ample time, and savings to be able to travel and be interested in it.

Global healthcare programs specifically address the healthcare affordability challenges posed by GASB 45. The cost savings associated with receiving medical care outside the United States are so significant that public-sector employers can reduce retiree health costs. At the same time, a network such as ours offers employers optional wraparound benefits options that can serve as an adjunct to existing benefit programs and can be implemented at a minimal monthly cost to the employer. Once the employer and the expatriate and retiree workforce has developed a familiar comfort level and confidence in our vetted and inspected providers through Mercury Healthcare, we feel strongly that it won't take much to convince them to allow others from the domestic active workforce to make prudent purchasing decisions to receive care abroad when medically appropriate.

Although there are no easy solutions to overcoming the financial challenges GASB 45 poses to the public sector, global health care benefit programs for early retirees may be a concept more local and state government entities will be embracing in the years to come. For this particular group of lives, their dilemma is unique. Industry research from surveys of the 50 states and a large sample of local governments, shows that the majority of these jurisdictions continue to manage retiree health care obligations on a pay-as-you-go basis, giving little or no attention to the potential impacts of mounting unfunded obligations. Most states, and some local governments, have adopted incremental policies to contain, shed, and or share costs. In general, surveys demonstrate that states have been more responsive to the health care dilemma than municipalities and counties.

- Alterations in health care provisions are possible through contract negotiations, but unions are nearly certain to resist any reductions in healthcare benefits for present and future retirees.
- Nearly all states have created a statewide healthcare pool, providing uniform benefit levels for the active workforce and to all retirees residing in the state.
- Many state plans include teachers and provide a local option for local governments and special districts to participate.
- In the last five years, 10% of states have established a plan that limits the state subsidy for future retirees; 34% say they are likely to introduce such a plan in the next five years.

For domestic and foreign hospital administrators and other providers, the strategic implications are clear. Either set competitive rates and customer service in your sights for this special needs population or watch their shadow as they exit through the door to more prudent purchasing options. Keep in mind that this particular population, includes school teachers who have led exploratory field trips abroad with students, and who have enjoyed summers off during their entire career affording the option to travel both domestically and abroad, and who are worldly and experienced. They may not be as fearful of international travel as others in this age group who may have never left the neighborhood. This baby-boomer age group has the discretionary income, and is incentivized to be a prudent purchaser of wellness services, checkups, diagnostic procedures, and a host of other longevity and age-related services that are orthopedic and cardiologic in nature. Women may also seek elective services paid for out of pocket from providers with whom they have established a relationship for other covered services outside their hometown. Their husbands and partners may also be seeking men's health services and antiaging services to maintain youth and active lifestyles.

WELLNESS AND MEDICAL TOURISM

Chapter 22

Wellness and Medical Tourism

Idiomatic Challenges of Terminology, Culture, and History

The term "wellness" is used differently in languages throughout the world. Wellness and good health have historically been seen as freedom from "dis-ease." If one weren't ill or not at ease, then one was considered "healthy." We now know from published research that this frame of reference is changing. Although few will argue that absence of "ill-ness" and "dis-ease" is a primary component of being healthy, it doesn't, however, indicate anything about one's state of "well-being."

As a state of health, wellness is closely linked to one's lifestyle and the choices one makes about activity level, certain food choices, sleep habits, substance abuse, and so on. Each individual has a responsibility to him- or herself to maintain good health, including proper weight control, good nutrition, physical activity and exercise, and controlling of health risk factors such as tobacco use, and alcohol and drug use or abuse.

Internationally, wellness is a proactive and preventative approach that's designed to provide optimum levels of health, and emotional and social functioning. It involves recognition that we each have psychological, physical, spiritual, and social needs that are necessary in order to have higher levels of functioning and longevity, and the prevention of disease, and signs and symptoms of premature aging.

Wellness emphasizes the whole individual. It's the integration of the spirit, body, and the mind, and the understanding that everything we do, feel, think and believe has a direct impact on one's state of health.

Understanding Employer-Sponsored Wellness Initiatives in the United States

In the United States, we continually hear this word during the news, in conversations, at work, or read it in newspapers, magazines, and the like. Surprisingly, there's no definition of wellness that

Figure 22.1   Coffee cup illustration, Europe/LATAM. (Photos courtesy of Maria Todd.)

seems to be universally accepted. Nonetheless there is a set of general characteristics found in most good attempts to define wellness. We routinely see a reference made to wellness being a "state of well-being," which for Americans, is very vague. Not so in other parts of the world. Actually, if one understands paradigm shift, the conceptual framework is less vague. Because Americans are probably the one of the least-traveled among developed nations' populations, and less often exposed to other cultures of many demographic groups, the concept may be more difficult for them to explain in terms of well-being as it relates to lifestyles.

Here's an example. In Vienna or Budapest, one might find a coffee shop such as Costa Coffee, Starbuck's, or some other chain. However, you'll rarely see people walking the streets with cardboard coffee cups and plastic dome lids. Instead, coffee shops have little round tables that often seat two, serve coffee in ceramic cups with saucers, a little square napkin or doily, and a cute little spoon to stir in sugar and milk or cream. The saucer is perfectly sized to accommodate a cookie or tiny biscotti and it is always served with a small glass of water. (See Figure 22.1.)

In Europe and Latin America, the cultural norm is to take time to relax over a cup of coffee alone or with a friend. Most of that population would find the habit of driving a car or walking down a sidewalk with a cardboard cup of coffee in hand, no cookie, and no water, extremely gauche and uncivilized.

As Mercury Healthcare travel coordinators generally issue a local mobile phone for emergencies to our health travel clients, they load it with photos of common items so that a client can easily point to what it is they want. When they loaded a coffee cup photo, originally, they loaded the image seen in a picture of Starbucks coffee. That presented a problem in certain countries, where Starbucks is not present and the frame of reference for coffee is completely different.

Many routinely refer to wellness as a "state of acceptance or satisfaction with their present condition." That can mean different things to different individuals. Charles B. Corbin from Arizona State University defined wellness as a "multidimensional state of being describing the existence of positive health in an individual as exemplified by quality of life and a sense of well-being."

If one defines wellness as an active process of becoming aware of and learning to make choices (healthy choices) that lead toward a longer and more successful existence, one gets closer to the less U.S.-centric definition of an employer–employee relationship and an employer-sponsored initiative centered around reduction of healthcare costs and return on investment (ROI) in healthcare coverage savings, and moves closer to the conceptual frame of reference in Europe, Asia, Latin America, and other nations where wellness refers to personal initiatives for health improvement, health improvement, continuously seeking more knowledge about how one can improve health status, range of motion, pain and stress reduction, antiaging, and other options and choices in one's own best interest.

In the United States, employer-driven wellness programs are currently underway where the objective is health status improvement through the use of a Health Risk Assessment (HRA), usually completed online, and complemented by an array of other services, coordinated by insurance companies and other "wellness program vendors" for a monthly fee per employee. They generally include the following.

Health Screening Services

These tests can take place in a number of locations. Customarily, they have taken place at a physician's office or hospital outpatient department. More recently with the advent of executive health programs and concierge/corporate physician services, some of the screening programs have taken place at a worksite for the convenience of a company's employees. These services can include fitness assessment, body composition analysis, osteoporosis screening, foot screening, hearing evaluations, vision screening, vaccines (especially if the workforce travels internationally to "hot zones"), blood testing, blood pressure screening, facial sun damage screening, tuberculosis testing (PPD), and random drug screening.

More extensive testing, such as bone density imaging, cardiac imaging, periodic colonoscopies, CT and MRI scans, nuclear studies, and so on, that may be necessary, are impossible to do outside a hospital setting. Dental exams often cannot be performed outside the dental office setting unless a mobile dental clinic is available.

Health risk screening programs should be carried out on a one-on-one basis by trained health care professionals. Health risk measures should include the following:

- Blood pressure (BP) measurements: at least two blood pressure measurements taken during the screening period.
- Blood pressure treatment status: ascertain whether the participant is under a physician's care, on any medication, following a prescribed diet, or any other kind of treatment for hypertension.
- Blood cholesterol measurement: sum cholesterol and HDL-cholesterol taken either using a properly tested and maintained tabletop blood analyzer, providing immediate feedback to the patron, or sending blood to a laboratory providing feedback using a method that is as effective as immediate feedback.
- Cholesterol treatment status: ascertain whether the client is under a physician's care, on any medication, on a prescribed diet, or any other kind of treatment for high cholesterol. In addition, personalized drug effectiveness testing may be carried out using the new tools that provide insight and information and data from the patient, such as the genotype or the gene expression profile and other clinical data, in order to establish the patient's risk, stratify the diagnostic, provide a prognostic, select the medication, prescribe this medication, or introduce preventive measures with the objective that all these actions are specific for each subject/patient.
- This sort of testing helps health professionals to select and prescribe the most adequate treatment for each patient, which can increase the chances of success of a medication, reduce the probability of side effects, and possibly reduce healthcare costs through both the control of the dosage and the reduction of the side effects, and minimizing possible iatrogenic complications, reducing also the number of visits and hospital costs related to adverse effects of the drug or to a worsening of the condition of the patient. With these tests, the screening participant's doctor will receive genetic counseling that will inform him or her about the polymorphisms

and the phenotypic interpretation. This counseling will also include suggestions on the dosage, as well as comprehensive recommendations regarding the prescribed medication.

■ Obesity: utilize an accepted method for estimating obesity. The tool may assess participant's height and weight and benchmark against an accepted reference height/weight chart or use body mass index scores. These often identify people 20% percent or more above their ideal weight and target them for campaigns promoting weight loss or bariatric surgery in cases of morbid obesity and the presence of other health risk factors.

■ Smoking status: assess whether the participant currently smokes cigarettes, whether the customer has quit or never smoked, and the number of cigarettes smoked/day.

■ Exercise habits: screening questions may be limited to frequency and duration of exercise, whether participants exercise in a moderately vigorous fashion at least three times per week for 30 minutes or more.

■ Diabetes: whether the patron has diabetes, and whether it's currently under control. A blood glucose could be also be done via finger stick and desktop analyzer. Several manufacturers make cassettes available that include cholesterol and glucose measurements.

■ Cerebrovascular disease or occlusive peripheral vascular disease (PVD): done to ascertain if the customer has had a stroke or other kind of capillary disease.

■ Family history of cardiovascular disease: ascertain whether any of the participant's parents or siblings had a heart attack or sudden death due to heart disease before age 55.

■ Coronary artery disease (CAD): ascertain if the customer has had a heart attack or other kind of coronary heart disease.

■ Stress: participant's assessment of stress in work or personal life. A series of well-tested and validated questions reviewing levels of stress are available from the employee assistance program vendors.

■ Participant release form: a release form is required in which the participant authorizes the wellness program to draw blood for testing, to send information to the participant's medical care provider if medical risks are identified, and to obtain information from the provider about diagnosis and prescribed treatment.

■ Participant interest survey: if an assessment of interest has not been gathered previously, the screening activity must assess levels of interest in health promotion programs such as weight control, tobacco use cessation, fitness or exercise, stress management, nutrition, self-care, cholesterol control.

■ Health education: the screener must review with the participant his or her identified health risks and what they mean to the participant's overall health, and give the participant a written record of the blood pressure, sum cholesterol, and any other test results.

■ Referral of participants for treatment: participants with elevated risks should be referred to appropriate sources of diagnosis and possible treatment, following nationally or locally recognized guidelines for such referral. This either happens at the time of the exam or later through targeted messages and campaigns that use predictive modeling, disease management, and case management. These may also be tied to incentives such as health travel and other program participation designed to reduce healthcare costs for chronic disease management for both the worker and the employer, and to improve worker productivity, longevity, and premature aging.

■ Demographic information should include location of the screening, workplace, program participant's name, address, identification number, home and work phone numbers, gender, race, date of birth, relevant job information, duties and essential job functions, department number, and work shift.

Training and Education

In addition to screening exams, history, and physical exams, a wellness program also includes time for patient education and training. These programs can educate your employees on the benefits of living a healthy lifestyle. These programs can come in the form of booklets, newsletters, private websites, or even as a scheduled seminar. The goal is to teach employees about healthy living, which will directly benefit both the employee and the company at which they are employed.

Online Health Management

Often, employees are provided a special website where they can log in and view creative and informative content that will get them on the way to healthy living. They will have access to thousands of articles, charts, and unique health tracking software applications. They may also incorporate a health risk assessment that is simple to complete and provides them with assessments created by artificial intelligence algorithms that create personalized results and health status improvement plans.

Onsite or Nearby Fitness Center Memberships

Employers often designate a place on the worksite that is converted to a gymnasium or fitness center, and may include open areas that can be used to perform yoga, tai chi, Pilates or other forms of stretching and movement activities. Alternatively, an employee discount may be arranged at a nearby gym or fitness center to encourage use.

Incentive Programs

These are often designed to offer rewards that include vacation days, trips, cash, and other goal-setting programs, or offer points toward prizes.

Activity Promotions

These are designed to increase awareness, encourage movement, flexibility, stress reduction, and usually are a good laugh or to produce recognition for the participants.

Encouraging Participation

A major concern in wellness programming is attracting staff members to participate and maximizing participation. When introducing a wellness program, a letter briefly explaining the wellness program signed by the president or CEO is a great endorsement.

Utilizing posters, newsletter articles, and flyers are excellent means of promoting the health promotion program. Other promotional methods to consider are e-mail and announcements at staff meetings. Ask wellness committee members to recruit participants.

Once the wellness program is kicked off, you may want to provide an incentive for any staff member who recruits another staff member to any of the wellness program offerings.

For personality types that include nonjoiners, loners, introverts, and some people with disabilities, programs may create uncomfortable situations for the participant who may be unwilling or uncooperative participating in a group setting. Don't despair or interpret this as a program failure. Instead maximize that which you can.

Examples of Programs

- Urge workers to walk during lunch or break times. Post a "steps accumulated" map on a workplace wall where workers can log their steps or miles.
- Encourage joggers, walkers, and those who enjoy other forms of exercise to form fitness groups to meet before work, at lunch, or after work.
- Promote the use of stairs rather than elevators. Place bulletin boards, art contests, and so on in stairwells.
- Sponsor "Bike-to-Work" or Walk-to-Work week.
- Schedule five-minute desk stretching at the worksite. This can relieve repetitive motion issues as well as eye and back strain.
- Organize a personal challenge exercise such as "Climb a Mountain" or "Swim a Sea." This is an honor system program in which participating employees are awarded minutes, steps, or miles credit for cardiovascular exercise (swimming, walking, running, skiing, biking, stair stepping, aerobics, etc.). The object of this type of challenge is to accumulate the equivalent mileage it would take to reach the top of a famous mountain, span a body of water (swim the nearby river), or reach a distant city/county. Try personalizing the challenge as much as possible to individual interests or area geographical matches close to the workplace.

Marketing Medical Tourism Wellness Offers

As you develop your strategy for wellness offers, take care to consider the idiomatic differences in your marketing language and your audience. If your hospital, resort, spa, health retreat, or hotel offers treatments to clientele other than Americans, you may find you need two different promotional collateral pieces. Having traveled with Americans who were spa savvy from an American standpoint, they were initially lost in the spas in Europe when the staff spoke of "cures," wellness, and even massages, which were different, more limited in scope and initially dismissed as inferior because expectations were not managed—by me—prior to arrival. Once they got into the groove of how it all worked, it was more difficult to get the three of them to leave.

Another problem we encountered in marketing was the problem of idiomatic translation of the words used in Europe, Latin America, and other locations back into English. For example, words such as "cure" in places other than litigious America, mean a treatment. In the United States, this word is reserved to describe an "outcome." Therefore if the anticipated outcome is not reached, no "cure" has been received, and liability and customer dissatisfaction could ensue.

Another big example was the use of the word "locomotor." In the United States and in spoken English, that term is, instead, "musculoskeletal." Locomotor is simply not used. Another I encountered was the use of "column" instead of spine, and so on.

Spend a small sum on idiomatic translation by translators who have the medical expertise. They are few and far between and often take the time and effort of both a professional translator, journalist, or linguist, and then secondary review by a person with medical knowledge to ensure that the translation is comprehensible by the intended audience. Mercury Healthcare Advisory Group consultants provide this service for hundreds of clients worldwide. We've seen some examples of other firms' work and we have to reserve our commentary and be careful not to show our chagrin on our faces, but sympathize with the client, as they often paid large sums of precious marketing dollars only to find out after paying for translation, layout, and four-color printing of thousands of copies of a booklet, brochure, or website, that it had to be tossed into the rubbish bin and completely redone.

Don't take the chance that your organization will give the impression of failure to pay attention to detail, illiteracy, or other fears such as "Will they be able to communicate with me if I go there?" simply because your product is described in what could be construed as shoddy advertising copy.

I have developed a glossary of terms in proper idiomatic English for the terms generally used to describe wellness treatments and procedures, and have included it in Appendix 2. I hope it helps you to save some money and time on translation, realize your investment in this handbook, and communicate more effectively with your English-speaking audience, to result in the outcome you are seeking: more patient referrals, bookings, and a polished and professional appearance in your marketing and promotional materials.

So much more could be written about the spa opportunities for program development in medical wellness tourism. I may consider dedicating one book just to medical spa tourism development in the next few years. I really cannot complain about the research and familiarization tours necessary in order to write the book from an authoritative perspective. It's hard work but someone has to do it!

Conclusion

Make It Happen

Thanks for hanging in there with me and for reading this far! When I run seminars or give presentations on medical tourism program development or conduct medical tourism facilitator skills training, this is the point where many people are excited to get out there and make it happen. They want to start building their organization or business right away or initiate an action plan to transform customer service and patient satisfaction goals to customer delight.

But in the audiences of my seminars and presentations there is always another group of people who tend to feel a bit overwhelmed. There is just too much information they say, or too many new and unfamiliar ideas. If you are in this category, you might be thinking that the people and organizations profiled in the book were able to figure things out that are just too complex and time-consuming for you to tackle, especially given your already hectic schedule. Let's face it, we all have too much stuff on our plates, and for most of us who don't have the luxury of delegation, implementing ideas in the book will represent an addition to our workloads. But here's one of the greatest things about the *Handbook of Medical Tourism Program Development*: you can implement these ideas in bits and pieces. In fact, I don't have any expectations that anybody will implement all the ideas here.

The healthcare environment today dictates that physicians enhance the roles of their playing and directing physician groups, not only from the contracting perspective but also from the management perspective. Physicians and dentists, among other providers, can no longer stand on the sidelines and permit other individuals to direct their fate. I hope that after reading this book you will decide to play a proactive role in ensuring that your voice, the voice of the patient advocate, is heard when policies and programs are being set that will govern your livelihood and have direct implications on patient care. Although it's very easy to take a passive position and assume that others will direct the healthcare system in a manner which recognizes the crucial role of the physician, it is not always true. Clinicians must prepare themselves for management responsibilities just as diligently as they went about preparing themselves for their clinical roles. This book presents many theories and principles that are crucial to the effective management of medical tourism programs. I encourage not only the clinicians, but also the administrators, to read this book and become familiar with its contents and benefit from the experience of others who've contributed to the manuscript.

My warmest regards and good wishes for your success!

Recommended Reading

If Disney Ran Your Hospital: 9 1/2 Things You Would Do Differently, Lee (2004, Second River Healthcare)

Why Hospitals Should Fly: The Ultimate Flight Plan to Patient Safety and Quality Care, Nance (2008, Second River Healthcare)

Putting Patients First: Best Practices In Patient-Centered Care, 2nd edition, Frampton and Charmel (2008, Josey-Bass)

Blue Ocean Strategy: How to Create Uncontested Market Space and Make Competition Irrelevant, Kim and Mauborgne (2005, Harvard Business School Press)

7 Habits of Highly Effective People, Covey (2004, Free Press)

Don't Make Me Think: A Common Sense Approach to Web Usability, 2nd edition, Krug (2005, New Riders Press)

The Managed Care Contracting Handbook, 2nd edition, Todd (2009, Productivity Press)

E-Health, Telehealth, and Telemedicine: A Guide To Startup and Success, Mahey, Whitten, and Allen (2001, Jossey-Bass)

Marketing for Health Care Organizations, Kotler and Clarke (1986, Prentice Hall)

Marketing for Hospitality & Tourism, 5th edition, Kotler, Bowen, and Makens (2009, Prentice Hall)

The Referral Engine: Teaching Your Business to Market Itself, Jantsch (2010, Portfolio)

Inspire! Why Customers Come Back, Champy (2009, FT Press)

Appendix 1: Mercury Healthcare Advisory Group—Business Model Development Worksheet

Key Partners

Create a table to

- List key partners
- List key suppliers
- List key resources you acquire from key partners
- List key activities that your key partners perform

Now describe:

- How does your organization motivate key partners to produce optimization and economy for you and for them?
- How does your organization reduce risk and uncertainty for your key partners and reduce it for your organization by their actions?
- How does your organization help key partners to acquire certain resources or activities? How do they reciprocate?

Value Propositions Supported by Key Activities and Resources

In order to demonstrate your value proposition to the marketplace, which key activities are required?

Which key resources are required for each (pair up physical, intellectual property, human capital, or financial capital, etc.)?

What are your distribution channels and how much business can you expect from each?

What resources do they require to maintain distribution (available beds, OR times, physicians, nurses who speak a certain language, etc.)?

List your key customer relationships—why are they classified as key relationships? What resources are required to maintain them?

Who else might be a key relationship? How can you get to them?

What diverse revenue streams can you create? Which ones would you rather not exploit and why?

What do you deliver to customers?

What problems are you solving for them?

What bundles of services can you offer to each customer segment?

Which customer needs are you solving?

Reduce These Thoughts to One Succinct Response

The newness of our product is demonstrated by _____

The performance of our product is measured by _____

The customization of our product is achieved through _____

We get the job done by _____

Our product design is unique because _____

Our brand means _____ to our customers

Our price is _____

We control costs for our purchasers through _____

We reduce risk for our purchasers by _____

We enhance or increase accessibility to our customers through _____

We offer convenience to our customers by _____

We offer utility to customers as demonstrated through _____

Customer Relationships

1. What type of relationship does our external customer (consumer) expect us to establish and maintain with them?

2. What type of relationship does our external customer (employer of expatriates) expect us to establish and maintain with them?

3. What type of relationship does our external customer (insurer or health plan) expect us to establish and maintain with them?

4. Which relationships have we established already? (add additional rows if necessary)

Name	Contract in Force	Expiration Date

5. Which relationships would we like to establish in the near term? (add additional rows if necessary)

Name	Advantage of the Relationship		Target Date
	To Us	To Them	

6. Who are our most important customers?
   - Mass market
   - Niche market
   - Market segments
   - Diversified Markets
   - Multisided platforms*

Customer Relationship Management and Key Performance Indicators

Through which marketing channels do your customers prefer to be contacted?

How are you contacting them now?

---

* A multisided platform brings together two or more distinct but interdependent groups of customers. Such platforms are of value to one group of customers only if the other groups of customers are also present. The platform creates value by facilitating interactions between the different groups. A multisided platform grows in value to the extent that it attracts more users, previously described in this chapter under the "Network Effect" model.

Are any of your channels integrated? How?

Which channels are proven performers? To what degree? Why do they work?

Which are not working? Why don't they work?

Which ones are most cost effective?

How are you creating awareness of your organization's products and services?

How do you help potential and existing customers evaluate your organization's value proposition?

How do you allow customers to purchase specific products and services?

How do you measure the actual value delivered to customers?

How do you provide postpurchase customer support, retention, and relationships?

Cost Management and Cost Containment

1. What are the most important costs that are integral to your business model?

2. Which key resources are the most expensive?

3. Which key activities are the most expensive? (Consider fixed costs, variable costs, economies of scale and scope among other characteristics.)

What Is Your Business Model?

Cost Driven? (leanest cost structure, lower price value proposition, automation intensive, outsourcing intensive, etc.)
Value Driven? (How do you create and demonstrate value and utility for money?)

Pricing

For what value are your customers willing to pay?

For what do they currently pay? How are they paying this?

Consumers
    Out of pocket
    Privately insured
    Government funded
    Charitable organization sponsors

Employers
    Defined benefit shared expense (employee/employer)
    Earmarked special funds
    Traditional health insurance policies
    Self-funded employer-funded trust

How would they prefer to pay?
    At the time of service
    Cashless
    Escrow
    Prepaid/Subscription

How much revenue does each revenue stream contribute to overall revenues?

Appendix 2: Glossary of Wellness Treatment Terms

A

Acupressure: A traditional Chinese pressure-point massage (massage where fingers are applied to key points on the body) used to stimulate energy flow in the body, ease muscle tension, relieve pain, and promote relaxation. Often referred to as "acupuncture without needles."

Acupuncture: This traditional Chinese healing technique is used to maintain or restore the body's balance of energy. Acupuncture is administered by properly trained and credentialed therapists who insert fine needles into energy centers (meridians) to stimulate energy flow. This therapy is used to treat underlying causes of conditions including addiction, asthma, carpal tunnel syndrome, fibromyalgia, headaches, lower back pain, menstrual irregularities, arthritis, allergies, high blood pressure, and sciatica.

Alexander Technique: Method of re-educating the mind and body to improve movement. The focus is on applying the appropriate amount of energy for each activity in order to improve posture and balance, and to eliminate stress-inducing habits.

Algotherapy: A seaweed (algae) bath that is a form of thalassotherapy.

A.H.A. Alpha Hydroxide: Alpha-hydroxy care exfoliates dead skin cells and decreases the depth of wrinkles and fine lines. Alpha-hydroxy also stimulates cell regeneration and clarifies the complexion. It transforms the appearance of skin, leaving it fresh and radiant.

Anaerobic: The opposite of aerobic exercise, anaerobic exercise—such as weightlifting and body-building—involves muscular work that causes the body to use more oxygen than it takes in.

Antiaging: A product or treatment that is meant to combat or defend against the effects of natural or premature aging processes.

Aqua Aerobics: Aerobic exercises performed in a pool using the support and resistance of the water to burn fat, strengthen bones, and increase cardiovascular health and endurance. The buoyancy of the water greatly reduces the chance of injuring joints or muscles.

Aromatherapy: Treatments such as massage, facials, body wraps, or hydrobaths that include the application of fragrant essential oils. Different oils are used for different therapeutic benefits.

Ayurvedic Massage: Deep therapeutic massage meant to release toxins, invigorate, and relax. Uses massage oils chosen to balance a person's doshas (see definition). Balancing the doshas is the basis of the ancient Indian system of Ayurvedic medicine, which incorporates nutrition, herbal medicine, aromatherapy, massage, and meditation.

B

Balneotherapy: The use of water, most often warm water, to restore and revitalize the body. Balneotherapy has been used for hundreds of years to improve circulation, fortify the immune system, and relieve pain and stress.

Behavior Modification: Change in personal habits through repetition of desired behaviors. Most spas incorporate behavior modification into their weight loss programs.

Bindi: A bodywork treatment combining exfoliation, herbal treatment, and light massage.

Biofeedback: Treatment method using real-time measurements of physiological functions (muscle tension or heart rate) to teach people how to consciously control them. Used to treat headaches, anxiety, pain, digestive disorders, high blood pressure, abnormal heartbeat, epilepsy, and more.

Body Conditioning: Any exercise program that focuses on overall conditioning of the body. A body-conditioning routine might combine exercises for strength and flexibility and use both strength-training equipment and floor exercises.

Body Sculpting: Fitness program using weight, flexibility, and endurance training; but not running or jumping, to shape hips, thighs, upper arms, and buttocks without creating bulk.

Body Wrap (also Herbal Wrap): Treatment in which strips of cloth are soaked in herbal teas and cocooned around the body.

Botox®: The most popular nonsurgical cosmetic procedure for the treatment of frown lines, forehead furrows, and crow's feet. One treatment produces results that can last up to four months. Botox® mark is owned by Allergan, Inc.

Brush and Tone: Through dry brushing of the skin, the therapist can remove dead layers and impurities while stimulating circulation. One of many exfoliating techniques used as a pretreatment for mud and seaweed body masks that are formed by the application of a moisturizing lotion.

C

Caldarium: The hottest room in ancient Roman baths where people would soak in steaming water to detoxify. Modern versions may not have a pool of hot water, but all use humidity or steam, sometimes infused with essential oils.

Champagne and Rosewater Facial: Splashes of complexion-toning champagne, paired with the long-known replenishing qualities of the rose, gently exfoliate and deeply hydrate the skin. Arms, neck, and shoulders are massaged with warm stones as a rejuvenating collagen mask is absorbed. Beautiful, petal-soft results for all skin types.

Chi Gong (also Qigong): Ancient Chinese method of maintaining health by guiding and balancing energy, or chi, through breathing, movement, and meditation.

Circuit Training: Exercise plan utilizing six to ten exercises that are completed one after another on weight-resistance equipment to increase mobility, strength, and stamina. Each exercise is performed for a certain number of repetitions.

Cold Plunge: A circulation-stimulating pool of frigid water designed to be used in conjunction with sauna or steam room sessions.

Collagen Mask: This is an exceptional treatment for fatigued or mature skin unable to retain sufficient moisture. The products used in this facial provide outstanding results in terms of epidermal regeneration, hydration, wrinkle smoothing and prevention, and scar treatment.

Collagen Therapy: Injection of collagen beneath the skin with a fine needle to fill out wrinkles and lines.

Colonic Hydrotherapy: An extended and more complete form of an enema as well as a method of removing waste from the large intestine without using drugs. Colon hydrotherapy is used to treat constipation or impaction, as preparation for diagnostic studies of the large intestine (barium enema, sigmoidoscopy, or colonoscopy), and as preparation before or after surgery. The procedure is also used for bowel training for paraplegics or quadriplegics, those with arthritis, and patients who have suspected autointoxication or intestinal toxemia.

Cosmeceuticals: Topical cosmetic–pharmaceutical combinations intended to improve health and appearance of skin. Not recognized or subject to review by the U.S. Food and Drug Administration.

Cranio–Sacral Therapy: Treatment that aims to improve function of the central nervous system by balancing the fluid and membranes that surround the brain and spinal cord. Performed through gentle palpitations of specific areas. Used to treat a range of conditions, including stress, insomnia, headache, anxiety, fibromyalgia, and head, neck, and back pain.

D

Dead Sea Mud Treatment: Along the Dead Sea coasts there are deposits of black mud which is characterized as a mineral mud and supported by analysis of its chemical composition. In addition to inorganic compounds it contains water and organic compounds. Dead Sea Mud is an alluvial deposit from a larger prehistoric sea that once occupied this section of the Syro-African Rift Valley. Its solid phase contains very fine grains of silicates and carbonates. The watery phase resembles Dead Sea brine but, unlike the brine, contains sulfides from biological sources. It has an extremely high heat-retaining capacity. Mud from the Dead Sea coast has been proven to have great therapeutic value in the treatment of rheumatic diseases and skin disorders, as well as for the stimulation of various biological functions of the human body. In addition, the mud can serve as raw material for the preparation of cosmetic products for the treatment of acne, psoriasis and skin diseases, for improving the elasticity of the skin, and also against dandruff.

Deep-Tissue Massage: Massage method focusing on aligning the deep layers of muscles and connective tissue (called fascia) through kneading and applying slow intense pressure. Benefits include improved range of motion and posture, and stress and pain relief.

Dermabrasion: A surgical procedure that involves the controlled abrasion (wearing away) of the upper layers of the skin with sandpaper or other mechanical means. It is common to use

CO2 or Erbium YAG laser as well. The procedure requires a local anesthetic. Afterward, the skin is very red and raw-looking, and it takes several months for the skin to rejuvenate and heal. The purpose of dermabrasion is to smooth the skin and, in the process, remove small scars (as from acne), moles (nevi), tattoos, or fine wrinkles. The mechanical method remains popular because it is the most affordable and has practically the same results as the laser method.

Diatomaceous Earth (Kieselguhr): Diatomaceous earth, or Kieselguhr, is composed of the siliceous shells of fossil diatoms (minute unicellular plants), or of the debris of fossil diatoms. It has similarities and uses to a material known as Fuller's Earth. It is listed in the British Pharmacopoeia and according to the Pharmaceutical Codex of 1923 is used for the preparation of absorbent and emollient dusting powders. Apart from having the ability to absorb essential oils and other active materials, it is also well known as a filtering agent. It is used as an absorbent for nitroglycerin, after which it becomes known as dynamite!

DNA Analysis: Any number of procedures that collect and analyze an individual's DNA and compare it against known genetic markers to recommend lifestyle and nutritional changes. Also referred to as personalized medicine.

Duo Massage: A massage treatment performed simultaneously by two therapists.

E

Effleurage: Massage technique involving quick long strokes used at the beginning and end of certain treatments.

Electrolysis: This technique employs electricity to permanently remove human hair. The actual process of removing the hair is referred to as electrolysis. The practitioner slides a solid hair-thin metal probe into each hair follicle. Proper insertion does not puncture the skin. Electricity is delivered to the follicle through the probe, which causes localized damage to the areas that generate hairs, either through the formation of caustic lye (galvanic method), overheating (thermolysis), or both (blend method). Three methods or "modalities" are used in electrolysis: galvanic, thermolysis, and blend; all have their own merits, and one method is not better than another. The success depends on the skill of the technician, the type of hair being removed, the condition of the skin and the pain threshold of the client. All three methods, when properly performed, can be thorough at destroying the hair matrix cells, and leaving follicles incapable of regrowing hair.

Endermologie: A French massage therapy performed as a cellulite treatment makes use of a unique machine providing both positive and negative pressure to reduce and smooth cellulite.

Erbium-YAG—Cutaneous Laser Resurfacing,: Lasers currently available for cutaneous resurfacing include a high-energy pulsed or scanned carbon dioxide laser, a short-pulsed erbium:yttrium-aluminum-garnet (Er:YAG), and modulated (short-and-long-pulsed) Er:YAG systems. High-energy pulsed or scanned carbon dioxide laser skin resurfacing can achieve excellent clinical improvement of damage to skin surfaces from overexposure to the sun, skin wrinkles (rhytides), and atrophic scars. However, this resurfacing is associated with an extended skill cell generation (re-epithelialization) period and, in some cases, prolonged redness (erythema) that may persist for several months. Of greater concern is the potential for delayed permanent lighter-toned skin areas (hypopigmentation) seen in as many as 20% of patients when multiple-pass carbon dioxide resurfacing is performed. The demand for less aggressive modalities for skin rejuvenation led to the development of the Er:YAG laser

Essential Oils: Aromatic liquids extracted from flowers, grasses, fruits, leaves, roots, or trees. The oils maintain the odors and tastes, and thus the essence, of the plant they are extracted from.

European Facial: Treatment that begins with deep cleansing, steam, exfoliation, and professional massage of the face, shoulders, and chest area, followed by a special mask that hydrates the skin.

Exfoliation: Procedure to slough the top layer of dead skin cells off the face or body. Dry brush, loofah scrub, and salt glow are among the techniques used in conjunction with ingredients including grape seed, sugar, clay, and salt.

F

Facial: Generic term for treatment of skin in the face that usually includes massaging, cleansing, toning, steaming, exfoliating, and moisturizing.

Fango: Italian for "mud." Treatment in which mineralized mud, mixed with oil or water, is applied to the body as a heat pack to detoxify skin, stimulate circulation, and soothe muscles.

Feldenkrais: The Feldenkrais method is named for its Russian-born originator, Dr. Moshe Feldenkrais. An education-based system for restoring physical function to a burdened or impaired body, the method consists of intensive verbal and touch-therapy workshops designed to reorganize the body's fundamental movements and relationship with the central nervous system. Certified practitioners must complete 800–1,000 hours of training in a three- or four-year period.

Fitness Profile/Assessment: A test administered by a fitness instructor to evaluate aerobic capacity, flexibility, and strength, as well as resting heart rate, resting blood pressure, and body composition.

Frigidarium: A room in ancient Roman baths where bathers plunged into a cold pool of water to refresh and close pores after visiting the warmer areas. Modern versions similarly revitalize visitors after they undergo heat treatments.

G

Glycolic Peel: Used on the face, neck, and décolletage, this natural acid provides deeper exfoliation to stimulate collagen production, soften fine lines, and enhance hydration. Skin is silky to the touch.

Gommage: Cleansing, rehydrating treatment using creams that are applied in long movements, similar to a massage.

H

Hammam (also Turkish Bath): A traditional Middle Eastern bath house. Modern versions involve a series of steam rooms of increasingly elevated temperature, wherein bathing rituals often include a massage, a cold shower, or time in a relaxation area.

Hair Extensions: Synthetic fibers or real human hair that is woven (sewn) or braided into existing hair to increase length, volume, or color.

Hatha Yoga: Branch of yoga that is devoted to the physical processes (as opposed to others that focus on wisdom, meditation, service, etc.) and involves breathing and physical exercises. There are many types of physical yoga.

Herbal Wrap: Treatment using strips of cloth soaked in a heated herbal solution to wrap around the body. It is used for relaxation and said to eliminate impurities and detoxify.

Holistic Medicine: System of heath care that looks at the entire person, taking into account physical, nutritional, environmental, emotional, social, spiritual, and lifestyle values, and avails itself of all modes of diagnosis and treatment including drugs and surgery in the absence of a safe alternative. The patient is urged to make personal efforts to achieve balance and well-being.

Homeopathy: Form of medicine based on the principle that "like cures like." To stimulate healing, patients are treated with minute quantities of natural substances that cause symptoms much like those of the disease they are meant to cure.

Hormone Replacement Therapy: Medication containing one or more female hormones (usually estrogen) used to treat women experiencing symptoms of menopause or amenorrhea, or women who have had a partial or full hysterectomy. Medical opinion about the risks of this kind of therapy is divided.

Hot Stone Therapy: A variation of a traditional massage, a heated stone massage utilizes hot stones, that are generally heated in 120–150°F water. A massage therapist then massages oils into the skin utilizing Swedish massage techniques. This relaxes and makes it easier for the body to absorb heat from the stones. A massage therapist then places a variety of stones at focal parts of the body such as the upper and lower back. The stones release heat, and calm and relax the muscles. When stones cool, they are replaced with other heated ones during the duration of a massage. This may also be followed with a traditional massage.

Hydrolifting: The use of a hydrolifting mask moisturizes and firms the skin. Composed of biotechnological extracts and hyaluronic acid, the mask is a powerful moisturizer and an exceptional lifter.

Hydrotherapy: General term for therapeutic procedures that use water for a variety of purposes, from relaxation to disease treatment. Methods can include Kneipp baths, underwater jet massage, specialized or experience showers, mineral baths, thalassotherapy, and more.

Hypoallergenic: Cosmetic products alleged by manufacturer to create fewer allergic reactions among those who are sensitive. However, no federal standards govern the use of this term.

I

Intense Pulsed Light (IPL): A technology aimed at producing light of high intensity during a very short period of time. It involves specific lamps together with capacitors whose rapid discharge provides the high energy required. It is a method of hair removal from the body most commonly employed by medical practitioners and estheticians. It involves the use of a specially constructed xenon flash lamp and focusing optics. Cheaper and faster than laser hair removal, the IPL removal procedure has become very popular. IPL can also be used as a skin treatment in a process known as photo rejuvenation.

Indian Head Massage: Massage therapy based on Ayurvedic principles that focuses on the scalp, face, neck, and shoulders to relieve stress and tension, and nourish the scalp.

Infrared Treatment: Treatment that uses far-infrared light to mimic sunlight without the exposure to harmful ultraviolet light. Applied using lamps or through infrared saunas to relieve sore muscles and joints and to detoxify.

Injectables: General term for fillers consisting of collagen, biologic acids, or synthetic compounds that are injected under the skin to eliminate small wrinkles and plump facial and bodily contours. Results are temporary.

Inhalation Therapy: Steam vapor treatments that are deemed especially helpful for those suffering from impaired respiratory function due to illness or a smoking habit. Vapor is often mixed with herbal elements such as eucalyptus and chamomile. This form of therapy is often found at spas with access to a mineral or thermal spring.

Iridology: The study of patterns and structures in the iris (colored part of the eye) to diagnose disease. Although the practice is disputed by most in the mainstream medical field, many holistic health professionals claim that the response of nerves in the iris to bodily phenomena (including disease) can be interpreted through close scrutiny of visible features in the eye. Some even believe that iridology can prevent the onset of disease by discerning warning signs in the iris.

ISPA: International Spa Association, a professional organization representing all aspects of the spa industry: club spas, cruise ship spas, day spas, destination spas, resort/hotel spas, medical spas, and mineral springs spas.

J

Jacuzzi: The first free-standing whirlpool bath was introduced by Roy Jacuzzi in 1968, of the famous inventing Jacuzzi family, whose members are also responsible for advances in agriculture and aviation. Although many companies manufacture whirlpool baths today, Jacuzzi is the trademarked name for the invention.

Japanese Furo Bath (also Ofuro): A hot, bubbling bath used for relaxation and usually enjoyed in the nude at a Japanese sento (public bath) or onsen (hot spring).

Juice Fast: A short-term diet regimen consisting of only fresh fruit or vegetable juices. Advocates of the juice fast claim it detoxifies the body.

Juvéderm™: Formulated for versatility in contouring and correcting facial lines and folds, this smooth-consistency injectable gel produces a smooth natural look and feel that is sustained for up to a year. The Juvéderm™ mark is owned by Allergan, Inc.

K

Kneipp Bath: Water therapy originated in the mid-1800s by Germany's Father Sebastian Kneipp, a holistic teacher and proponent of natural remedies. Originally involving dips in the icy Danube, the modern version involves immersion in both warm and cold water, movement therapies, massage, herbal medicine, and nutrition.

Krauter Bath: Based on a German natural remedy, this is a strong, aromatic herbal bath solution.

Kur: German for "cure." A planned course of spa treatments that typically involves soaking in mineral waters, mud baths, body wraps, and massage. "Taking the kur" might be a process lasting 10 to 20 days.

L

Laconium: Hot room with relatively low humidity that was part of ancient Roman baths. Milder than a Finnish sauna, the laconium helps users eliminate toxins through perspiration. Similar to a sweat lodge in Native American cultures.

Lactic Acid Peel: Used on the face, neck, and décolleté, lactic acid's anti-inflammatory ingredients make this peel perfect for sensitive skin types. Evens out skin tone and boosts cell renewal.

Laser Hair Removal: Through the use of selective photothermolysis (SPTL), the matching of a specific wavelength of light and pulse duration to remove hair on targeted tissue with minimal effect on surrounding tissue. Lasers can cause localized damage by selectively heating dark target matter, such as melanin, in the area that causes hair growth, the follicle, while not heating the rest of the skin. Light is absorbed by dark objects, so laser energy can be absorbed by dark material in the skin, but with much more speed and intensity. This dark target matter, or chromophore, can be naturally occurring or artificially introduced.

LaStone Therapy: Relaxing, therapeutic treatment in which dark smooth stones heated in hot water or hot spring pools are placed or stroked with light pressure on areas of the body such as the back, in the palms, and between the toes. Cold stones may also be used.

Lomi Lomi: Hawaiian massage technique derived from ancient Polynesian cultures. Sometimes referred to as the "loving hands" massage because of its gentle, continuously flowing and rocking motion. May include gentle stretches and joint rotation, as well as traditional rituals or prayers.

Loofah Scrub: Exfoliation with a sponge made of the fibrous skeleton of the loofah, a vegetable from the gourd family. Loofah is used extensively in Europe and Asia because of its effectiveness in removing dry skin and stimulating circulation.

Lulur: Body treatment, evolved from a traditional Javanese wedding ceremony, that typically involves a coconut oil massage, exfoliation with a mix of rice and fragrant herbs, a floral bath, and a yogurt moisturizer.

Lymphatic Drainage: Therapeutic massage technique intended to increase circulation and drain trapped water and toxins from the body through the lymphatic system using delicate wavelike movements on the face and neck or entire body. Used to reduce swelling, detoxify, regenerate tissue, and relieve pain and stress.

M

Marine Glacial Clay: This clay originates from a remote estuary on the west coast of Canada, and is harvested by hand. It is washed by a 10-foot tide every day in the unpolluted water of the northwest coast of British Columbia. Marine Glacial Clay can be used for the face and entire body. In its natural state this clay was used by the native Indian people for centuries for its curative and therapeutic properties and has been used successfully for burns, scalds, cuts, athlete's foot, chicken pox, eczema, and other topical skin conditions with very promising results. It contains 37 minerals and trace elements, including silicon, aluminum, iron, calcium, sodium, magnesium, and potassium. It also contains 29 minor minerals including traces of rare earths: pH: 6.5–7.3.

Massage: Manipulation of tissues, usually manually, to improve health and well-being by relaxing muscles, relieving tension, and improving circulation.

Medical Spa: Destination or day spa that offers traditional and complementary medical services supervised or administered by medical professionals. A spa may specialize in diagnostic testing, preventive care, cosmetic procedures, or a combination.

Meditation: Practice of using mental skills to perform such feats as focusing attention on a single object for a long period of time; cultivating compassion, which involves the transforming of negative events; and creating a state of pure awareness of thoughts, emotions, and sensations without reacting. Meditation is said to increase emotional well-being and is being studied for alleged benefits to physical health.

Mineral Spring: A source of thermal water containing naturally occurring elements from surrounding rocks, sand, and soil, that is used in hydrotherapy treatments.

Microdermabrasion: Facial exfoliation procedure in which the top layer of skin is abraded away with ultrafine crystals of aluminum oxide or other ingredients. Microdermabrasion improves and smoothes the skin's surface and can minimize imperfections like blemishes, fine lines, and signs of sun damage.

Mineral Springs Spa: Spa offering an on-site source of mineral-rich thermal or seawater that is used in hydrotherapy or thalassotherapy.

Mocktail: Nonalcoholic drinks made with fresh fruit and vegetables.

Moor Mud: Mud harvested from a moor or peat marsh that is rich in proteins, organic matter, and minerals. Used as a body or facial treatment to hydrate and exfoliate the skin and in a bath to ease aches and pains.

Moor Peat Baths: Uses mud harvested from a moor or a peat marsh that is rich in proteins, organic matter, vitamins, and minerals. It is used as a body or facial treatment to hydrate and exfoliate the skin and in a bath to ease aches and pains.

N

Naturopathy: Holistic medical system based on the healing power of nature and the ability of the body to heal itself. Naturopathy focuses on prevention and treating causes, not symptoms, using natural foods, vitamins and supplements, exercise, herbal medicine, lifestyle changes, homeopathy, hydrotherapy, and mind-body therapies.

Neuromuscular Integration: Body work and exercise system that focuses on the interaction between the central nervous system and the muscles of the body.

NIA (Neuromuscular Integrative Action): Hybrid form that combines the grace and spontaneity of dance, the power and explosiveness of martial arts, and the stillness and concentration of yoga and tai chi in an energetic, low-impact full-body cardiovascular workout.

Nutraceuticals: Natural chemical compounds added to foods to prevent or treat disease and improve health. Also known as functional foods, or phytochemicals.

O

Oxygen Infusion Facial: This treatment delivers an infusion of both oxygen and collagen within one service. First, a collagen serum is applied to promote firmness and elasticity. Next, a steady mist of pressurized oxygen is sprayed directly on the skin, delivering oxygen deep into the cellular layers which immediately plumps the skin. The deep infusion of oxygen and collagen revives and replenishes skin cells, leaving skin instantly hydrated and younger looking. The result is a complexion that looks rejuvenated, radiant and glowing.

P

Panchakarma: Cleansing and rejuvenating program for the body, mind, and consciousness based on Ayurvedic medicine and meant to clear the body of toxins, restore balance, strengthen the immune system, and promote calm. May involve massage, sweat therapy, yoga, diet, and the like.

Parafango: Volcanic mud is mixed with paraffin wax to alleviate aches and pains caused by such illnesses as rheumatism and arthritis.

Paraffin Treatment: Heated paraffin wax is brushed over the body to soothe muscles and, by drawing out the dirt, removing the dead skin, and drawing out perspiration through the head, leave skin clean and soft.

Photo Rejuvenation: Series of gentle laser treatments that stimulate new collagen, smooth fine wrinkles, and diminish the appearance of age spots, broken capillaries, and rosacea.

Pilates: Body-conditioning program meant to develop flexibility and strength via a system of controlled exercises. Developed by Joseph Pilates in the early 1900s, it can be performed on a mat or on specially designed equipment.

Polarity Massage: Therapeutic, relaxing treatment involving hands placed along the energy meridians, stretching, and light rocking to bring the body's own energy into balance.

Preventive Medicine: A holistic approach to health in which a combination of conventional, traditional, and alternative methods are employed to stave off or reverse disease, as opposed to a solely conventional medical model that seeks to cure existing maladies.

Q

Qi Gong (also Chi Gung or Chi Kung): From qi (energy) and gong (the achievement that comes from practice), a group of Chinese self-healing exercises. They combine simple movement, breathing, and mental imagery to relax and strengthen the body and the mind.

R

Rassoul (also Rhassoul): Traditional Arabic cleansing ritual in which the body is coated in mineral-rich Moroccan mud that exfoliates and draws out impurities. Followed by relaxation in a steam room and rinsing mud off in a warm shower. Rassoul or Rhassoul mud was created at the piedmont of the Atlas mountains in Morocco, Formed in deposits during the Jurassic period in the Mesozoic era, 208 to 144 million years ago. This detoxifying clay is mined from 2.5 miles within the Atlas Mountains. Its purity is renowned throughout history going back as far as 2,500 B.C. Rhassoul contains lithium as well as magnesium and other trace elements such as iron, potassium, copper, and zinc. The mud has been used since the twelfth century; Moroccans used Rassoul as a daily therapeutic source for skin cleansing and purification, dermatitis, sensitivities, smoothing rough or scaly skin, seborrhea, and skin and scalp and hair treatments. The underground mining of Rassoul originally commenced with ancient North African civilizations.

Reflexology: Introduced as zone therapy to the West in 1913 by Dr. William Fitzgerald, reflexology is based on ancient techniques that use pressure-point massage, usually on the feet but also on the hands and ears, to restore the flow of energy throughout the body.

Practitioners believe that areas on the feet and hands correspond to other areas throughout the body. Used to relieve symptoms of such conditions as back pain, migraines, arthritis, sleep disorders, injuries, and stress.

Reiki: Spiritual Japanese healing technique in which practitioners lay hands on areas of the body to channel energy and promote deep relaxation, stress reduction, and well-being.

Repaichage: Full-body treatment that uses a combination of clay, herbs, seaweed, and mud to deal with the differing cleansing and moisturizing needs of different parts of your body and face.

Restylane®: The first cosmetic dermal filler made of non-animal-based hyaluronic acid, which exists naturally in the human body. This enhancement restores volume and fullness for six months or longer and does not require allergy testing. Restylane is a registered trademark of HA North American Sales AB, a subsidiary of Medics Pharmaceutical.

Restorative Yoga: Passive yoga poses lasting up to 20 minutes, supported by pillows, towels, and so on, and meant to encourage relaxation via the release of tension in the muscles and spine. Also quiets the mind, rejuvenates the body–mind connection, and doesn't require the flexibility or athletic ability of other forms of yoga.

Rolfing: Deep massage system developed by Dr. Ida Rolf to achieve changes in posture and structure by manipulating the body's muscular–skeletal system. She believed proper alignment would relieve pain and chronic stress. Treatments progress from localized areas to larger body segments.

Roman Bath: A complex of hot, warm, and cold pools and rooms where ancient Romans would go to communally bathe and socialize. (See also caldarium, frigidarium, laconium, and tepidarium.)

S

Sauna: An enclosed, heated room designed to promote sweating and boost circulation, relax muscles, and release toxins. Often followed by a shower or a dip in a pool to cool off. The Finnish sauna, which is heated by hot rocks, is the most common; other cultures have similar concepts, including Native American temazcals, Turkish hammams, and Roman laconiums and caldariums.

Sclerotherapy: A procedure in which a solution is injected into spider veins, causing them to collapse and disappear, often delivered in a series of treatments.

Scotch Hose: Water massage through high-pressure hose while client is standing. The therapist alternates hot and cold and fresh or salt water to relieve sore muscles and stimulate circulation.

Scrubs and Wraps

Cream and Sugar Scrub: A gentle sugar exfoliation followed by a hydrating body massage with cream, intensifies moisture absorption for lasting softness. Sensitive skin friendly.

Detoxifying Seaweed Wrap: A warm seaweed body mask draws out toxins and restores skin vitality. Cocooned in warmth, enjoy a relaxing scalp massage.

Phyto Organic Shea Butter Wrap: Antioxidant olive oil exfoliation prepares skin for a moisture-drenched warm shea butter wrap. The ultimate in hydration, skin is fully refreshed and supple.

Purifying Mud Wrap: The body is enveloped in rich crème mud to eliminate impurities and replace minerals. Enhances cell turnover and texture for total skin rejuvenation.

Salt Glow: Body treatment in which skin is rubbed with coarse salt, sometimes in combination with fragrant oils, to exfoliate and stimulate circulation.

Seaweed Wrap: Body treatment using concentrated seawater and seaweed that contains nutrients including minerals, rare trace elements, vitamins, and proteins. Said by proponents to detoxify, increase circulation, and improve appearance of cellulite.

Sugaring: Ancient depilation process that involves applying a sugar-containing sticky paste to the skin, then pressing on a cloth or paper strip and quickly removing it to remove unwanted hair. Estheticians in some states must be licensed to perform this procedure.

Sensory-Deprivation Flotation Capsule: Enclosed tank filled with warm water and Epsom salts in order to create a dark peaceful environment, similar to that in the womb, to promote total relaxation.

Shiatsu: A form of therapy of Japanese origin based on the same principles as acupuncture, in which pressure is applied to certain points on the body using the hands.

Shirodhara: Ayurvedic treatment lasting 7 to 10 minutes during which stream of oil is poured in the center of your forehead (on your "third eye") in order to help you focus, concentrate, and relax your mind and body.

Spinning: Indoor cycling on stationary bikes that allow riders to adjust resistance to make pedaling easier or harder. Class instructors guide students through a virtual hilly course and cue students about adjusting resistance.

Steam Room: Room where temperatures are kept at 110 to 130° F and humidity is generated in order to soften the skin, clean the pores, calm the nervous system, and relieve tension.

Step Aerobics: Low-impact aerobic activity performed by stepping on and off a platform that usually ranges from four to ten inches high to tone hips, legs, and buttocks.

Stress Management: Combination of physical exercise, deep relaxation techniques, and visualization techniques meant to reduce the ill effects of stress on the body.

Stretching: Extending and lengthening muscles slowly, then in a static manner when hitting resistance. Meant to increase flexibility and relieve stress by improving circulation, and facilitating blood flow to the muscles, heart, and brain.

Swedish Massage: Classical European massage technique manipulating muscles with the use of massage oils and five different movements: long strokes, kneading, tapping, friction, and vibration. Used to soothe tense muscles, increase circulation and flexibility, and de-stress.

Sweat Lodge: Traditional Native American place for ceremonial purification and meditation involving the use of intense heat in a sauna-like environment.

Swiss Shower: Treatment that involves powerful shower jets directed at the body from various heights and at different temperatures to simulate an invigorating massage.

T

Tai Chi (also Tai Chi Chuan): Chinese martial art in which practitioners move slowly and gracefully through a series of postures coordinated by their breath. Used to reduce stress and improve flexibility, strength, energy, agility, and well-being. Often described as "meditation in motion."

Temazcal: Traditional steam bath used by indigenous Mexican and Central Americans consisting of a domelike structure built around a pit where water is poured over hot rocks.

Induces sweating, relaxation, and detoxification. Herbs are often heated on the rocks to create aromatic steam for medicinal purposes. Also known as a sweat lodge among indigenous North American peoples.

Tepidarium: Warm room in ancient Roman baths where visitors would prepare for bathing. The modern version is a heated lounge area with comfortable furniture where guests can relax before and after treatments.

Thai Massage: Full-body treatment that involves passive, yoga-like stretching and pressure-point massage along the body's major energy channels to release blocked energy, relieve tension, align the skeletal structure, and increase flexibility. Traditionally done on the floor with client wearing loose clothing.

Thalassotherapy: Umbrella term describing variety of treatments that use seawater, seaweed, and other natural elements from the ocean for therapeutic benefits. Treatments include underwater jet massage, different types of showers, mineral baths, and seaweed or algae wraps. (See also hydrotherapy.)

Threading: This secret of smoothing began in India and the Middle East, and can be used on the entire face. A precise and intricate art, threading hair removal uses twists of cotton thread to trap unwanted hairs and remove them from the root. Inexpensive, quick and easy, threading assures perfect lines, and hair that grows back slower and thinner.

Traeger Massage: Therapy developed by boxing trainer Milton Treager, MD, that uses gentle, rhythmic movements to relieve tension, ease movement (especially in joints), and induce relaxation. Compressions, elongations, and light bounces as well as rocking motions are involved.

Transcendental Meditation: Simple means of meditation that allows you to quiet the mind through repetition of a personal mantra (word or phrase given you by an instructor) for 20 minutes once or twice a day.

Tui Na: Chinese therapy used to balance energy in the body and release toxins with massage and acupressure techniques. An important component of traditional Chinese medicine.

Turkish Bath (also Hammam): Bathing procedure that involves going through a series of steam rooms of increasing elevated temperature, followed by a rubdown and massage and finished off with a cold shower.

U

Ultrasound: Ultrasound spa treatments use low-frequency sound waves to promote subcutaneous rejuvenation by causing friction beneath the surface of the skin. This technique is employed in several areas of spa aesthetics, from facials to cellulite reduction. Many spa professionals claim that ultrasound treatments tend to be even more effective and efficient than similar treatments without ultrasound.

V

Vichy Shower: A type of shower in which large quantities of warm water are poured over a spa patron while he or she lies in a shallow wet bed, similar to a massage table, but with drainage for the water.

Vinothérapy: Skin treatments that use antioxidant-rich grape skins, seeds, and extracts in a variety of scrubs, baths, and masks. (The term vinothérapie® is trademarked by the beauty products company Caudalie.)

Vitamin C Treatment: This facial includes the use of a reactivating treatment designed to rejuvenate your skin by stimulating collagen and elastin synthesis. Vitamin C Treatment provides excellent skin lifting, toning, oxygenative and clarifying effects.

W

Watsu: Combining the words water and shiatsu, this healing massage treatment is performed in a warm pool in which a therapist supports the client and administers rhythmic movements, pressure-point massage, and stretches. The watsu is designed to relieve stress, muscle tension, and pain, and promote deep relaxation.

Waxing: Depilation process that involves application of warm wax followed by a strip of cloth quickly pulled away from skin to remove unwanted hair.

Weight Training: Use of free weights or weight machines in a series of repetitive exercises meant both to tone the body and add or replace lean muscle mass and also to raise metabolism.

Whirlpool: Whirlpool baths can supplement spa services by providing stress-relieving, therapeutic hydromassage. Regular uses of whirlpools are often prescribed by doctors to patients experiencing chronic pain or recovery from injury. Most baths are equipped with hydrojets utilizing electric pumps and automated air vents to soothe muscle tension, aches, and pains with streams of heated water that can be directed by the bather(s).

I've also included in Appendix 3 some descriptions of spa terminology regarding the different kinds of spas that are out there at the time I write this. Terms continue to evolve based on new and creative business models. I've also given some of the locations I've visited of each type without using the names of the spas, but a quick search on your favorite search engine or one of my websites will show you informative examples and the variety among the options. Although the terminology is grouped into categories, each example and each spa within the category is as unique as a flower.

Appendix 3: A Glossary of Spa Types

Adventure Sport Spas: These types of spas offer adventure in the day, and then the opportunity to unwind at night in thermal waters and often followed by a massage. They offer the traditional treatments to help you feel relaxed and pampered, but also much, much more. In addition to offering skydiving, hang gliding, trekking, and other similar activities, these spas offer hearty meals and local wines with dinner, if desired. Adventure spas offer more specific, educational, or extreme adrenaline rush adventures. They may also feature other packages for those persons who aren't up for an extreme adventure, but also don't want to visit a spa just for the pampering treatments. This might include sports performance (golf swings, tennis serves, baseball batting, cycling, running, or certain high-altitude activities) clinics that focus on developing endurance or technique.

Bed & Breakfast (South Africa, Whidby Island, and Victoria, BC): Spa guest accommodations include a sleeping room and morning meal, prepared and served on the premises often in a quaint cottage-like setting either in one's sleeping room or in the dining room with other guests, if present, or the proprietor. In some of the larger properties, breakfast may be in the form of a buffet in a restaurant-like setting. (Thanks very much to my hosts John and Anna Thacker, in South Africa (http://www.fairlawns.co.za/) and Ms. Cornell Culverwell, of Travel Metier, who personally and meticulously managed all the travel and transfer arrangements, in a professional and at the same time spontaneously warm manner. I shall never forget my incredible experience there!)

Cosmetic Spa (Hungary, Spain, Colombia, Brazil, California, Denver, Florida): This spa primarily offers aesthetic/cosmetic and preventive health and wellness procedures. Services are available such as facials, peels, waxing, and other noninvasive procedures that are within the scope of practice of its certified estheticians, but do not require on-site medical supervision by a licensed physician. An increasing number of cosmetic spas are being opened as a sideline business operation by plastic surgeons, ear, nose, and throat specialists, and dermatologists, as well as many of these physicians creating signature cosmetic lines and registering patents for them.

Cruise Ship Spa (All Ocean Routes): A spa aboard a cruise ship providing a variety of spa, fitness, cosmetic, esthetic, and wellness services may offer reduced calorie spa cuisine menu choices. Nearly all cruise lines now have a spa aboard ship, my favorites being Holland America, Crystal, and Seabourn because of the quality of their spa therapists and estheticians. To get ideas about wellness cruises, search the term "theme cruises" on your favorite search engine. They generally range in the $1000–$1500 range for seven days, and provide passengers with the opportunity to learn about health, wellness, nutrition, and offer mixers with other wellness-oriented passengers, special menus for weight loss, cooking demonstration classes, and take-home logo-imprinted mementos. Cosmetic procedures are also now performed aboard ship. The most popular nonsurgical cosmetic procedure on land, Botox®, was rolled out last year on several ships in the Norwegian Cruise Line, the first cruise line to offer the injections. Celebrity, Royal Caribbean, and Princess Cruise Lines followed Norwegian's lead. The wrinkle-reducing injections, which also include dermal fillers, were being performed on at least 21 ships back in late 2009 according to Steiner Leisure Limited, which operates the medical spa program for at least four cruise lines. *(*www.steinerleisure.com) No newcomer to the spa industry, Steiner has been in business since 1901.

Culinary Spa (Napa, Spain, Vermont, Baja, Oaxaca): This is a destination spa that offers nutrition seminars, preparation demonstrations, or cooking classes. The activities focus on meals that are healthy, low fat, high protein, or meet special dietary needs. I had the opportunity to visit the Lake Austin Spa Resort in Texas while there on a speaking engagement. I changed my ticket and extended my stay to enjoy the spa for a few days. The Culinary Experience™ at Lake Austin Spa Resort is designed to provide guests with a rich and interactive cooking school experience. The program has been a huge success among food enthusiasts, or "foodies," and novices in the kitchen. It's a great way to explore new things about preparing and eating different foods, as well as a great opportunity to take your culinary experience at Lake Austin Spa Resort home with you through learning. The Culinary Experience™ is offered for one week out of every month, year-round, and features special guest chefs from around the country. A sample Culinary Experience™ at Lake Austin Spa Resort week might include:

> All About Herbs
> Boat, Hike, and Breakfast Cookout
> Cheese Sampling
> Hands-On Spring Rolls and Sushi
> Garden Tea and Tour
> Kitchen Gadgets
> Party Planning
> Remodeled Recipes
> The Chocolate Mystique
> Wine Tastings
> Additional Daily Cooking Classes

Day Spa (Worldwide): Spa services available to guests on a day-use basis. Most offer facials, massage, peels, wraps, and endermologie services.

Dental Spa (Hungary): A spa focused on a variety of services by licensed dental professionals as well as relaxation and aesthetic treatments designed to relax the patient before or after dental services.

Destination Spa (Worldwide): A destination spa with an average length of stay of five to seven days. I just did one of these visits in Hungary with three of our clients, my husband, and our managing director from London. The feel is very different than most spas. The average age of the clientele was estimated by me to be about 30 years our senior during the week (very similar to week-long cruises) and then trended considerably younger over the weekend. These spas typically offer a comprehensive program that includes physician checkup, medical history review, along with prescribed thermal spa, balneotherapies, thalassotherapies, rehabilitation, and spa services, physical fitness activities, wellness education, healthful cuisine, and esthetic and cosmetic services and other special theme programs. (A thank you goes to Hunguest Helios Thermal Spa General Manager, Mrs. Adele Joos, and her staff at both the Helios Hotel and the Panorama in Heviz, Hungary for their courtesy and kindnesses. All enjoyed their stay and cannot wait for the opportunity to return to their favorite little "village" on Lake Heviz.)

Detox Spa (Europe): A detox spa is a facility that offers support and encouragement as guests follow either a "Detox Diet" or special dietary plan which typically eliminates sugars, caffeine, processed foods, additives, tobacco and alcohol, or may include dietary fasting.

Eco Spa (Peru, Wyoming, India, Colombia, South Africa, Morocco, Austria, Ireland, Costa Rica, California, Chichén Itzá, Maldives): An eco spa is a facility that offers an ecologically sustainable environment and strives to carry out predominantly ecologically and environmentally friendly practices. Here you'll likely find natural and organic meal ingredients rather than synthetic ingredients in treatments; organic and natural textiles, and the use of alternative energy and power; recycling programs; and pollutant reduction practices. If you are looking for a serious adrenalin boost, fresh air, and some of Colombia's beautiful flora and fauna, go to the Montevivo reservation in Santa Elena, only 30 minutes outside Medellin. You can speed above the forest on five different zip lines; one route is 400 meters, one of the longest in the world. Equipped with a security belt, helmet, and gloves, the adventure begins with a hike through Colombia's diverse flora and fauna. Gazing at palm trees and orchids, butterflies and eagles, time flies by and you will reach the platform in a blink. After a brief lesson you can jump into velocity, and speed freely above the trees. If you chicken out during the ride, just grab the line with a gloved hand and you'll slow down. The adventure ends after only 45 seconds but the adrenalin pumping will make you smile for the rest of the day. What's that old saying? If it doesn't kill you, it makes you stronger? Yeah, right! For those who are not into speed but into heights, you can visit the climbing park and swing from tree to tree. And for the lazy ones that just want to relax: check out the eco spas in the area, and the restaurants and accommodations next to a lake and dotted around the reservation or the first preserve nearby.

Fly-In Spa Resort (Florida, Canada, Vermont, Wisconsin, Wyoming, Michigan, Oregon, Minnesota, Oklahoma, Pennsylvania, Texas, Egypt, Brazil, Hungary): A resort usually in a remote area that features a private airstrip or heliport for arrivals and departures. I have been aware of fly-in spas in Florida since the 1970s when I worked for the American Automobile Association's Worldwide Travel Department as a travel agent. At that time, I visited many properties published in the Association's *Tourbook*®, for both personal familiarity with the properties and because I used to skydive and many of them offered lift flights for jumpers combined with a spa stay.

Medical Spa (worldwide): Medical spas are often a concession at a hotel or resort operated by a full-time, on-site licensed healthcare professional. The physician or allied health professional often provides comprehensive medical and wellness care combined with integrated spa services. Often, medical spas incorporate a variety of traditional, complementary, or alternative therapies and treatments. In addition to the Helios Spa in Heviz, I have had the good fortune to find myself in San Sebastian, Spain, where kind, skilled massage and rehabilitation therapists at La Perla Spa worked on my trochanteric bursitis, which flared after walking stairs and climbing curbs throughout Spain on sidewalks and ancient buildings full of stairs. After seven major knee surgeries on my left knee, my right trochanteric area was in agony. I could barely walk, and couldn't sleep comfortably on the Spanish (European, no fair picking on just Spain for this!) beds that are considerably harder and with thinner mattresses than those to which I am accustomed at home (http://www.la-perla.net/ingles/home.htm). The La Perla Thalassotherapy Centre opened during San Sebastián's Belle Époque period. Over a century ago, Queen María Cristina chose the city as the royal house summer venue. Bathing in the sea was one of the refined pleasures enjoyed by vacationers, combining therapeutic effects with relaxation and well-being. The original wooden La Perla spa, was substituted on La Concha, as it was designated the "Royal Beach" in 1912. La Perla del Océano went on to make the most of the location to spread health and serenity. Today, situated on the magnificent La Concha Bay, the La Perla Thalasso-Sports Centre combines the benefits of the sea with a healthy body. Its location is unique in Europe because seawater is the medium used to achieve truly relaxing therapeutic effects. La Perla is a place where you'll find the high-technology physical/sports rehabilitation equipment, therapists with excellent skills, and opportunities for relaxation and stress reduction programs.

Ranch Spa (Wyoming, Santa Fe, California, Colorado, Australia, New Zealand, Arizona, Canada, Kansas, Montana, Texas): A ranch resort or lodge which offers as its primary recreation a menu of outdoor activities including horseback riding, fishing, hiking, camping, swimming, and trail walking, and, dining is more rustic and hearty, often outdoors or on the trail. After the activities, guests often enjoy traditional spa resort services of massage, soaks, sauna, esthetic and cosmetic services, yoga, and other stretching programs.

Thermal Spa (Hungary, Switzerland, Colombia, Spain, Germany, Japan, Colorado, and more): This is a spa offering an on-site source of natural minerals, salts, mud, thermal waters, springs, or seawater used in hydrotherapy treatments.

Resort/Hotel Spa (Worldwide): A spa located within a resort or hotel providing a variety of relaxation, skin care, esthetic and cosmetic services, fitness, nutrition, and wellness services. Some spas offer nonguests access.

Salon Spa (Worldwide): A beauty salon that primarily offers services for cutting, grooming, and styling hair for men and women, and also offers certain spa services. In some strip malls in Las Vegas, one can find three and four of them in one place. I just wonder how they all make money in such stiff competition in difficult financial times, when discretionary income dwindles.

Spiritual Spa Retreat (Worldwide): A spiritual spa retreat is a wellness destination with overnight accommodations (lodge rooms, bunkhouse, dorm, cabins, or guesthouses) at a retreat center (e.g., farm, monastery, school) conducted by individuals who encourage the use of personal reflection, prayer, or meditation, as well as offering body and wellness services which could include yoga, massage, hydrotherapy, colon therapy, steam and sauna, and more.

Vinotherapy Spa (Hungary, Spain, Colombia, Napa, France, Italy): Vinotherapy is a therapeutic treatment in which either the residue of wine making (the seeds and pulp) are incorporated into skincare and body care treatments (scrubs and masks) because the pulp is believed to have antioxidant, antiaging, and exfoliating qualities, or wine (as a beverage) is added to a hydrotherapy treatment to soften the skin. Increasingly, the incorporation of grapeseed oil, a natural antiseptic, ground grape seeds as a "scrub," and wine extracts and scents in lotions and potions are also being described as "vinotherapy" as well, although this is more pleasurable than therapeutic.

Weight Loss Retreat (Spain, California, Colorado, Texas, Hilton Head, Vermont, Utah): A weight loss retreat offers medical supervision by a licensed professional, which may include a medical doctor, dietician, or nutritionist, whose primary purpose is dietary and nutritional education, counseling, and programming in order to assist guests in achieving healthy weight goals. Some of the facilities and programs are geared toward the needs of children, teenagers, and young adults.

Index